Ireland

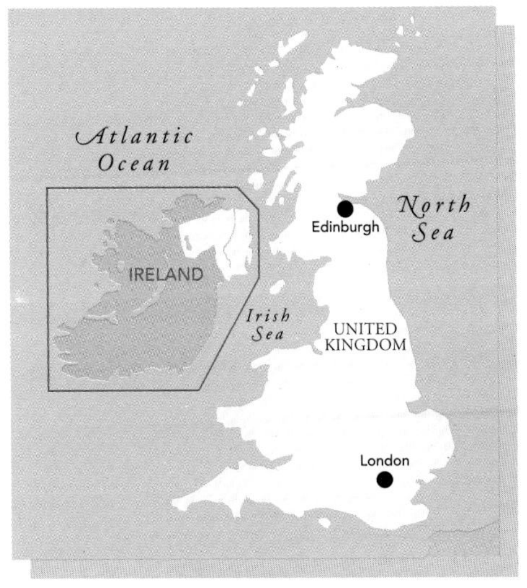

HarperCollins*Publishers*

Dunguaire Castle, Co. Galway

YOUR COLLINS TRAVELLER

Your Collins Traveller Guide will help you find your way around your chosen destination quickly and easily. It is colour-coded for easy reference:

The blue section answers the question 'I would like to see or do something; where do I go and what do I see when I get there?' This section is arranged as an alphabetical list of topics. Within each topic you will find:

- A selection of the best examples on offer.
- How to get there, costs and opening hours for each entry.
- The outstanding features of each entry.
- A simplified map, with each entry plotted and the nearest landmark or transport access.

The red section is a lively and informative gazetteer. It offers:

- Essential facts about the main places and cultural items. What is La Bastille? Who was Michelangelo? Where is Delphi?

The gold section is full of practical and invaluable travel information. It offers:

- Everything you need to know to help you enjoy yourself and get the most out of your time away, from Accommodation through Baby-sitters, Car Hire, Food, Health, Money, Newspapers, Taxis, Telephones to Youth Hostels.

Cross-references:

Type in small capitals – CHURCHES – tells you that more information on an item is available within the topic on churches.

A-Z after an item tells you that more information is available within the gazetteer. Simply look under the appropriate name.

A name in bold – **Holy Cathedral** – also tells you that more information on an item is available in the gazetteer – again simply look up the name.

CONTENTS

CONTENTS

PRACTICAL INFORMATION GAZETTEER

CONTENTS

Dingle Harbour

INTRODUCTION

On a globe Ireland is just an undefined blob, a tiny island on the western extremities of Europe. On investigation, however, its 32,524 sq. miles encompass some of the world's most unspoiled scenery, most ancient remains, and the most historic and homely cities. It is an island where the past and present are interwoven – with varied success – and few people are immune to the spell it casts.

The island is divided first into four provinces – Leinster, Munster, Connacht and Ulster – and then into the 32 counties. In a further sub-division, six of the nine Ulster counties make up Northern Ireland, part of the United Kingdom. Together, the two Irelands house a population of about 4.3 million, of which 3.5 million live in the Republic. Much of the land, however, is sparcely inhabited and only large urban areas continue to expand – 1 million people live in and around Dublin.

This homeland is predominantly a country of contrasts. Spectacular cliffs tower above the harsh Atlantic Ocean; green rolling pastures are sprinkled with cattle and sheep; mountains loom over rugged coasts and tranquil lakes; flat midland plains and bogs stretch for miles; and while its metropolises buzz and hum with activity, little has changed in fifty years or more in hundreds of remote villages.

But it is also a somewhat shabby country, with many internal problems, social and economic. Visitors are often taken aback by its cities' grey urban sprawl and by the ugly bungalows and huge modern houses which have erupted alongside country roads leading into tacky, fly-blown towns. Crime is also a growing problem in urban centres, and the days are gone when tourists could set up camp anywhere and not be troubled.

It can all be a bit of a shock for first-time visitors who arrive unprepared for the 'real Ireland'. Some expect to find a nation of redheads eating potatoes, swinging shillelaghs and living in thatched cottages, with 'pigs in the parlour' and a castle round the corner. Others associate Ireland with bombs and terrorism. And neither is close to the true picture. For though a certain amount of 'shamrockery' is to be found, it's often just a show for the tourists. You're unlikely to hear anyone say 'begorra' but you are likely to be beguiled by the turn of phrase in the spoken language of many areas and in the vibrant literature of Ireland, past and present.

The Guildhall, Derry

Meanwhile, though most of its residents still want peace, it is only in some parts of Northern Ireland that bombs, terrorism, sectarianism and discrimination have become a feature of life, on both sides of the political divide – Nationalist and Unionist. Both sides have endured countless atrocities, while many abominable actions have been committed and condoned over the decades on all fronts. It is a complex and tragic situation, one that cannot be brushed aside but one that deserves not to be dealt with briefly. All that can be said is that crossing the border into Northern Ireland is disturbing. It is nerve-racking to be challenged, albeit politely, by armed soldiers. The sporadic security checkpoints, military patrols, cordoned-off city streets and barricaded police stations are also daunting but Northern Ireland, despite the so-called 'Troubles', is a marvellous part of the island, rich in scenery, antiquities, historic homes and top-of-the-range tourist amenities.

In both parts of Ireland tradition and custom still play an important role, particularly in rural areas. Midsummer fires are lit in the West, masked children invade Dublin's streets at Hallowe'en and ceilidh dancing is still popular, while the mummers and 'wren-boys' make their rounds in some districts on St. Stephen's Day (Boxing Day). And,

not surprising in a country where Roman Catholicism is the dominant religion (Northern Ireland excepted), religious customs are still vibrant. Holy wells are visited, the 'stations' (the celebration of Mass on a rota basis in the houses of rural communities) are held, pilgrimages are made to shrines or up Croagh Patrick, and in many Catholic homes you will still see a St. Brigid's Cross made of rushes or a red lamp flickering under a picture of the Sacred Heart (of Jesus).

One custom peculiar to Northern Ireland is the annual marches. On 12 July every year Ulster's Orangemen march, wearing bowler hats and orange sashes, playing pipes and beating the magnificent but menacing Lambeg drums. They walk to commemorate William of Orange's victory over James II at the Battle of the Boyne in 1690, just as Derry's Apprentice Boys march on 12 August in memory of the 13 apprentices who shut the city gates against James' forces. The Catholic equivalent of the Orangemen, the Ancient Order of Hibernians, does its marching on 15 August, the Feast of the Assumption of the Blessed Virgin.

Remains of habitation have been found in Ireland dating back to almost 9000 BC, and the Irish today, as throughout the centuries, are a motley mix of races and nationalities. Among the earliest inhabitants were the

Fir Bolg – the belly men – and the mythical Tuatha de Dannan, while later centuries brought – by invasion, invitation and accident – races and groups including the Beakers, Celts (from whom the Gaels descended), Vikings, Normans, Anglo-Normans, English, Spaniards, Huguenots and Scottish Presbyterians.

Almost all of Ireland's inhabitants from Mesolithic times onwards have left their architectural mark on the landscape, be it passage graves, cooking pits, crannogs or burial mounds. The early Christian monks left behind their oratories, round towers, high crosses and of course the most ancient of all ecclesiastical remains, the beehive huts, of which the best known are on Skellig Michael off the Kerry coast.

The invasion of the Anglo-Normans in the late 12thC launched a trend of castle building, of which the oldest are fortified mounds or mottes. Later castles were usually square stone towers. The 12thC also saw the beginning of elaborate monastic settlements founded by different religious orders, and impressive remains can still be seen at Holy Cross Abbey in Co. Tipperary and Clonmacnoise in Co. Offaly.

And while centuries of colonization and rule left behind some unhealed scars, they also bequeathed to the country many well-planned and picturesque garrison and Plantation towns. In addition, the 18thC and the Protestant ascendancy saw the erection of some of the country's most lovely architecture, particularly Georgian, which still stands proud in most of the country's cities.

Ireland also strives, against many odds and often in a half-hearted fashion, to be Europe's 'green' country. Its potential continues to attract visitors and immigrants, particularly from northern Europe, who see an opportunity to enjoy the 'good life'.

But most of all, this is not a country to rush through. Take time to savour your surroundings and unwind, even if it means shortening your itinerary. Golf, fish, sail, cruise on the splendid inland waterways, sip a pint and enjoy the 'crack'. But most of all, remember to relax – you're in the Emerald Isle!

Westport House, Co. Mayo

Glencolumbkille, Co. Donegal

BAILEYS
ORIGINAL IRISH CREAM
FLORIST

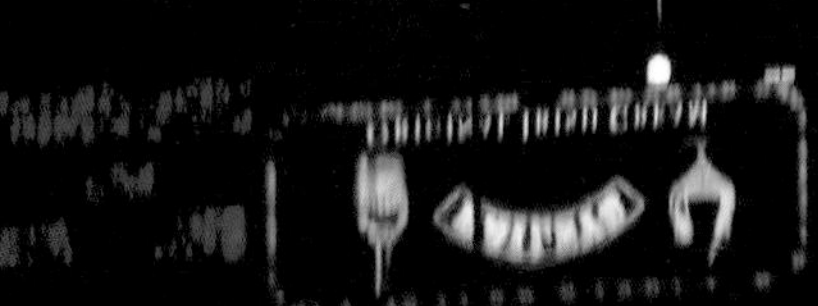

Dublin City & The East

COUNTIES

Dublin, Wicklow, Kildare, Meath & Louth

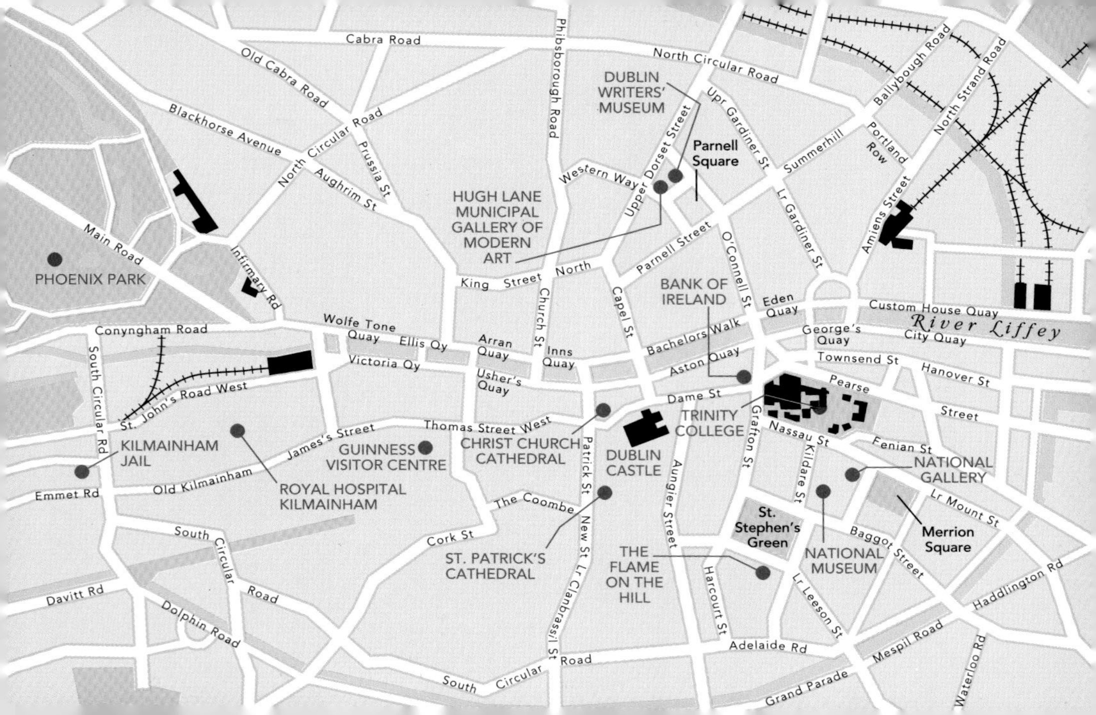
River Liffey
PHOENIX PARK
DUBLIN WRITERS' MUSEUM
Parnell Square
HUGH LANE MUNICIPAL GALLERY OF MODERN ART
BANK OF IRELAND
TRINITY COLLEGE
DUBLIN CASTLE
CHRIST CHURCH CATHEDRAL
GUINNESS VISITOR CENTRE
KILMAINHAM JAIL
ROYAL HOSPITAL KILMAINHAM
ST. PATRICK'S CATHEDRAL
THE FLAME ON THE HILL
St. Stephen's Green
NATIONAL MUSEUM
NATIONAL GALLERY
Merrion Square
Cabra Road
Old Cabra Road
Blackhorse Avenue
North Circular Road
Prussia St
Aughrim St
Main Road
Infirmary Rd
Phibsborough Road
Western Way
Upper Dorset Street
Upr Gardiner St
Summerhill
Portland Row
Ballybough Road
North Strand Road
Amiens Street
Lr Gardiner St
Parnell Street
O'Connell St
North King Street
Church St
Capel St
Eden Quay
Custom House Quay
George's Quay
City Quay
Townsend St
Hanover St
Pearse Street
Bachelors Walk
Aston Quay
Wolfe Tone Quay
Ellis Qy
Arran Quay
Inns Quay
Victoria Qy
Usher's Quay
Conyngham Road
St. John's Road West
South Circular Rd
Dame St
Grafton St
Nassau St
Kildare St
Fenian St
Lr Mount St
Baggot Street
Lr Leeson St
Haddlington Rd
Mespil Road
Waterloo Rd
Grand Parade
Adelaide Rd
Harcourt St
Aungier Street
Patrick St
New St
Lr Clanbrassil St
South Circular Road
Thomas Street West
James's Street
Old Kilmainham
Emmet Rd
The Coombe
Cork St
South Circular Road
Davitt Rd
Dolphin Road

DUBLIN CASTLE Dame St, tel: 01-777580/777129.
■ 1000-1215, 1400-1700 Mon.-Fri., 1400-1700 Sat. & Sun. Closed on State occasions. ● £1, child 50p.
An architectural, historical and artistic treasure house. See **A-Z**.

TRINITY COLLEGE College Green, tel: 01-772941. ■ Daily. Library 0930-1645 Mon.-Fri., 0930-1245 Sat. ● College free. Library £1.75.
The Long Room in the Library was Europe's biggest reading room when built in 1712. Among its treasures is the Book of Kells *(see* **A-Z**). *An audiovisual show telling Dublin's story is open May-Sep. See* **A-Z**.

CHRIST CHURCH CATHEDRAL Christ Church Pl., tel: 01-778099. ■ 1000-1700. ● Donation.
In 1038 Sitric, King of the Dublin Norsemen, founded the first cathedral. Rebuilt by 'Strongbow' in the 12thC, it was restored in the 19thC.

ST. PATRICK'S CATHEDRAL St. Patrick's Close, tel: 01-754817.
■ 0830-1800 Mon.-Fri., 0830-1600 Sat., 1000-1630 Sun. ● Donation.
Ireland's largest church on Dublin's oldest Christian site. The 5thC church was replaced by the current building in 1191. Nearby is Marsh's Library, Ireland's oldest public library.

BANK OF IRELAND College Green, tel: 01-776801.
■ Bank opening hours. Guided tours 1030, 1130 & 1345 Tue. ● Free.
Built in 1729 to house the Irish parliament and used until 1800, when the British and Irish parliaments were united. The entire front portico was built without windows to prevent distractions from outside.

THE FLAME ON THE HILL St. Audoen's Church, High St, tel: 01-6791855/6791018. ■ 1000-1700. ● £1.30, child 80p.
Multivisual presentation telling the story of Ireland before the Vikings. The church stands on the site of the first Viking settlement in the area.

PHOENIX PARK
The largest city park in Europe. Its 1750 acres include sports grounds, a peoples' garden, deer herds, the zoo and the president's residence.

GUINNESS
PORTER
GUINNESS IS GOOD FOR YOU

KILMAINHAM JAIL Inchicore Rd, tel: 01-535984. ■ 1100-1800 June-Sep., 1400-1800 Wed. & Sat. (Oct.-May). ● £1.50, child 60p.
Largest unoccupied jail in Ireland and Britain. The leaders of the Easter Rising (see **A-Z***) were executed here. Political prisoners included Emmet (see* **A-Z***) and Parnell (see* **A-Z***). Guided tours and audiovisual show.*

ROYAL HOSPITAL KILMAINHAM St. John's Rd, tel: 01-718666. ■ 1200-1800 Tue.-Sun. Guided tours 1200-1700. ● Free Tue., £1 Wed.-Fri., £1.50 Sat. & Sun.
Built for Charles II's old soldiers by William Robinson who modelled it on Les Invalides. Renovated to house an arts centre. Cellar restaurant.

NATIONAL MUSEUM Kildare St, tel: 01-618811. Also at 7-9 Merrion Row. ■ 1000-1700 Tue.-Sat., 1400-1700 Sun. ● Free.
Wonderful collection of prehistoric, Bronze-Age and early-Christian artefacts, including the Ardagh Chalice and the Tara Brooch.

NATIONAL GALLERY Merrion Sq., tel: 01-615133. ■ 1000-1800 Mon.-Sat. (until 2100 Thu.), 1400-1700 Sun. Guided tours 1430, 1515 & 1600 Sun. Lecture 1500 Sun. ● Free.
Houses a collection of over 2000 paintings from all the European schools, as well as Irish artists Barrett, Yets, Osborne, Lavery and Orpen.

DUBLIN WRITERS' MUSEUM 18-19 Parnell Sq. North, tel: 01-722077. ■ 1000-1700 Mon.-Sat., 1400-1800 Sun. ● £2, child 50p.
Traces Irish literature from the Book of Kells *(see* **A-Z***) to the modern day. Explains the lives and works of Jonathan Swift (see* **A-Z***), W. B. Yeats (see* **A-Z***), Brendan Behan (see* **A-Z***), James Joyce (see* **A-Z***), etc.*

GUINNESS VISITOR CENTRE Hop Store, Crane St, tel: 01-538364. ■ 1000-1500 Mon.-Fri. ● £1, child 50p.
Brewing museum, video show and a free glass of Guinness (see **A-Z***).*

HUGH LANE MUNICIPAL GALLERY OF MODERN ART
Parnell Sq., tel: 01-741903. ■ 0930-1800 Tue.-Sat., 1100-1700 Sun.
19th-20thC paintings shared with London's National Gallery.

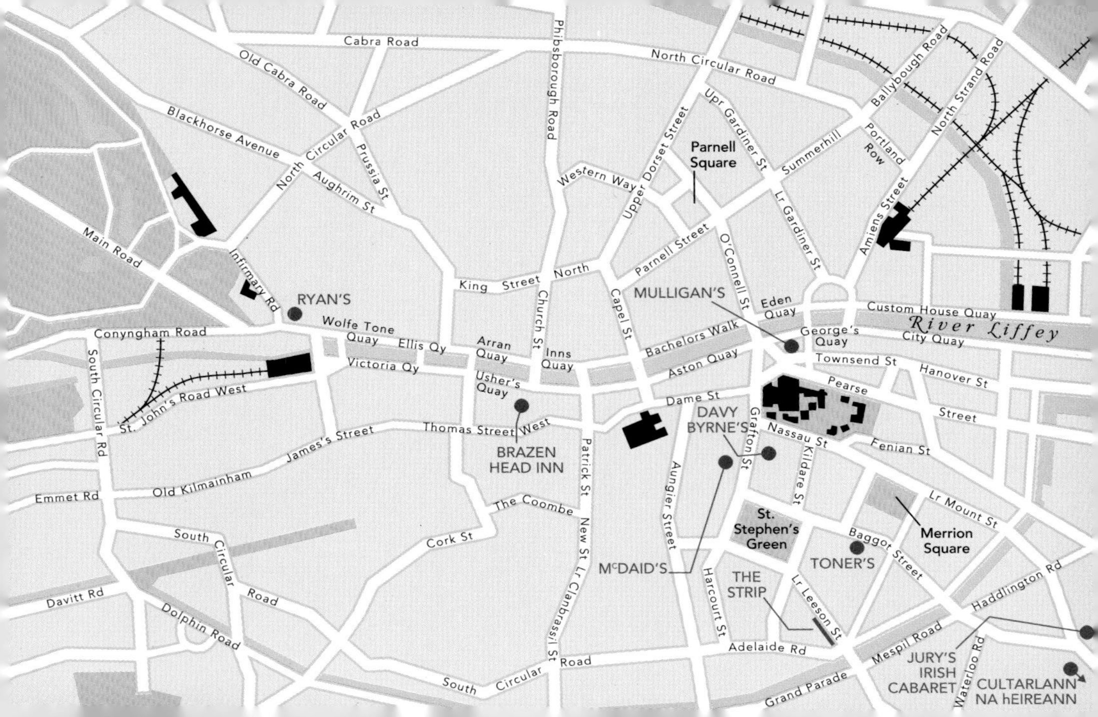

Cabra Road
North Circular Road
Old Cabra Road
Blackhorse Avenue
North Circular Road
Prussia St
Aughrim St
Phibsborough Road
Western Way
Upper Dorset Street
Upr Gardiner St
Parnell Square
Summerhill
Portland Row
Ballybough Road
North Strand Road
Amiens Street
Lr Gardiner St
Parnell Street
O'Connell St
Main Road
Infirmary Rd
RYAN'S
King Street North
Church St
Capel St
MULLIGAN'S
Eden Quay
Custom House Quay
River Liffey
George's Quay
City Quay
Conyngham Road
Wolfe Tone Quay
Ellis Qy
Arran Quay
Inns Quay
Bachelors Walk
Aston Quay
Townsend St
Hanover St
Victoria Qy
Usher's Quay
Pearse Street
St. John's Road West
South Circular Rd
Dame St
DAVY BYRNE'S
Grafton St
Nassau St
Fenian St
Thomas Street West
James's Street
BRAZEN HEAD INN
Patrick St
Aungier Street
Kildare St
Old Kilmainham
Emmet Rd
The Coombe
St. Stephen's Green
Lr Mount St
Merrion Square
Cork St
New St Lr Clanbrassil St
Baggot Street
TONER'S
South Circular Road
McDAID'S
Harcourt St
THE STRIP
Lr Leeson St
Davitt Rd
Dolphin Road
Haddington Rd
Adelaide Rd
Mespil Road
Waterloo Rd
JURY'S IRISH CABARET
CULTARLANN NA hEIREANN
South Circular Road
Grand Parade

JURY'S IRISH CABARET Jury's Hotel, Pembroke Rd, Ballsbridge, tel: 01-605000. ■ 1915 (dinner), 2000 (cabaret) Tue.-Sun. (May-Oct.). ● Expensive.
The longest-running dinner/cabaret in Dublin, with leading Irish acts.

CULTARLANN NA hEIREANN Belgrave Sq., Monkstown, tel: 01-2800295.
Headquarters of Comhaltas Ceoltoiri Eireann (see **A-Z***). Regular cabaret-type show during the summer. Also ceilidh dancing and music sessions.*

'THE STRIP' Lower Leeson St.
Packed with (very) late-night basement wine bars and discos. No cover charges but a bottle of plonk may leave you with a sore head and *a sore pocket. Two of the longest-running are Buck Whaley's and Suesy Street.*

BRAZEN HEAD INN 20 Lower Bridge St, tel: 01-6795186.
The oldest pub in Dublin, first licensed in 1666 but said to date back to the 13thC. Traditional music every night.

RYAN'S 28 Parkgate St, tel: 01-776097.
Virtually unchanged since the turn of the century, including the snugs.

MULLIGAN'S Poolbeg St, tel: 01-775582.
Dating from 1845 and mentioned in Dubliners *by James Joyce (see* **A-Z***). Dowdy but extremely popular. The clocks run 15 min fast.*

DAVY BYRNE'S 21 Duke St, tel: 01-711298.
Joyce's Leopold Bloom dined here (see **Bloomsday***). Good bar menu until 2100 specializing in seafood.*

McDAID'S 3 Harry St, off Grafton St, tel: 01-6794395.
A favourite with Brendan Behan (see **A-Z***). The perfect spot for a lunch-time sandwich or an afternoon drink when you tire of the shops.*

TONER'S 139 Lower Baggot St, tel: 01-763090.
Only pub reputed to have served W. B. Yeats. He had one sherry and left!

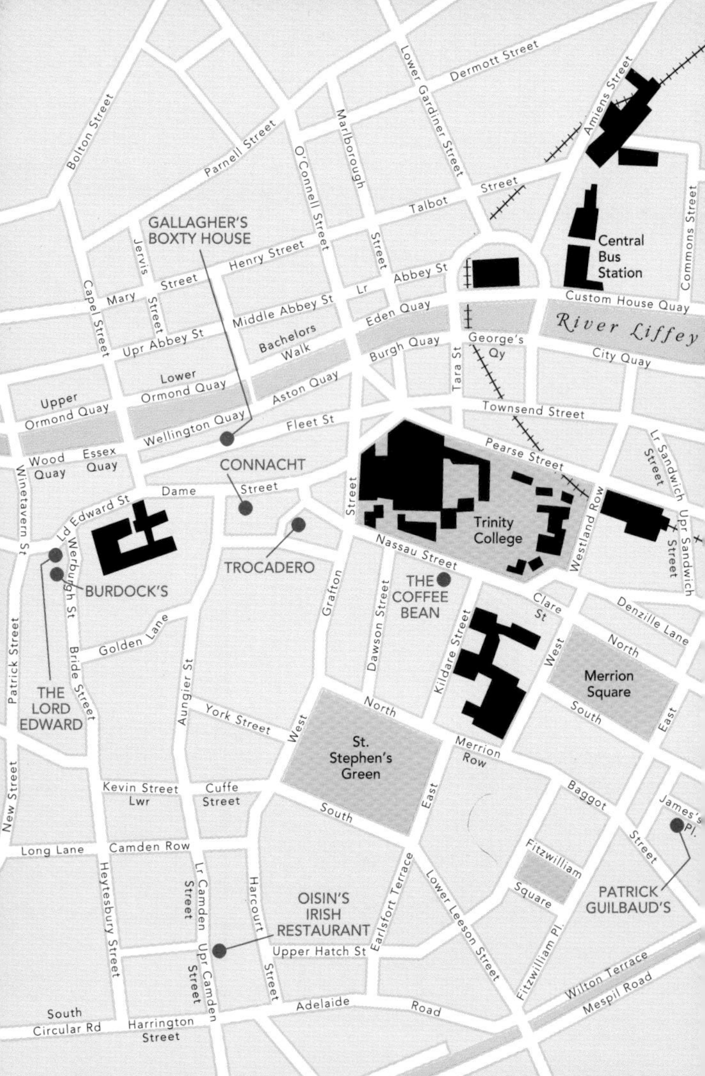

GALLAGHER'S BOXTY HOUSE
CONNACHT
TROCADERO
BURDOCK'S
THE LORD EDWARD
THE COFFEE BEAN
Trinity College
Central Bus Station
River Liffey
Merrion Square
St. Stephen's Green
OISIN'S IRISH RESTAURANT
PATRICK GUILBAUD'S
Fitzwilliam Square
Dermott Street
Lower Gardiner Street
Amiens Street
Parnell Street
Bolton Street
Marlborough
O'Connell Street
Talbot Street
Henry Street
Mary Street
Jervis Street
Capel Street
Abbey St
Lr
Middle Abbey St
Upr Abbey St
Bachelors Walk
Eden Quay
Burgh Quay
Custom House Quay
City Quay
George's Qy
Tara St
Commons Street
Lower Ormond Quay
Upper Ormond Quay
Aston Quay
Wellington Quay
Fleet St
Townsend Street
Pearse Street
Lr Sandwich Street
Upr Sandwich Street
Westland Row
Wood Quay
Essex Quay
Dame Street
Ld Edward St
Winetavern St
Werburgh St
Nassau Street
Grafton Street
Dawson Street
Kildare Street
Clare St
Denzille Lane
North
West
South
East
Golden Lane
Bride Street
Patrick Street
Aungier St
York Street
Merrion Row
Baggot Street
James's Pl.
Kevin Street Lwr
Cuffe Street
New Street
Long Lane
Camden Row
Heytesbury Street
Lr Camden Street
Upr Camden Street
Harcourt Street
Earlsfort Terrace
Lower Leeson Street
Fitzwilliam Pl.
Upper Hatch St
Adelaide Road
Wilton Terrace
Mespil Road
South Circular Rd
Harrington Street

PATRICK GUILBAUD'S 46 James Pl., off Lower Baggot St, tel: 01-764192. ■ 1230-1400 Tue.-Fri., 1930-2215 Tue.-Sat. ● Very expensive. *Regarded as one of Dublin's finest restaurants. French cuisine. A place to dress up and relish every pricey morsel.*

OISINS' IRISH RESTAURANT 31 Upper Camden St, tel: 01-753433. ■ 1830-2230 Mon.-Sat. Reservations. ● Expensive. *An intimate restaurant where Irish stew, Dublin coddle, colcannon (see* **Food***) and corned beef feature regularly on the menu. Excellent seafood.*

THE LORD EDWARD 23 Christ Church Pl., tel: 01-752557. ■ 1230-1415 Tue.-Fri., 1800-2230 Tue.-Sat. ● Expensive. *Highly-regarded seafood restaurant.*

TROCADERO 3 St. Andrew St, tel: 01-775545/6792385. ■ 1800-0030 Mon.-Sat., 1800-2330 Sun. ● Moderate-expensive. *Cosy bistro-type restaurant. Popular with theatrical people.*

CONNACHT 14 Dame Court, off Dame St, tel: 01-6793550. ■ Lunch Mon.-Sat., dinner Tue.-Sat. (until 2400 Thu.-Sat.). ● Moderate. *Friendly service. Traditional Irish cooking, steaks and seafood.*

GALLAGHER'S BOXTY HOUSE 21 Temple Bar, tel: 01-772762. ■ 1230-2330. ● Inexpensive-moderate. *Reservations are not accepted at this relaxed restaurant but even the wait for a table across the road in the Auld Dubliner pub makes it worth a visit. Try the colcannon (see* **Food***), bacon and cabbage, boxty (Irish potato bread), and Bailey's and brown bread ice cream.*

THE COFFEE BEAN 4 Nassau St, tel: 01-6797140. ■ 1030-1530 Mon.-Sat. ● Inexpensive-moderate. *Serves filling lunches and specializes in vegetarian and wholefoods.*

BURDOCK'S Werburgh St, near Christ Church Cathedral. ■ 1700-2245 Mon., Wed. & Fri., 1730-2245 Thu. & Sat. ● Inexpensive. *A Dublin institution. Takeaway fish and chips cooked to perfection.*

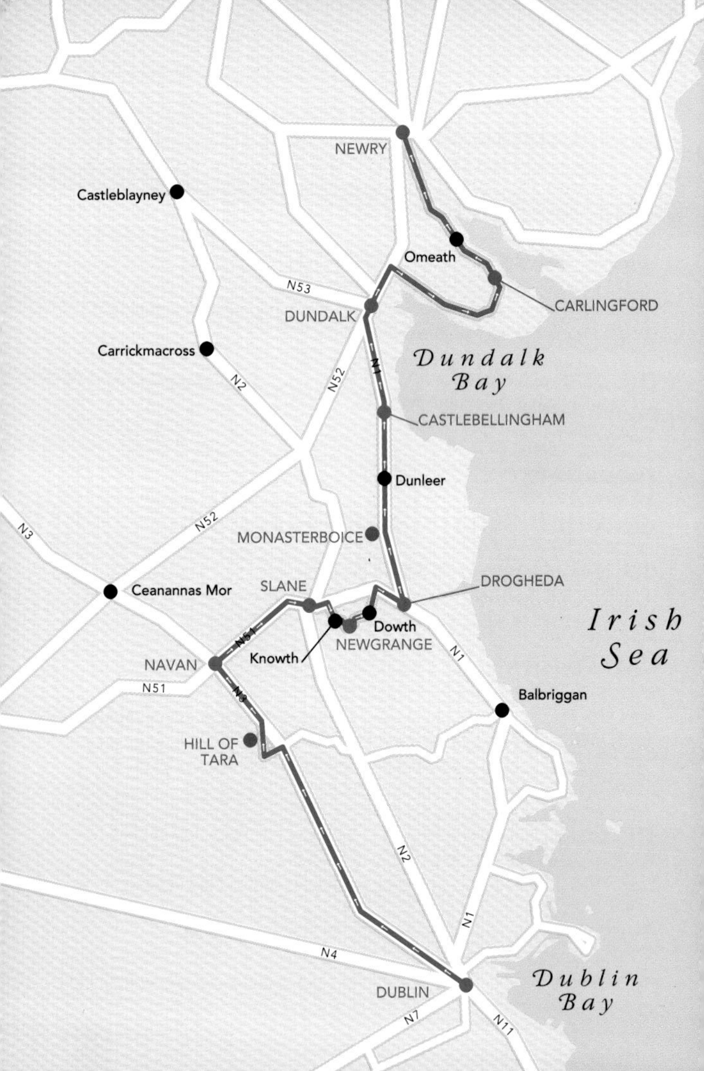

NEWRY
Castleblayney
Omeath
CARLINGFORD
N53
DUNDALK
Carrickmacross
Dundalk Bay
N1
N52
N2
CASTLEBELLINGHAM
Dunleer
N3
N52
MONASTERBOICE
DROGHEDA
SLANE
Ceanannas Mor
Irish Sea
Dowth
N51
NEWGRANGE
Knowth
N1
NAVAN
N51
N3
Balbriggan
HILL OF TARA
N2
N1
N4
Dublin Bay
DUBLIN
N7
N11

East Coast

Dublin city–Newry. Duration: 1 day.

Leave Dublin (see **DUBLIN CITY**, **A-Z**) on the N 3, turning left after 24 miles, signposted Tara.
25 miles – Hill of Tara (see **A-Z**). The site entrance is to the left past the shop. A map inside the gate shows the area's layout. Turn down the road opposite the shop. On reaching the N 3, turn left towards Navan.
31 miles – Navan (An Uaimh). The county town of Meath, at the confluence of the Boyne and Blackwater rivers, was of strategic importance during Anglo-Norman times when it was defended by a castle. This has now disappeared but a large motte, built by Joceline de Angulo, can still be seen on the west side of the town. Turn right over the bridge, crossing the Boyne, signposted Slane/Drogheda/Kingscourt. Drive up Flower Hill and turn right again, signposted Slane/Drogheda, on the N 51. The road skirts the Boyne valley. After about 6 miles it begins to descend past the Slane Castle estate (1400-1800 Sun., Mar.-Oct.; £1.60, students £1), seat of Lord Henry Mountcharles, who has staged huge rock concerts in front of the house. The Gothic gates on the right mark the entrance to the estate. There is no general admission to the castle, designed by James Wyatt in 1785, but it does have a basement restaurant (1200-2230 Wed.-Sat., 1200-2200 Sun.), and there are guided tours of some of the rooms, including one used by U2 while recording *The Joshua Tree*.
39 miles – Slane. A neat little village, set on a steep hillside running down the Boyne. In the village centre at the corners of a crossroads are four almost identical three-storey 18thC houses.
DETOUR: Take a left at the crossroads to Slane Hill, where St. Patrick (see **A-Z**) lit the first paschal fire in AD 433, to herald the arrival of Christianity in Ireland. The ruins of a 16thC friary and college building remain on its summit.
Keep straight on, passing the restored cottage of poet Francis Ledwidge, who died on a Flanders battlefield in 1917. After 2.5 miles turn right for the megalithic tombs of Knowth, Dowth and Newgrange, part of the huge collection of tombs and monuments in this area known as Brugh na Boinne. Follow the signposts for Newgrange.
DETOUR: If you have time visit Knowth, a Neolithic burial site 500 years

older than Newgrange. Two passage graves within its mound are still under excavation and 18 satellite tombs have been found. There is evidence of occupation here from 3000 BC to AD 1200.

34.5 miles – Newgrange (see **A-Z**).

DETOUR: A right turn leads to Dowth half a mile on. Dowth is a chambered burial mound, currently closed to the public, with a nearby medieval church and castle. The road, with views ahead of Townley Hall, leads across the Boyne to the Drogheda road. This is one of the areas where the Williamite forces rested during the Battle of the Boyne (see **A-Z**). On the left are Townley Hall Woods, which are popular for walks. It is possible to continue along the road to Drogheda but if it is not dark and road conditions are good, turn right across the bridge to Oldbridge – where King William's main force crossed to cut off the Jacobites' communications – and follow the narrow road which skirts the Boyne. Veer left after 2 miles.

42 miles – Drogheda (see **A-Z**). Take the Belfast road north. About 4 miles out a papal cross commemorates a Mass attended by half a million people in nearby fields during the visit of John Paul II in 1979. Two miles further take a left turn for Monasterboice, making another left turn after half a mile. Follow the road round to the site.

48 miles – Monasterboice (open all year; free). This early monastic site is renowned for its high crosses and is reputed to have been founded by St. Buithe, who died in AD 521. The most famous character in its history is Flann Mainistreach, who died in 1056 and is said to have written extensive verses on the Tuatha de Dannan (see Introduction) and the kings of Tara. The remains at the site consist of two 13thC churches, a pre-Gothic sundial, an early cross-decorated slab, a 110 ft round tower and three high crosses. Return to the main road and turn left.
57 miles – Castlebellingham. A picturesque spot. The converted mill on the left now contains the Olde Mill Restaurant. The An Sos Coffee Shop and Craft Centre is open in summer for snacks and lunches. Continue on the N 1.
65 miles – Dundalk. Pop: 24,000. Tourist Information, Market Sq., tel: 42-35484. Louth's county town and not as desolate a spot as many people believe. A settlement first sprang up here in the 12thC. During the Middle Ages it was an important border fortress for the English pale and a base for English attacks on Ulster. The New Queen pub and restaurant on Market Sq. serves food all day. Cellars, Backhouse Centre, Clanbrassil St serves home-cooked food with a vegetarian emphasis. Turn left past the 19thC courthouse and St. Nicholas' Parish Church, which incorporates the remains of a 13thC church. Cross over the river and continue along the N 1. About 2 miles outside the town take a right turn signposted Ballymascanlon House Hotel. Pass the hotel, which has a well-regarded, if expensive, restaurant. The Cooley mountains are to the left. Continue into Carlingford, keeping left.
82 miles – Carlingford (see **A-Z**). Continue north round the lough for 12 miles, via Omeath, to Newry (see **EXCURSION 15**) (94 miles).

The Southeast

COUNTIES

Wexford, Waterford, Carlow, Kilkenny & Tipperary

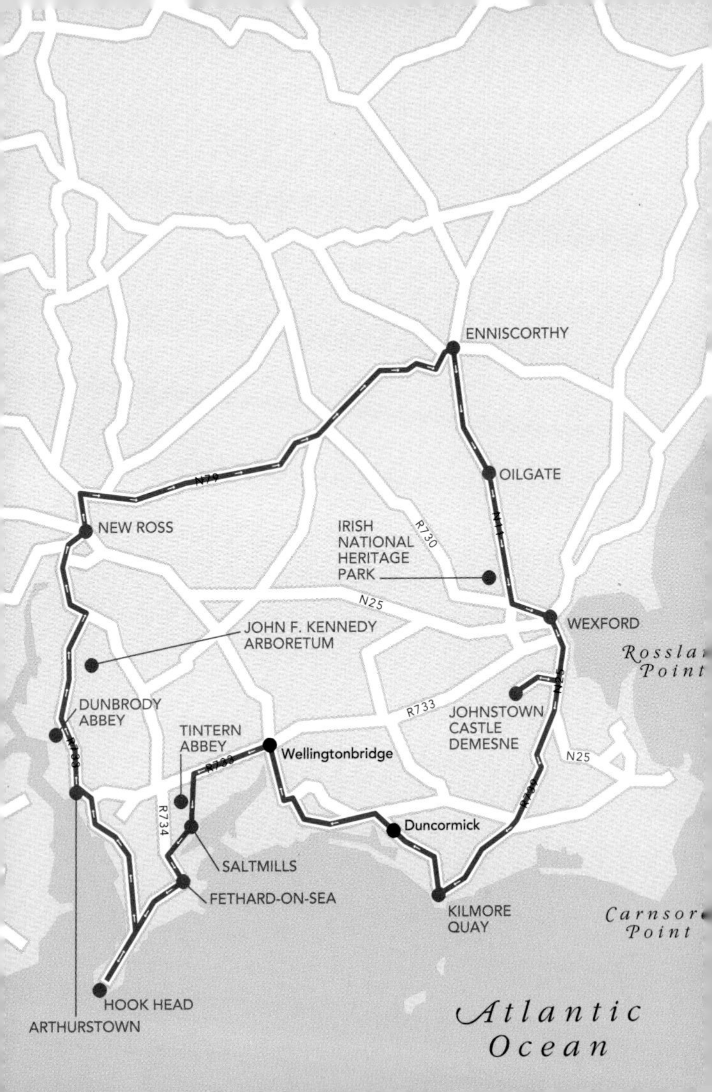
ENNISCORTHY
OILGATE
N79
NEW ROSS
IRISH
NATIONAL
HERITAGE
PARK
R730
N11
N25
WEXFORD
JOHN F. KENNEDY
ARBORETUM
Rosslare
Point
N25
R733
JOHNSTOWN
CASTLE
DEMESNE
DUNBRODY
ABBEY
R733
TINTERN
ABBEY
R733
Wellingtonbridge
N25
R739
R734
Duncormick
SALTMILLS
FETHARD-ON-SEA
KILMORE
QUAY
Carnsore
Point
HOOK HEAD
ARTHURSTOWN
Atlantic
Ocean

Southeast Coast

Wexford town–Hook Head–Enniscorthy–Wexford town.
Duration: 1-2 days.

Wexford Town (see **A-Z**). Leave on the Rosslare road (N 25). A mile outside the town is a left turn for Johnstown Castle Demesne and Agricultural Museum (0900-1900 Mon.-Fri., 1400-1900 Sat. & Sun., April-mid Nov.; 0900-1700 Mon.-Fri., mid Nov.-Mar.; grounds £2.30 per car, pedestrians £1.20, child 60p; museum £1.50, child 75p). Return to the N 25 and turn right after 4 miles, signposted Kilmore. The road winds through a number of small settlements.
11 miles – Kilmore Quay. A fishing village, made picturesque by its thatched cottages and whitewashed walls, which boasts a sandy beach. It hosts a seafood festival in July which includes a trawler race around the nearby Saltee Islands. A maritime museum is sited on the lightship *Guillemot* berthed in the stone harbour (1400-2000 June-Sep.; £1, child 50p). The Wooden House Bar on the way to the pier serves seafood. Follow signposts for Wellingtonbridge at the harbour. After 3 miles take a left turn and then another left 2 miles further on. Pass through Duncormick, turning left outside the village. Ballyteige Bay is on the left. Four miles out take the left turn at the crossroads for Wellingtonbridge. Two miles on the road begins to skirt Bannow Bay, affording lovely views. In Wellingtonbridge keep left and follow signposts for Arthurstown. About 4 miles on take a left turn at the crossroads, signposted Hook Peninsula. After half a mile a right turn leads to Tintern Abbey.
34 miles – Tintern Abbey (grounds open all year). Built in 1200 by William Marshall, Earl of Pembroke, who, when caught at sea during a storm, vowed to build an abbey on the spot the stricken vessel landed, if it were saved. The ship drifted around Carnsore Point, past Kilmore and up the channel into Bannow Bay. The presbytery is based on the abbey's famous namesake in Wales. The abbey, which was converted to a dwelling house in the 16thC, was vacated in 1960 and is currently being renovated by the Office of Public Works. Return to the road and keep right. Cross Bannow Bay into the village of Saltmills and keep left following signposts for Hook Peninsula. Saltmills itself is a 'transferred' community. The generous Colcloughs, Protestant landlords who were

granted Tintern Abbey after the Dissolution in 1583, relocated the people of the village which had grown up around the abbey, and maintained a school for Catholics here.

38 miles – Fethard-on-Sea. This ancient seafaring settlement is now a thriving summer resort. It was once a bishop's seat. Turn right in the village, signposted Ring of Hook, beside the tennis court. Follow signposts for the Ring. After 5 miles turn right for Hook Head. Loftus Hall on the right has a dubious claim to fame: the devil, it is alleged, appeared here!

46 miles – Hook Head. This is the site of one of Europe's oldest lighthouses. Since early Christian times a beacon was attended by monks, beginning with the Welsh missionary Dubhan (*dubhan* is the Irish word for 'hook'). Monastic cells at the base of the current tower (built on its Norman predecessor) can be examined with permission from the lighthouse attendants. Retrace the route, turning left after 3 miles at a petrol station, and follow signposts for Duncannon. Turn left on entering the village and follow the coast to Arthurstown.

57 miles – Arthurstown. The local sandy beaches make this a good stop for a swim.

DETOUR: A regular drive-on, drive-off 10 min ferry service to Passage East for Waterford city (see **A-Z**) operates from nearby Ballyhack, site of a Knights Templar castle which guarded the head of the harbour. Follow signposts for New Ross. Two miles out on the left is Dunbrody Abbey. A sign on the gate gives directions to the keyholder for this impressive Cistercian monastery founded in 1210.

DETOUR: After 3 miles turn right for the John F. Kennedy Arboretum (1000-2000 May-Aug., 1000-1830 April & Sep., 1000-1700 Oct.-Mar.; car £2-8). Dedicated to the memory of the late US president, its extensive grounds include signposted walks, a narrow-gauge railway and visitor centre. Continue through agricultural land, entering New Ross along the banks of the River Barrow.

69 miles – New Ross. A steep-streeted settlement built as an inland port, with some lovely views after a climb to the top of the town. St. Mary's Abbey Church is a 13thC parish church, of which the transepts and chancel remain. The town's *tholsel* (tollhouse) in South St was built in 1749 and its turret replaced at the end of the 18thC. Opposite is a

1798 memorial (see **1798 Rebellion**). The Galley Cruising Restaurant, which has an office on the quay near Bridge St, operates river trips up the Barrow and Nore as far as St. Mullins (see **A-Z**) and Inistioge (see **A-Z**), or south to Cheekpoint. Leave on the N 79 to Enniscorthy via Clonroche and The Leap.

89 miles – Enniscorthy (see **A-Z**). Leave on the Wexford road, passing after 7 miles through Oilgate, for centuries a centre of intense devotion to St. David, patron saint of Wales. Six miles further is a right turn for the marvellous 30 acre Irish National Heritage Park.

103 miles – Irish National Heritage Park (0900-1700 April-Oct.; £2; guided tours on the hour). The park, on the River Slaney, contains full-size replicas, built using archaeological and historical information, of sites and buildings dating from man's first settlement in Ireland to the 12thC. Reproductions include a crannog (see **A-Z**), dolmen, Viking longboat house and early monastery. An original round tower and Norman watchtower are located nearby. Also included are an exhibition of ancient artefacts – some found on site – and an impressive audiovisual show. Continue on the main road for 2 miles, following signposts for Wexford town (105 miles).

Thurles
N8
KILKENNY
N10
N76
R691
N10
N9
N8
CASHEL
N9
N24
N76
N8
N24
CAHIR
N8
N24
Clonmel
River Suir
WATERFORD
N9
Clogheen
N24
N25
CAPPOQUIN
TRAMORE
LISMORE
Annestown
N72
DUNGARVAN
River Blackwater
Helvic Head
N25
Atlantic Ocean
Ram Head

Cahir & Cashel

Waterford city–Kilkenny city. Duration: 1-2 days.

Leave Waterford city (see **A-Z**) on the R 675, following signposts for Tramore.
8 miles – Tramore. A busy seaside resort with amusements, a 3 mile sandy beach, racecourse, golf course, and Celtworld, a three-dimensional audiovisual show dedicated to Irish legends. South along the Doneraile Cliffs is the 'Metal Man', a gigantic iron figure which serves as a marker for ships. According to tradition young women who manage to hop around its base three times without allowing their other foot to touch the ground, will be married within a year! Take the coast road to Dungarvan, passing through Fennor after 4 miles. Three miles further on is a car park and a lovely spot for a coast walk just before Annestown. The road offers some breathtaking views. Seven miles on is a wood-turning shop, and 2 miles further an old mine – *not* a good spot for walking as there are a number of uncovered shaft openings. The coastline becomes more rugged on the descent into Bunmahon but the road veers inland again. Turn right outside the village. Follow signposts for Dungarvan on this twisting road. The Monavullagh and Comeragh mountains are to the right after about 10 miles. Cross the harbour and go back onto the coast before entering the outskirts of Dungarvan.
36 miles – Dungarvan. This busy and beautifully-sited market town is the administrative centre of Co. Waterford. The ruins of a castle erected by King John in 1185 can be seen on the banks of the Colligan River, and in Abbeyside on the east bank are the remains of a castle and Augustinian priory founded by the McGrath family in the 13thC. Remnants of the original town walls can be seen on the 'Dead Walk'.
DETOUR: Two and a half miles outside the town, on the N 25, is a left turn for An Rinn, part of the Deise Gaeltacht (see **A-Z**), and impressive Helvic Head.
Turn right in The Square, signposted Clonmel/Cappoquin, taking the R 672 and N 72. In Cappoquin (see **A-Z**) turn left, then left again for Lismore across the Blackwater River.
51 miles – Lismore (see **A-Z**). Retrace the route and turn left for Clogheen, following the river bank and ascending into the heart of the Knockmealdown mountains. The rhododendron-lined roads, which

should not be attempted at night, pass through Lismore Woods and offer a series of spectacular views on entering Co. Tipperary, with the Galty mountains ahead. The road continues to Clogheen.

DETOUR: Leave the route and follow signposts for Mitchelstown Cave (see **A-Z**) and Ballyporeen, the ancestral home of former US president Ronald Reagan, before rejoining the excursion at Cahir.

Turn right in Clogheen for Ballylooby. In Ballylooby turn right.

75 miles – Cahir. The town is built on the River Suir. Cahir Castle (see **A-Z**) is to the right. In the town centre turn right, following signposts for Swiss Cottage, and watch out for a right turn after about 1.5 miles. Swiss Cottage (1000-1800 Tue.-Sun., mid June-Sep.; 1000-1700 Sat. & Sun., Oct.-early Nov.; £1, child 70p, family £3) is a restored 19thC building situated in the beautiful demesne of Cahir Park. It was built on the estate of the earls of Glengall to a Swiss design by Regency architect John Nash. Return to the town and veer right on the N 8.

88 miles – Cashel. Tourist Information, Town Hall, tel: 062-61333. In medieval times this was the ecclesiastical capital of Munster and the small market town is still renowned for its variety of secular and ecclesiastical monuments. The most famous is of course the Rock of Cashel (see **A-Z**), or St. Patrick's Rock, which is probably one of Ireland's most

Kilkenny Castle

spectacular sites, no matter from which angle it is approached. Follow signposts for access to the rock. In the town, the GPA Bolton Library in the grounds of St. John's Church is also worth a visit (0930-1730 Mon.-Sat., 1430-1730 Sun.; £1, child 70p). A selection of ancient manuscripts, rare maps and literary treasures is usually on display. Also of interest are Cashel Folk Village (0930-2000 May-Sep.; 50p, child 30p) in the town centre, St. Dominic's Abbey and Hore Abbey. To leave Cashel, turn right after the tourist office, passing the Presentation convent and turning right shortly afterwards, signposted Palm Grove B&B. This third-rate road takes you to Kilkenny city (see **A-Z**) via Dually, Ballinure, Laffansbridge, Killenaule and Ballingarry, and a left turn on the N 76 (123 miles).

The Southwest

COUNTIES

Cork & Kerry

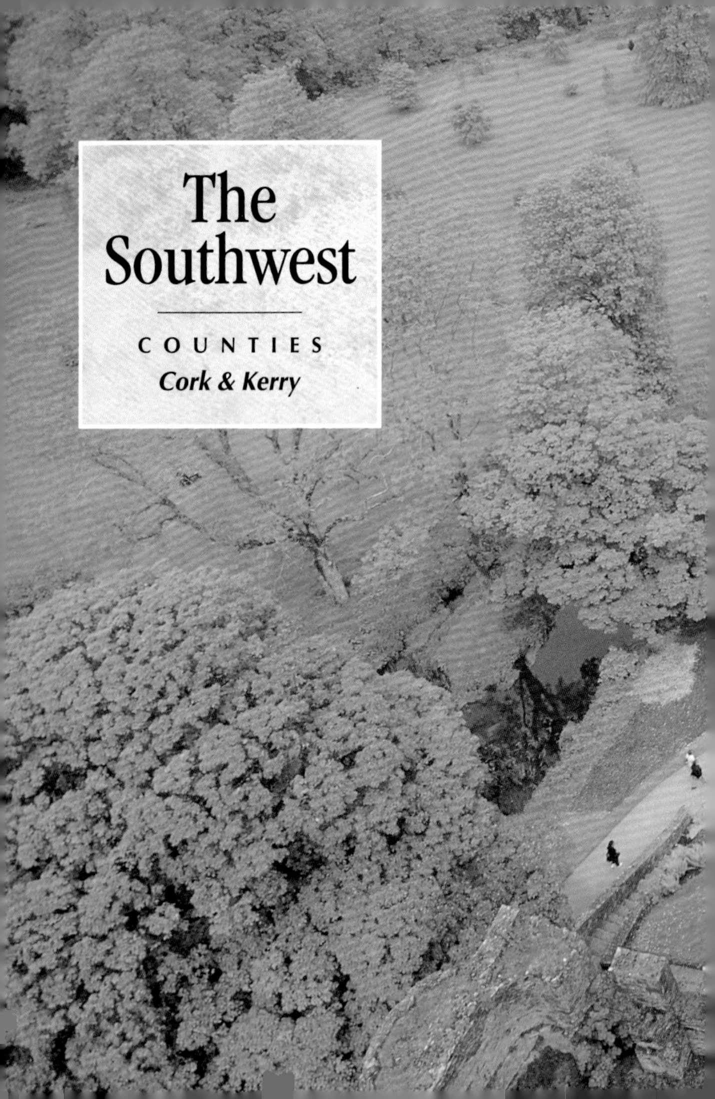

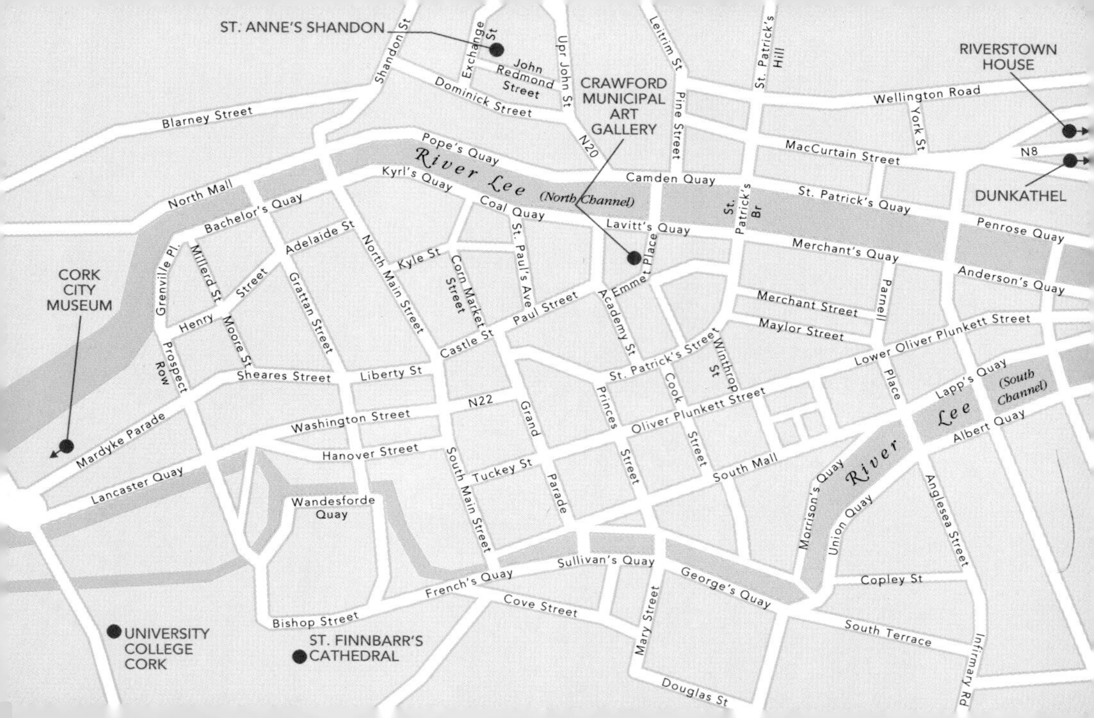

ST. ANNE'S SHANDON
Shandon St
Exchange St
John Redmond Street
Upr John St
CRAWFORD MUNICIPAL ART GALLERY
Leitrim St
St. Patrick's Hill
RIVERSTOWN HOUSE
Dominick Street
Pine Street
Wellington Road
York St
Blarney Street
N20
MacCurtain Street
N8
Pope's Quay
River Lee
(North Channel)
Camden Quay
DUNKATHEL
Kyrl's Quay
St. Patrick's Quay
North Mall
Coal Quay
St. Patrick's Br
Bachelor's Quay
Lavitt's Quay
Penrose Quay
Merchant's Quay
CORK CITY MUSEUM
Grenville Pl
Millerd St
Adelaide St
North Main Street
Kyle St
Corn Market Street
St. Paul's Ave
Emmet Place
Anderson's Quay
Street
Grattan Street
Paul Street
Academy St
Merchant Street
Parnell
Henry
Moore St
Castle St
Maylor Street
Lower Oliver Plunkett Street
St. Patrick's Street
Winthrop St
Prospect Row
Sheares Street
Liberty St
Cook Street
Place
Lapp's Quay
(South Channel)
N22
Grand Parade
Princes Street
Oliver Plunkett Street
Lee
Washington Street
Mardyke Parade
Albert Quay
Hanover Street
South Main Street
Tuckey St
South Mall
River
Morrison's Quay
Lancaster Quay
Wandesforde Quay
Union Quay
Anglesea Street
Sullivan's Quay
Copley St
French's Quay
George's Quay
Cove Street
Bishop Street
South Terrace
Mary Street
UNIVERSITY COLLEGE CORK
ST. FINNBARR'S CATHEDRAL
Douglas St
Infirmary Rd

ST. ANNE'S SHANDON Shandon. ■ 1000-1800 Mon.-Sat. (June-Sep.); 1030-1600 Oct.-May. ● £1 bells, £1.50 bells & tower.
The 'pepperpot' steeple of St. Anne's, built in 1750, with its 11 ft salmon weather vane, dominates the north side of Cork city. Visitors can ring the eight 18thC bells with the help of music cards. Two sides of the tower are faced in red sandstone and two in white – the colours of Cork.

ST. FINNBARR'S CATHEDRAL Dean St. ■ Daily. ● Donation.
The 19thC cathedral stands where the saint first established his monastic school in the 7thC. The triple-spired building has a fine rose window, mosaic pavements and elaborate carvings.

UNIVERSITY COLLEGE CORK Western Rd, tel: 021-276871.
This Tudor-Gothic university has a particularly attractive riverside quadrangle. The Honan Chapel is modelled on Cormac's Chapel on the Rock of Cashel (see **A-Z***).*

CORK CITY MUSEUM Fitzgerald Park, Mardyke. ■ 1100-1300, 1415-1700 Mon.-Fri., 1500-1700 Sun. ● Free Mon.-Fri., 20p Sun.
Displays include local historical finds, silver and lace.

CRAWFORD MUNICIPAL ART GALLERY Emmet Pl., tel: 021-273377. ■ 0900-1700 Mon.-Sat. ● Free.
Collection of 19thC and contemporary Irish art. A varied sculpture collection includes some Rodin bronzes. See **CORK CITY-RESTAURANTS**.

DUNKATHEL Glanmire, 3 miles east on the N 8, tel: 021-821014. ■ 1400-1800 Wed.-Sun. (May-mid Oct.). ● £1.50, child 50p.
Built by wealthy Cork merchant Abraham Morris, the house dates from the late 18thC and has some outstanding 19thC decoration. There is some fine period furniture and a rare 19thC barrel organ.

RIVERSTOWN HOUSE Glanmire, near Dunkathel on the N 8, tel: 021-821205. ■ 1400-1800 Thu.-Sat. (May-Aug.). ● £1.50.
Italian stuccodores *Paolo and Filippo La Franchini carried out their first work in Ireland here. Beautifully restored plasterwork.*

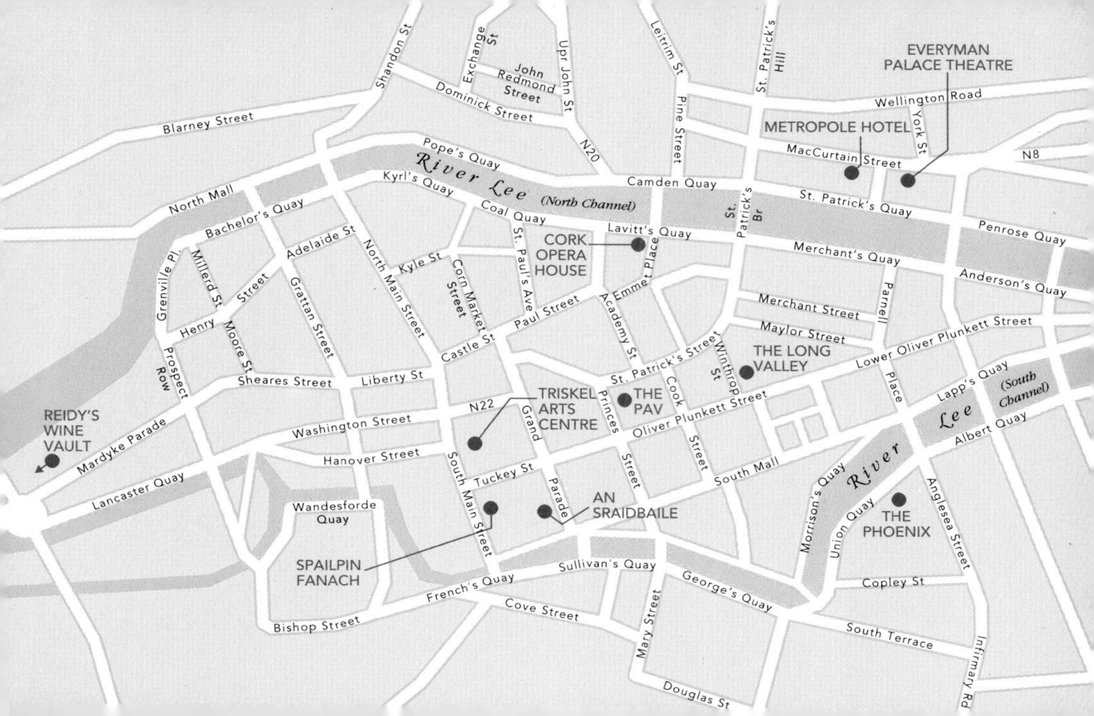

EVERYMAN PALACE THEATRE
METROPOLE HOTEL
CORK OPERA HOUSE
THE LONG VALLEY
TRISKEL ARTS CENTRE
THE PAV
REIDY'S WINE VAULT
AN SRAIDBAILE
SPAILPIN FANACH
THE PHOENIX
Shandon St
Exchange St
John Redmond Street
Upr John St
Leitrim St
St. Patrick's Hill
Dominick Street
Blarney Street
Pine Street
Wellington Road
York St
MacCurtain Street
N8
N20
Pope's Quay
River Lee (North Channel)
Camden Quay
Kyrl's Quay
Coal Quay
St. Patrick's Quay
St. Patrick's Br
North Mall
Bachelor's Quay
Lavitt's Quay
Penrose Quay
Merchant's Quay
Anderson's Quay
Adelaide St
St. Paul's Ave
Emmet Place
Grenville Pl.
Millerd St
Street
Kyle St
Corn Market Street
Grattan Street
North Main Street
Merchant Street
Parnell Place
Paul Street
Academy St
Maylor Street
Lower Oliver Plunkett Street
Henry
Moore St
Castle St
St. Patrick's Street
Winthrop St
Prospect Row
Sheares Street
Liberty St
Lapp's Quay
(South Channel)
Cook Street
Oliver Plunkett Street
N22
Princes Street
Grand Parade
Washington Street
Lee
Albert Quay
Mardyke Parade
Hanover Street
South Mall
River
Morrison's Quay
Tuckey St
Union Quay
Lancaster Quay
South Main Street
Anglesea Street
Wandesforde Quay
Sullivan's Quay
Copley St
George's Quay
French's Quay
Cove Street
Bishop Street
South Terrace
Mary Street
Infirmary Rd
Douglas St

CORK OPERA HOUSE Emmet Pl., tel: 021-276357.
Hosts drama, classical and popular concerts, ballet and opera.

EVERYMAN PALACE THEATRE MacCurtain St, tel: 021-501673.
Local drama, pantomime and visiting theatre companies.

TRISKEL ARTS CENTRE Tobin St, off South Main St, tel: 021-272022. ■ Food 1100-1800.
Exhibitions, films, poetry and drama. Hot and cold snacks and lunches.

AN SRAIDBAILE Grand Parade Hotel, Grand Parade, tel: 021-274391. ■ June-Sep. ● £14 inc. dinner.
A re-created century-old Irish village scene with turf fires, a storyteller and set dancing. Lively sessions three times a week in summer. The hotel also contains a nightclub with disco and regular live music.

SPAILPIN FANACH 28 South Main St, tel: 021-277949.
Bar food served daily. Traditional and folk music nights. Mixed clientele.

THE PHOENIX 3 Union Quay, tel: 021-964275.
Live bands and traditional music. Vegetarian restaurant upstairs.

THE LONG VALLEY Winthrop St, tel: 021-272144.
Wonderful pub with great sandwiches, where the bar staff wear white coats and the Muzak dates from the 1930s and '40s.

REIDY'S WINE VAULT Western Rd, tel: 021-275751.
Spacious pub in old wine vault with antique Victorian bar. Popular with local business people. Home-cooked food daily, including Irish stew and seafood.

METROPOLE HOTEL MacCurtain St, tel: 021-508122.
Live music most nights and Sun. jazz sessions.

THE PAV Off St. Patrick's St, tel: 021-276330.
The *place to nightclub in Cork. Big dance floor. Not for teenyboppers.*

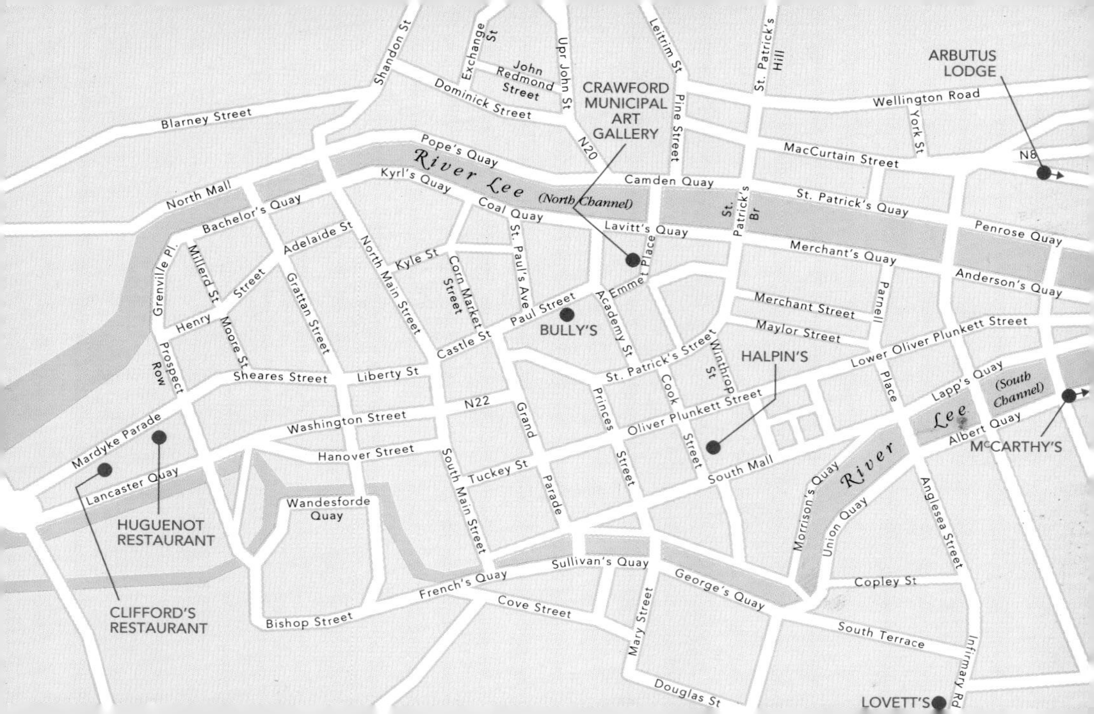

ARBUTUS LODGE
CRAWFORD MUNICIPAL ART GALLERY
BULLY'S
HALPIN'S
McCARTHY'S
LOVETT'S
HUGUENOT RESTAURANT
CLIFFORD'S RESTAURANT
River Lee (North Channel)
River Lee (South Channel)
Shandon St
Exchange St
John Redmond Street
Upr John St
Dominick Street
Blarney Street
Leitrim St
Pine Street
St. Patrick's Hill
Wellington Road
York St
MacCurtain Street
N8
N20
Pope's Quay
Kyrl's Quay
Camden Quay
St. Patrick's Quay
St. Patrick's Br
Penrose Quay
North Mall
Bachelor's Quay
Coal Quay
Lavitt's Quay
Merchant's Quay
Anderson's Quay
Grenville Pl.
Millerd St
Street
Adelaide St
Kyle St
St. Paul's Ave
Corn Market Street
North Main Street
Grattan Street
Henry
Moore St
Paul Street
Emmet Place
Academy St
Merchant Street
Maylor Street
Parnell Place
Lower Oliver Plunkett Street
Prospect Row
Sheares Street
Liberty St
Castle St
St. Patrick's Street
Winthrop St
Cook Street
Lapp's Quay
Albert Quay
N22
Washington Street
Grand Parade
Princes Street
Oliver Plunkett Street
Mardyke Parade
Hanover Street
South Main Street
Tuckey St
South Mall
Lancaster Quay
Wandesforde Quay
Morrison's Quay
Union Quay
Anglesea Street
Sullivan's Quay
French's Quay
George's Quay
Copley St
Cove Street
Bishop Street
Mary Street
South Terrace
Infirmary Rd
Douglas St

ARBUTUS LODGE Middle Glanmire Rd, Montenotte, tel: 021-501237. ■ 1300-1400, 1900-2130 Mon.-Sat. ● Expensive.
Still probably Cork's most renowned restaurant. Vegetarian meals available. The Gallery Bar is cheaper than the main restaurant (lunch only).

CLIFFORD'S RESTAURANT 18 Mardyke Parade, tel: 021-275333. ■ 1230-1430 Tue.-Fri., 1900-2230 Tue.-Sat. ● Expensive.
In a former library. Superb menu adds new dimension to old favourites.

LOVETT'S Churchyard Lane, off Well Rd, Douglas, tel: 021-294909/362204. ■ 1230-1400 Mon.-Fri., 1900-2200 Mon.-Sat. ● Expensive.
French cuisine. Fresh fish and game a speciality.

McCARTHY'S Blackrock Castle, Blackrock, tel: 021-357414. ■ 1230-1430 daily, 1900-2230 Wed.-Sun. ● Moderate-expensive.
Dine in old-world style as the ships glide by on the River Lee.

HUGUENOT RESTAURANT French Church St, Mardyke Parade, tel: 021-273352. ■ 1230-1430, 1800-2230. ● Moderate-expensive.
Excellent food and atmosphere. Pre-theatre specials before 1930.

HALPIN'S Cook St, tel: 021-277853.
■ 1200-2400. Self-service & waitress service until 1730. A la carte until 2400. ● Inexpensive-moderate.
Large, bustling, informal restaurant. Sandwiches, salads, lasagne, steaks, daily specials and good Sun. lunches.

CRAWFORD MUNICIPAL ART GALLERY Emmet Pl., tel: 021-274415. ■ 1030-1700 (lunch 1200-1430) Mon.-Sat., 1830-2130 Wed.-Fri. ● Inexpensive-moderate.
Offshoot of the renowned Ballymaloe House Restaurant. Outstanding cooking. Classical music Wed.-Fri. nights. *See* CORK CITY-ATTRACTIONS.

BULLY'S 40 Paul St, tel: 021-274415. Also in Douglas village, tel: 021-892415. ■ Daily until 2330. ● Inexpensive-moderate.
A good selection of pizzas, pastas and fish dishes.

Lough Leane
KILLARNEY
N72
N20
N71
MUCKROSS HOUSE & GARDENS
Muckross Lake
Upper Lake
N22
CORK
KENMARE
R569
Macroom
R618
N70
N22
R600
R584
N71
GLENGARRIFF
N71
N71
R572
KINSALE
BANTRY
N71
R600
R586
Bantry Bay
ROSSCARBERRY
CLONAKILTY
Timoleague
LEAP
N71
Old Head of Kinsale
BALLYDEHOB
N71
SKIBBEREEN
GLANDORE
R595
Galley Head
Atlantic Ocean

Southwest Coast

Cork city–Killarney. Duration: 1-2 days.

Leave Cork past the airport on the R 600 following signposts for Kinsale. After 7 miles take a left turn through Riverstick and Belgooley.
16 miles – Kinsale (see **A-Z**). Leave on the R 600 signposted Ballinspittle and turn left over the new bridge.
DETOUR: After about 4 miles turn left for the Old Head of Kinsale, a bird sanctuary and a good spot for a blustery walk.
After 6 miles the road passes a grotto built in honour of the Blessed Virgin Mary; it was here that hundreds of people reported seeing the statue move in the mid-1980s. In Ballinspittle turn left, following signposts for Clonakilty. After about 9 miles the road, which is right on the seashore, becomes extremely narrow and it is necessary to drive with caution. In Timoleague keep on the R 600 signposted Clonakilty.
42 miles – Clonakilty. This market town is rapidly becoming one of the area's liveliest spots and now boasts its own festival and agricultural show in July and busking festival in Aug. For live music sessions try Shanley's in Rossa St and De Bara's on Pearse St. An Sugan serves hot bar food all day. Nearby Inchydoney Strand is one of the district's best beaches. Take the N 71 via Lissavairy and Rosscarberry, an important monastic centre for many centuries, with a little museum housed in the Protestant cathedral. There are some lovely beaches nearby, and Tonn Cliodhna (pronounced 'cleena'), the 'roar of Cliodhna's wave', can sometimes be heard as the water rushes into the sea caves. In traditional mythology Cliodhna was a powerful goddess and the Tonn Cliodhna was one of the three great magical sounds. In the town take the R 597 left to Glandore, a quiet fishing village.
DETOUR: Four miles outside Rosscarberry is a left turn for the Drombeg Stone Circle, a druidic circle dating from about 150 BC. Next to the circle is an open-air cooking pit which was filled with water and heated by throwing in stones from a fire.
The road winds around the bay where there are two islands known as Adam and Eve. Sailors entering the bay were given the instructions, 'Avoid Adam and hug Eve'. Keep straight on at the bridge. The pine trees on this stretch give the area an almost alpine feel. Turn left in Leap (pronounced 'lep') for Skibbereen. In times gone by the area west of

here was regarded as dangerous country for travelling, and the saying was, 'Beyond the Leap, beyond the Law'.

63 miles – Skibbereen (see **A-Z**). Leave on the N 21, signposted Bantry.

DETOUR: Go south on the R 595 for the picturesque harbour village of Baltimore (see **A-Z**), where ferries run to Cape Clear (see **A-Z**) and Sherkin Island (see **A-Z**), and the R 596 to Castletownshend, a sleepy village centred on one steep street, and the home of Somerville and Ross, the authors of *The Irish RM* series.

After 11 miles keep straight on at the bridge before Ballydehob, signposted Bantry.

DETOUR: Ballydehob itself, which has a thriving artistic community, can be reached by crossing over the humpback bridge. This detour also leads on to the delights of Skull, the beaches of Barleycove and Crookhaven, and Mizen Head, Ireland's most southerly point.

After 6 miles the road ascends into forest and then descends. Five miles further, as you enter Bantry, is the entrance to Bantry House and Gardens (0900-1800, till 2000 summer; £2, child £1). Built c. 1750, the house is the seat of the earls of Bantry and looks over Bantry Bay. The impressive contents include part of a tapestry made for Marie Antoinette as a wedding gift, mosaics excavated from Pompeii and priceless Russian icons. The house also contains an exhibition about an ill-fated French Armada invasion in 1798.

86 miles – Bantry. At the head of beautiful Bantry Bay, this busy market town and fishing port includes a local museum, off Wolfe Tone Sq., filled with historical trivia (1500-1730 Tue.-Fri., June-Sep.). The Oriada Gallery, New St, which houses temporary exhibitions of local art, is just one of the craft shops and galleries worth a visit. For food try O'Connor's Seafood Restaurant and Bar. Bowls (see **A-Z**) is often played on roads around the town at weekends. Keep straight on for Glengarriff via Ballylickey on the N 71, from where there are views of Bantry Bay.

97 miles – Glengarriff. Picturesque but commercialized. A boat trip to the Italian Garden on Garinish Island (see **A-Z**), however, though expensive (haggle with the boatmen) is a 'must'.

DETOUR: Take the R 572 left for the Beara peninsula (see **A-Z**).

Follow signposts for Killarney. The road ascends into the Caha mountains, offering breathtaking views but drive with extreme caution. Pass

through Turner's rock tunnel into Co. Kerry.
114 miles – Kenmare (see **A-Z**). Follow signposts for Killarney. After 6 miles is Moll's Gap. There is a viewing area opposite the shop. The gap in the distance is the Gap of Dunloe, and the furthest and highest mountain in view is Purple Mountain. MacGillicuddy's Reeks begin on the left side of the Gap of Dunloe. The Owenreagh River is below to the left. Turn right for Killarney. After 2 miles is Looscaunagh Lough. Pass the beginning of the Upper Lake below and arrive at Lady's View, another viewing spot. This is a popular place for proposals of marriage but not when the tourist season is in full swing, though even coachloads of tourists milling in and out of the nearby café and shop cannot detract from the views. The road continues to wind as it descends, passing through a small tunnel. To the left is the Long Range, a narrow strip of water which links the Upper Lake, Muckross Lake and Lough Leane.
WALK: Five miles after Lady's View is a car park and walking track to Dinis Cottage. It is possible to walk all the way to Muckross House (see below) from Dinis, though the track is somewhat overgrown in parts. Keep on the N 71.
130 miles – Torc Waterfall. A car park on the right marks the best spot for ascending to the waterfall; it's only a short climb.
131 miles – Muckross House & Gardens (0900-1730 Sep.-June, 0900-1900 July & Aug.; £2, child £1). On the left is the vehicle entrance to the estate. (Pedestrian and jaunting car entrances are further along the road.) During the summer a regular bus service operates from Killarney to the car park at the house. Situated on the shores of Muckross Lake, this expansive estate includes a ruined but beautifully preserved 15thC abbey and a furnished Elizabethan-style mansion. The stables now house craft workshops, and the grounds encompass an extensive range of scenic walks and nature trails, including one of the area's loveliest spots, The Meeting of the Waters. Continue along the N 71 for 3 miles into Killarney (see **A-Z**) (134 miles).

Feohanagh
GALLARUS ORATORY
BALLYFERRITER
Sybil Point
Slea Head
FAHAN
OGHAM STANDING STONES
DINGLE
Stradbally
Tralee Bay
R559
BLENNERVILLE
N69
TRALEE
N21
N22
N23
Anascaul
INCH
R561
CASTLEMAINE
N70
FARRANFORE
Dingle Bay
KILLORGLIN
Glenbeigh
Lough Caragh
KILLARNEY
Lough Leane
CAHIRCIVEEN
N71
KENMARE
WATERVILLE
Lough Currane
R568
SNEEM
CAHERDANIEL
Bolus Head
Kenmare River

Ring of Kerry

Killarney–Waterville–Dingle–Tralee–Killarney. Duration: 2-3 days.

Leave Killarney (see **A-Z**) on the N 71 to Kenmare (see **A-Z**), reversing the final 20 miles of **EXCURSION 4**. In Kenmare follow signposts for Waterville, with views across the Kenmare River to the Caha mountains. To the right are the hills of Letter South and Knocknaskill. Pass through Tahilla. Two miles outside the tiny village is a bird sanctuary on the left, and the entrance to just one of the Parknasilla Wood walks on the right. Continue along the tree-lined road.

36 miles – Sneem (The Knot). Spectacularly situated on the estuary of the Sneem River and a popular walking base. The mountains which circle the town are dominated by Coomcallee on the left. There are a number of interesting craft shops. Continue along the N 70 to Castlecove.

DETOUR: Here a small unclassified road leads to Staigue Fort, one of Ireland's best-preserved ring forts, dating from c. 1000 BC.

Continue along the coast road, which skirts the foot of Eagles Hill, to Caherdaniel, and turn left for Derrynane House.

51 miles – Derrynane House (0900-1730 Nov.-mid Mar., 0900-1800 mid Mar.-June, 0900-1900 July & Aug., 0900-1700 Sep. & Oct.; £1, child 40p). The home of Daniel O'Connell (see **A-Z**), set in 120 hectares of impressive parkland. Return to Caherdaniel and turn left. The road rises again, passing beneath Cahernageeha and Farraniaragh mountains and through the Coomakesta Pass with wonderful sea views. The road descends into Waterville, affording views of Ballinskellings Bay and Bolus Head on the left and Lough Currane on the right.

63 miles – Waterville. Beautifully sited between lovely Lough Currane and Ballinskelligs Bay, this is a famous salmon fishing resort. It recently became a location for Club Med holidays, yet it can nonetheless be a desolate spot in winter. Follow signposts for Cahirciveen.

DETOUR: Three miles outside the town turn left for the villages of Ballinskelligs (see **A-Z**) and Portmagee, Valentia Island (see **A-Z**) and The Skelligs (see **A-Z**).

72 miles – Cahirciveen. There are plenty of bars serving pub food, and small restaurants. The Roman Catholic church here was erected to the memory of Daniel O'Connell in 1888 and both the cornerstone and arch keystone were a gift from the Pope. Continue on the N 70, with

2267 ft Knocknadobar to the left. Pass through Kells. A little further on, Kells Bay opens onto Dingle Bay on the left with views across the Dingle peninsula. Pass through Glenbeigh.
DETOUR: If it's a warm sunny day a visit to Rossbehy beach, a 4 mile sandy stretch, is a lovely way to spend a few hours relaxing. Take a left turn as you enter Glenbeigh. Keep on the N 70 to Killorglin.

99 miles – Killorglin. This small town on the River Laune derives its fame from the annual three-day Puck Fair (see **A-Z**). Nick's Bar and Restaurant has a well-deserved reputation for good food. In the village cross over the bridge and turn left, signposted Castlemaine. The Slieve Mish mountains are to the left across Castlemaine Harbour. Continue to Milltown and turn left to Castlemaine (famed in song by *The Wild Colonial Boy*), then following the signposts for Dingle.
ALTERNATIVE: Continue straight on for Tralee (see page 56).
After 2 miles, in Bolteens, there are views left across the bay towards MacGillicuddy's Reeks. Nine miles on is Inch, where there is a beautiful 4 mile strand. Keep on the coast road for about 6 miles then veer inland before taking a left turn outside Anascaul, signposted Dingle. Continue via Lispole, passing Dingle racecourse after another 4 miles.

123 miles – Dingle (see **A-Z**). Follow signposts for Ventry/Ballyferriter, turning right after about quarter of a mile. Continue alongside Dingle Harbour, home of Fungi the dolphin, into Milltown and turn left across the Milltown River, signed Murreagh. Follow signposts for Slea Head, skirting the harbour. There are views of Mount Eagle ahead across Ventry Harbour, and three ogham (see **A-Z**) standing stones on the right. In Ventry turn left and keep following signposts for Slea Head.

143 miles – Fahan. Only a hamlet but Dunbeg Promontory Fort is a short distance to the left. A mile outside Fahan is a right turn for the Fahan prehistoric beehive huts, just some of 400 *clochans* or huts in the area. Drive round Slea Head, in the shadow of Mount Eagle, with spectacular views of the Iveragh peninsula, The Skelligs and The Blaskets (see **A-Z**), and continue along the road into Coumeenoole, the site of yet more *clochans*, including one small modern hut. Continue into

Dunquin, turning left at the village crossroads. Clogher Head is on the left in just over a mile. Here the views stretch across the bay to Sybil Point, and in the distance are The Three Sisters, a strange rock formation. At the T-junction turn right, following signposts into Ballyferriter, a summer resort and Gaeltacht (see **A-Z**) village. The old schoolhouse is now a heritage centre. Keep straight on in the village, following signposts for Murreagh and Dingle. Cross a bridge and keep straight on. After another mile turn left, signposted Gallarus Oratory. The road now passes through a barren landscape dotted with ancient monuments. Turn right at the T-junction.

153 miles – Gallarus Oratory. This beautifully preserved oratory, measuring 10 ft x 15 ft inside, is one of the most important pieces of early Christian architecture in Ireland, dating possibly from the 9thC. The walls are 3.5 ft thick and so well fitted together that they have not fallen in. Traces of mortar have been found between the stones. There is a 4 ft cross pillar in the graveyard. Less than a mile west are the ruins of Gallarus Castle, which was once a Fitzgerald stronghold. Return to the T-junction and turn right. In the village of Murreagh – Smerwick Harbour is on the left – turn right and follow signposts for Feohanagh, passing a transmitter for Radio na Gaeltachta on the left. Drive past Ardamore and follow the road for views of the Cliffs of Dooneen on the left. Continue

via Feohanagh then take a sharp left, passing Ballydavid Head on the left before entering Ballycurrane. Half a mile on, turn right for Dingle. The road ascends with views of the Brandon mountains to the left, and at its highest point along the valley of the Milltown River to Dingle Harbour. Pass through Milltown again to return to Dingle.

166 miles – Dingle. Take a left turn at the Small Bridge Bar at the bottom of Main St and then take the right fork in the road, signposted Connor Pass Summit. This road should not be attempted except in the best of weather conditions and if possible should be traversed early in the morning when tourist traffic is at its lightest. Sheep traffic, however, is always heavy so drive slowly. Be prepared also to reverse, as many sections of the road are too narrow for cars to pass in opposite directions and, despite the hazards, bus tours continue to cross the pass. Nonetheless, in clear conditions the views are superb on the 4 mile ascent to the summit. After four more miles the white line reappears on the road.

DETOUR: A mile further a left turn takes you to beautiful Brandon Point and Brandon Mountain, overlooking Brandon and Tralee bays.

The road continues via Ballyduff into Stradbally overlooking Brandon Bay, with views out to the Seven Hogs or Magharee Islands.

DETOUR: To reach the seaside resort of Castlegregory and the narrow isthmus which separates Brandon and Tralee bays, take a left turn a mile outside Stradbally.

Continue along the main road into Blennerville, where there is a chance to stop at a renovated windmill (0930-1800 May-Nov.; £1). A restored narrow-gauge railway also operates here. Continue on the R 559.

196 miles – Tralee (see **A-Z**). Follow signposts for Killarney, taking the N 22 via Farranfore, where Ulick's bar and restaurant is a popular eating and night spot.

ALTERNATIVES: Take the N 69 for north Kerry, Listowel, the Tarbert ferry, Foynes (see **A-Z**) and Limerick city (see **LIMERICK CITY**, **A-Z**); or take the N 21, turning left in Castleisland (see **A-Z**) for Limerick city.

Continue to Killarney (216 miles).

King John's Castle

Shannon
COUNTIES
Clare & Limerick

Thomond Br
THE TREATY STONE
KING JOHN'S CASTLE
Athlunkard Street
Bridge St
ST. MARY'S CATHEDRAL
Clancy Strand
N18
River Shannon
Baal's Br
George's Quay
Charlotte Quay
Lock Quay
Ennis Rd
Broad St
HUNT MUSEUM
Callaghan Strand
Sarsfield Br
Donans Quay
Patrick Street
Michael Street
Ellen Street
John St
Sarsfield Street
Denmark Street
Mungret Street
Bedford Row
Henry Street
O'Connell Street
Robert St
John's Square
William Street
High Street
LIMERICK MUSEUM
Shannon Street
Thomas Street
Lr Gerald Griffin St
Lr Cecil St
Anne St
Wickham Street
Upr William St
Upr Cecil Street
Roches Street
Catherine Street
Lr Mallow Street
Henry Street
Glentworth Street
Sexton Street
Mulgrave St
Parnell Street
O'Connell Street
Mallow Street
Roxboro Road
Hartstonge Street
Upr Mallow St
Pery Square
CITY ART GALLERY
Rail & Bus Terminal
Barrington St
N20
People's Park
Botherbuoy

ST. MARY'S CATHEDRAL Bridge St, tel: 061-310293.
■ 0900-1300, 1430-1730 summer, 0900-1300, 1415-1700 winter.
Son et lumière 2115 mid June-mid Sep.
Founded in the 12thC in the oldest part of the city, the King's Island. Originally the site of a palace owned by Donal Mor O'Brien, one of the kings of Munster, who donated it for use as a church in 1172. There are 15thC stalls in the choir and the nave, whose carved misericords are the only surviving examples in Ireland. The cathedral provides a wonderful setting for a 45 min son et lumière show outlining the history of the city.

KING JOHN'S CASTLE Beside Thomond Bridge, tel: 061-411201.
■ 0930-1630. ● £3, child £1.50, family £7.
Built after a visit by King John in 1210, this imposing edifice overlooks the Shannon from the heart of Englishtown, in what was the old walled city. Excavations have uncovered artefacts dating from the 7thC. Quaker William Penn, who founded Pennsylvania, served as an officer in the garrison here and evangelist John Wesley preached within the walls.

LIMERICK MUSEUM John's Sq., tel: 061-417826.
■ 1000-1300, 1415-1700 Tue.-Sat. ● Free.
Viking coins, Fenian memorabilia, artefacts from Lough Gur *(see* **A-Z***).*

HUNT MUSEUM Plassey House, University of Limerick, Castletroy, tel: 061-333644. ■ 0930-1730 May-Sep. ● £1.60.
Probably Ireland's finest collection of Celtic and medieval treasures outside Dublin, presented to the nation by the late John Hunt, art historian.

CITY ART GALLERY Pery Sq., tel: 061-310663.
■ 1000-1300 Mon.-Sat., 1400-1800 Mon.-Fri. ● Free.
Housed in the Carnegie Building at the People's Park (lovely except for the graffiti), which was opened as a library and museum in 1906. Permanent collection of Irish art from the 18thC. Temporary exhibitions.

THE TREATY STONE Clancy Strand, beside Thomond Bridge.
The Treaty of Limerick ended a bloody siege by the army of William III in 1691. This is the stone on which it was signed.

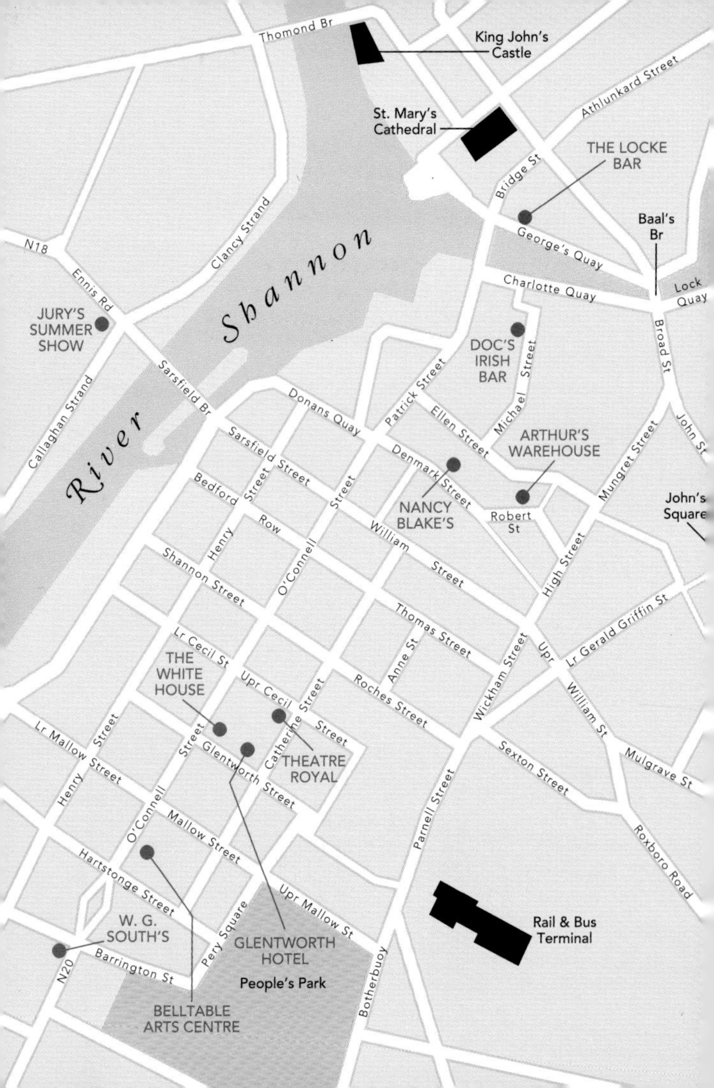

Thomond Br
King John's Castle
Athlunkard Street
St. Mary's Cathedral
THE LOCKE BAR
Bridge St
Baal's Br
George's Quay
Clancy Strand
N18
River Shannon
Charlotte Quay
Lock Quay
Ennis Rd
JURY'S SUMMER SHOW
DOC'S IRISH BAR
Broad St
Michael Street
Patrick Street
Sarsfield Br
Callaghan Strand
Donans Quay
Ellen Street
John St
ARTHUR'S WAREHOUSE
Mungret Street
Sarsfield Street
Denmark Street
Bedford Row
Henry Street
O'Connell Street
NANCY BLAKE'S
Robert St
John's Square
William Street
Shannon Street
High Street
Thomas Street
Lr Gerald Griffin St
Anne St
Lr Cecil St
Upr William St
THE WHITE HOUSE
Wickham Street
Upr Cecil Street
Roches Street
Catherine Street
THEATRE ROYAL
Lr Mallow Street
Glentworth Street
Sexton Street
Mulgrave St
Parnell Street
Mallow Street
Roxboro Road
Hartstonge Street
Upr Mallow St
W. G. SOUTH'S
Pery Square
Rail & Bus Terminal
GLENTWORTH HOTEL
Barrington St
N20
People's Park
Botherbuoy
BELLTABLE ARTS CENTRE

BELLTABLE ARTS CENTRE 69 O'Connell St, tel: 061-319886.
Drama, concerts, poetry readings and musical recitals. A season of Irish theatre is held during July and Aug.

THEATRE ROYAL Upper Cecil St, tel: 061-414244.
A full programme of drama, recitals and concerts.

JURY'S SUMMER SHOW Jury's Hotel, Ennis Rd, tel: 061-327777.
■ Wed. & Thu. evening, June-Sep. ● Moderate.
An evening of Irish music, song, dance and comedy. Choice of dinner and show, or show only.

GLENTWORTH HOTEL Glentworth St, tel: 061-413822.
Offers folk music Mon., Irish cabaret Tue. and ballroom dancing Wed. and Sun.

THE LOCKE BAR 3 George's Quay, tel: 061-413733.
Beautifully situated on the banks of the River Shannon. Regular traditional music and pub food.

DOC'S IRISH BAR Granary Courtyard, Michael St, tel: 061-417286.
In a renovated granary. Regular traditional music sessions. Popular with the younger age group.

ARTHUR'S WAREHOUSE 7 Robert St, tel: 061-417616.
Traditional music Mon. night. Restaurant. Bar food. Breakfasts served!

THE WHITE HOUSE (James Gleeson's), O'Connell St.
A genuine traditional pub. Usually a good bet for a peaceful pint.

NANCY BLAKE'S Denmark St, tel: 061-416443.
Traditional music Sun.-Wed., and a lovely spot for a quiet drink during the early evening or on music-free nights.

W. G. SOUTH'S The Crescent, tel: 061-318850.
A relaxed traditional-style pub.

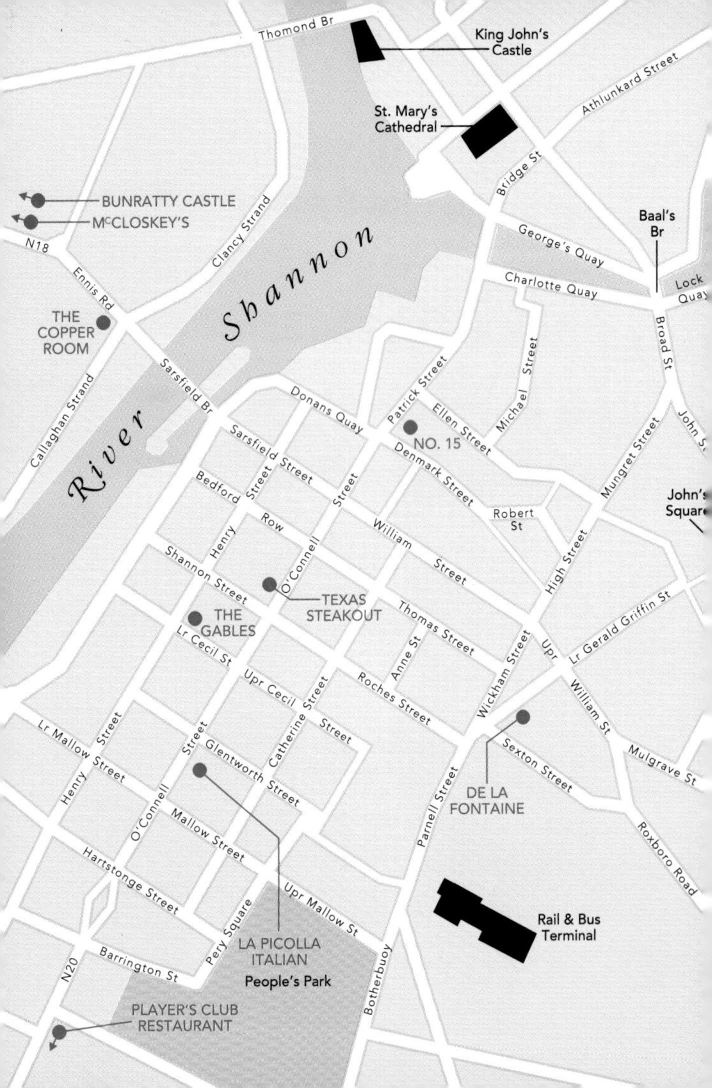
Thomond Br
King John's Castle
St. Mary's Cathedral
Athlunkard Street
Bridge St
BUNRATTY CASTLE
McCLOSKEY'S
Clancy Strand
Shannon
River
Baal's Br
George's Quay
Charlotte Quay
Lock Quay
N18
Ennis Rd
THE COPPER ROOM
Callaghan Strand
Sarsfield Br
Broad St
Patrick Street
Michael Street
Donans Quay
Ellen Street
NO. 15
John St
Sarsfield Street
Denmark Street
Mungret Street
John's Square
Bedford Row
Henry Street
O'Connell Street
Robert St
William Street
High Street
Shannon Street
TEXAS STEAKOUT
THE GABLES
Thomas Street
Lr Cecil St
Anne St
Wickham Street
Upr William St
Lr Gerald Griffin St
Upr Cecil Street
Catherine Street
Roches Street
Lr Mallow Street
Henry Street
Glentworth Street
Mulgrave St
Sexton Street
DE LA FONTAINE
Parnell Street
O'Connell Street
Mallow Street
Hartstonge Street
Roxboro Road
Upr Mallow St
Pery Square
Rail & Bus Terminal
Barrington St
N20
LA PICOLLA ITALIAN
People's Park
Botherbuoy
PLAYER'S CLUB RESTAURANT

THE COPPER ROOM Jury's Hotel, Ennis Rd, tel: 061-327777.
■ 1830-2200. ● Expensive.
French cuisine. The winner of award after award.

BUNRATTY CASTLE Bunratty, tel: 061-61788.
■ Details from tourist office. ● Expensive.
Medieval banquet with mead, music, song and dance. See **Bunratty**.

McCLOSKEY'S Bunratty House, Bunratty, tel: 061-364082.
■ 1900-2200 Tue.-Sat. (Feb.-Dec.). ● Expensive.
Excellent seafood, game and steaks. Well worth the drive. See **Bunratty**.

DE LA FONTAINE 10-12 Upper Gerald Griffin St, tel: 061-44461.
■ 1230-1430 Tue.-Fri., 1900-2200 Mon.-Sat. ● Moderate-expensive.
Beautifully cooked French cuisine. Very popular.

LA PICOLLA ITALIAN 55 O'Connell St, tel: 061-315844.
■ 1130-2400. ● Moderate.
Favourites like mushrooms in tomato and garlic, veal, pasta and chicken.

TEXAS STEAKOUT 116 O'Connell St, tel: 061-44440.
■ 1200-2330 Mon.-Sat., 1230-2330 Sun. ● Moderate.
Informal surroundings. Breaded mushrooms, chicken Milanese and steaks.

PLAYER'S CLUB RESTAURANT Punch's, Patrick's Cross, 1 mile on the N 20, tel: 061-27149/29588. ■ 1200-2200. ● Moderate.
Popular with business people. Also has a good bar food menu.

THE GABLES Lower Cecil St, tel: 061-42161.
■ 1100-2330 Mon.-Sat., 1300-2000 Sun. ● Inexpensive-moderate.
Home-made soups, roasts, daily specials and grills. Also Sun. lunches.

NO. 15 15 Patrick St, tel: 061-42200.
■ 1100-1800. ● Inexpensive.
Limited but enticing menu. Home-made soup, crepes, stir-fries, etc.

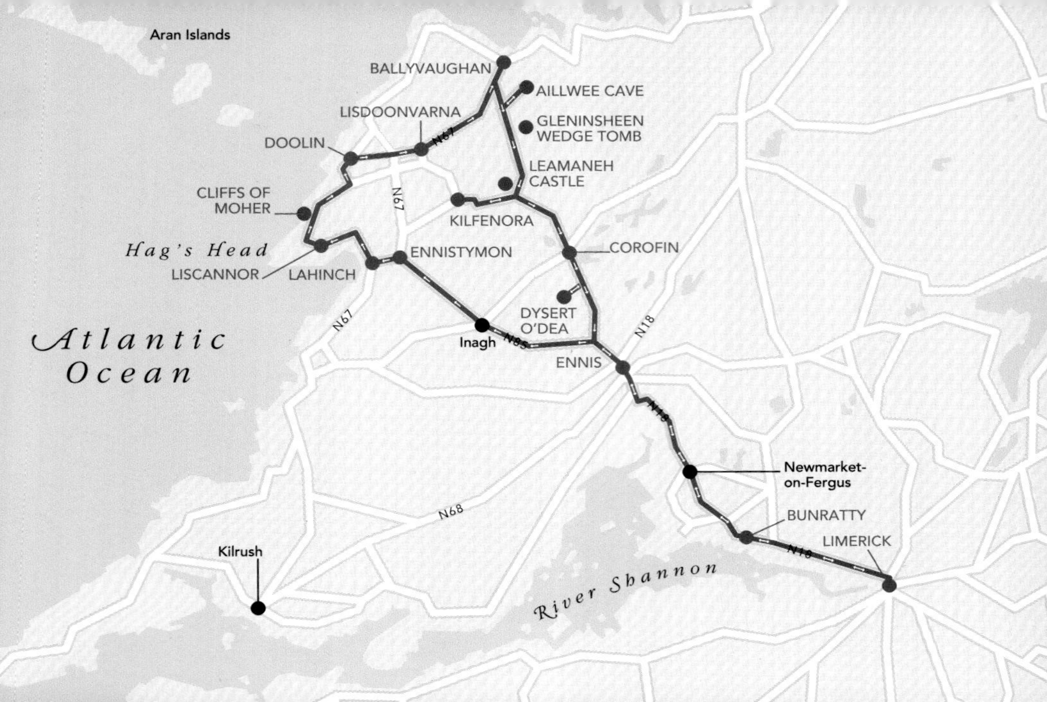
Aran Islands
BALLYVAUGHAN
AILLWEE CAVE
GLENINSHEEN
WEDGE TOMB
LISDOONVARNA
N67
DOOLIN
LEAMANEH
CASTLE
CLIFFS OF
MOHER
N67
KILFENORA
Hag's Head
ENNISTYMON
COROFIN
LISCANNOR
LAHINCH
N67
DYSERT
O'DEA
N18
Atlantic
Ocean
Inagh
N85
ENNIS
N18
Newmarket-
on-Fergus
N68
BUNRATTY
Kilrush
LIMERICK
N18
River Shannon

Cliffs of Moher

Limerick city–Ennis–Cliffs of Moher–The Burren–Limerick city.
Duration: 1-2 days.

Leave the city (see **LIMERICK CITY**, **A-Z**) on the N 18.
DETOUR: After 4 miles turn right for Cratloe Woods House (see **A-Z**).
On both sides is gently undulating agricultural and wooded land, and there are views of the Shannon estuary to the left.
8 miles – Bunratty (see **A-Z**). Continue on the N 18, following signposts for Ennis and Galway. Enter Newmarket-on-Fergus and turn left, and after 2 miles begin to skirt the walls of the Dromoland Castle (a luxury hotel) estate, which was the residence of Lord Inchiquin until 1962. The Fergus estuary is to the left. Continue past the walled estate of 17thC Carnelly House, through Clarecastle.
22 miles – Ennis (see **A-Z**). Leave on the N 85, veering left after 3 miles at Fountain Cross, signposted Ennistymon. The road passes a quarry and continues through hilly agricultural land into Inagh. A little further on there are views of small lakes to the left, while the Cullenagh River flows alongside below. On entering Ennistymon the ruined 16thC castle of Turlough O'Brien is on a hill to the left.
38 miles – Ennistymon. This market town, which still retains many outstanding old shop fronts, is noted for its fishing. The Cullenagh River rushes over slabs of rock but to see it at its most dramatic follow the Cascade Walk at the side of The Falls Hotel. Poet Brian Merriman, who wrote the celebrated satire *Cuirt An Mhean Oiche* (*The Midnight Court*), was born nearby c. 1757. There are a number of pubs here that seem to have been caught in a time warp, while others are filled with traditional music all year round. Turn left opposite O'Brien's Bakery, signposted Lahinch. After 2 miles the road ascends a hill and expansive views open up ahead.
40.5 miles – Lahinch. Very much a summer spot, when it buzzes with tourists, surfers, and families reopening their holiday homes or caravans. The golfers, however, tend to come year-round to play the championship course. The beach here is magnificent but swimming is not always safe, so check the lifeguards' flags. For food try the restaurant in the Atlantic Hotel or Mr Eamon's, which is beside the bakery on entering the town.

DETOUR: Follow the N 67 round the coast to the left for Milltown Malbay (venue for the Willie Clancy summer school of traditional music and dance) and peaceful Spanish Point, where many Armada vessels were wrecked in 1588.

Return to the roundabout on the town outskirts and follow the road past the golf course, signposted Liscannor. At O'Brien's Bridge, where the Dealagh River enters the sea, the road passes the ruins of Dough Castle, owned by Daniel O'Brien in the 17thC, and 15thC Kilmacreehy church. Donn, the Fairy King, is said to live in the sand holes round the castle! Ahead is the square tower of an ancient fort at Liscannor, formerly a stronghold of the O'Connors and the O'Briens. After about 2 miles there are views back across Liscannor Bay to Lahinch and the Rinneen Cliffs.

43.5 miles – Liscannor. It is this fishing village that gives Liscannor stone or slate (used in all the walls locally) its name. John P. Holland, the man who is attributed with inventing the submarine, was born here in 1841. He was a Fenian (see **A-Z**) and his work was financed in the USA by the Fenian movement, and intended for use against Britain. But after the US Navy used his model in 1900 the British built their first four submarines the following year, using Holland's design. Keep on the main road, with extensive sea views ahead, before it veers inland to Derreen.

DETOUR: Continue along the coast for spectacular Hag's Head, where the Cliffs of Moher begin.

The road cuts through stone-walled green pastures, and before long the walk to the summit of the Cliffs of Moher looms to the left ahead.

48 miles – Cliffs of Moher. Turn left into the car park beside the visitor centre, where there is the first taste of the rampant commercialization to come. Almost all the way up the trail to O'Brien's Tower there is someone trying to wheedle money. Any semblance of peace is usually shattered by the sound of 'entertainers' trying to flog tapes by playing their recordings at ear-piercing levels, while, for a charge, a man will allow you to photograph his tragic-looking dog perched on the back of his even sadder-looking donkey. The spectacular views, however, remain untainted, and you can walk away from the crowds along the cliffs, which stretch for 5 miles back to Hag's Head and ahead beyond O'Brien's Tower. The tower, which was erected as a teahouse in 1835 on the highest cliff, now houses a souvenir shop. On a clear day there are exceptional views of the Clare coast, the Aran Islands (see **A-Z**) and the mountains of Kerry and Galway. At their highest point the cliffs reach 668 ft. Return to the road and turn left. The walls made of Liscannor flagstone continue. After a mile, as the road descends, there are spectacular views stretching left to Inisheer and the other Aran Islands, down into Doolin, and across Galway Bay. Turn left after 3 miles, just past the petrol station. At the T-junction turn left.

54 miles – Doolin. The fishing village of Doolin, also known as Fisherstreet, is really a scattering of houses, pubs and hostels. This is one of two settlements in the area where people congregate, predominantly for music. In fact, without music Doolin would be just another dot on the map. The area is always mobbed throughout the summer but even in winter musicians and tourists come from far afield. In the lovely Ivy Cottage there are crafts for sale, while Lisa's Kitchen serves good home-cooking. Try O'Connor's for mussels, steak sandwiches, fresh fish, and music. Continue for another mile down to the pier, where it's less than a 30 min boat trip to Inisheer (up to 10 sailings daily, Mar.-Oct.). Do not attempt to swim here; there is a safe sandy cove nearby. Return past O'Connor's, keeping straight on at the T-junction for Doolin village. Here McGann's draws the crowds for pints, pub food and music. After less than a mile turn right, signposted Burren Tourist Trail/ Lisdoonvarna. The road leads through hilly land.

ALTERNATIVE: Keep straight on for a spectacular drive via Fanore and Black Head, meeting the excursion again at Ballyvaughan.

59 miles – Lisdoonvarna (see **A-Z**). To leave the town keep straight on at the crossroads. At the outskirts of The Burren (see **A-Z**) the fields become rocky. Flat-topped Slieve Elva is to the left. About a mile after passing a forest plantation The Burren opens up ahead, and the road winds treacherously down Corkscrew Hill with sea views of Ballyvaughan and Galway bays. Rocky outposts of The Burren flank the view ahead on both sides. Pass Greggan's Castle Hotel and at the next junction keep straight on, still flanked by the limestone hills.

70.5 miles – Ballyvaughan. This small fishing and market town is made picturesque by its thatched and slate cottages. The Burren Way walk is signposted from here. Monk's, on the quay, is an idyllic spot for lunch.

ALTERNATIVE: From here it is possible to follow the coast round to Galway city (see **GALWAY CITY, A-Z**).

Retrace the route for about a mile, watching out for signposts on the left to Aillwee Cave. Cross pastureland into the rocky Burren, turning left again after less than a mile and following signposts which point up a steep road to the cave. There are expansive views from the car park.

73 miles – Aillwee Cave (1000-1900 June-Aug., 1000-1800 Sep.-early Nov. & Mar.-May; £2.85, child £1.50). The centre which houses the entrance to this awe-inspiring two-million-year-old cave has been beautifully incorporated into The Burren landscape. Guided tours go about one-third of a mile into the cave, which features an underground river and a waterfall. If you are scared of the dark be prepared for a nerve-racking few minutes when the tour guide switches off the lights – pitch black is an understatement! The complex also contains a small restaurant and craft shop. Retrace the route, turning left, signposted Corofin. Almost immediately on the right, behind a wall, is an ancient earth ring fort, and within a few hundred yards another, just two of the hundreds of earthworks and monuments scattered throughout this barren region. Walls, incredibly, divide the landscape into stone fields. After about 2 miles Gleninsheen wedge tomb can be seen to the left. Keep following signposts for Corofin and after another mile the Poulabrone dolmen, the most famous of The Burren's portal dolmens, is on the left in front of a farm. It dates from 2500 BC. The road re-enters green but rocky pastureland before it goes left, signposted Corofin. After about a mile 15thC Carran church is on the left and the landscape begins to get bleak again. At the next junction keep straight on, signposted Corofin, flanked by hawthorn trees, turning right after 2 miles at Leamaneh Castle, signposted Kilfenora. The castle is a 17thC fortified house, which incorporates a 15thC O'Brien tower.

85 miles – Kilfenora. The Burren Display Centre helps to explain the archaeology, geology and legends of this fascinating area with the help of informative guides, displays and audiovisual presentations (1000-1300, 1400-1730 Mar.-May, Sep. & Oct., 0900-1900 June-Aug.; £2, child £1). The ruins of St. Fachtnan's Cathedral, built in the 12thC with 15thC alterations, are behind the centre. Among the contents of the cathedral is an effigy which is said to represent St. Fachtnan. In the

graveyard are three 12thC stone crosses. Of these the finest is Doorty Cross, which features some strange finger carvings. Return to Leamaneh Castle and veer right, signposted Ennis, driving though hilly grazing land. Pass through Killinaboy, with a ruined church on the right. A mile on there are sporadic views of beautiful Inchiquin Lough. It is the island, Inis Ui Chuinn, in the lake which gave the district and lake their name, and the O'Brien family its title (Lord Inchiquin).

94.5 miles – Corofin. Nestled between Inchiquin Lough and Lough Atedaun, this is a lovely fishing base. The Clare Heritage Centre is housed in a church off the Main St (1000-1800 April-Oct., 0900-1700 Mon.-Fri., Nov.-Mar.; £1). The centre's theme is 'Ireland West 1800-1860', covering the topics of famine (see **A-Z**), emigration and land tenure. There is also a genealogical research service. Follow the road through the village and past the lovely Old Schoolhouse. After 2.5 miles watch for a right turn, signposted Dysert O'Dea, and follow signposts for Dysert Archaeological Centre and Castle.

95.5 miles – Dysert O'Dea (see **A-Z**). Return to the road and turn right, following signposts for Ennis. From Ennis take the N 18 back to Limerick city (128 miles).

The West

COUNTIES

Galway, Mayo & Roscommon

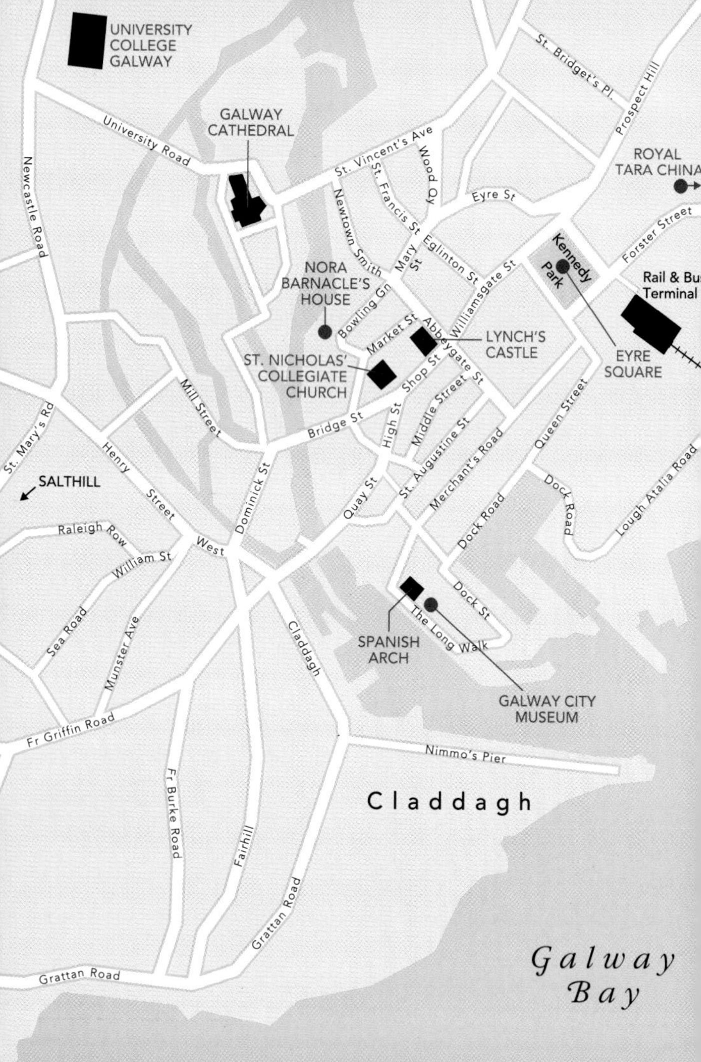

UNIVERSITY COLLEGE GALWAY
GALWAY CATHEDRAL
University Road
Newcastle Road
St. Vincent's Ave
Wood Qy
St. Francis St
Newtown Smith
Eyre St
St. Bridget's Pl.
Prospect Hill
ROYAL TARA CHINA
Forster Street
Kennedy Park
Rail & Bus Terminal
Eglinton St
Mary St
Williamsgate St
NORA BARNACLE'S HOUSE
Bowling Gn
Market St
Abbeygate St
LYNCH'S CASTLE
EYRE SQUARE
ST. NICHOLAS' COLLEGIATE CHURCH
Shop St
Middle Street
Mill Street
Bridge St
High St
St. Augustine St
Merchant's Road
Queen Street
St. Mary's Rd
Henry Street
SALTHILL
Dominick St
Quay St
Dock Road
Dock Road
Lough Atalia Road
Raleigh Row
West
William St
Sea Road
Munster Ave
Claddagh
SPANISH ARCH
The Long Walk
Dock St
GALWAY CITY MUSEUM
Fr Griffin Road
Nimmo's Pier
Claddagh
Fr Burke Road
Fairhill
Grattan Road
Grattan Road
Galway Bay

EYRE SQUARE
Originally an open space in front of the city's main gate, the square now includes the John F. Kennedy Memorial Park, developed in the mid-60s. Kennedy was the first American president to visit Ireland while in office, and received the freedom of Galway city a few months before his assassination in 1963. The Browne doorway, which was removed from the original Browne Mansion in Uppergate St in 1906, marks the entrance to the park. The centrepiece of the square is the Quincentennial Fountain, erected in 1984 to commemorate the 500th anniversary of Galway as a mayoral city. The fountain, designed by Eamon O'Doherty, depicts a Galway hooker, a traditional sailing boat. The cannon in the square were presented at the end of the Crimean War to the Connaught Rangers, British army recruits from the west of Ireland. In No. 19 Eyre Sq., a Bank of Ireland branch, the silver Sword of Galway (early 17thC) and the Great Mace (1710) are on display.

LYNCH'S CASTLE Junction of Shop St & Upper Abbeygate St.
■ Bank opening hours.
Dating from the early 16thC, this is one of the finest surviving town castles in Ireland and now houses a branch of the Allied Irish Bank. Though much altered, some features have been preserved, among them some gargoyles (a rare sight in Ireland), and the arms of Henry VII of England and the Lynch family.

ST. NICHOLAS' COLLEGIATE CHURCH Market St, tel: 091-64684. ■ 0900-1745 Mon.-Sat. (May-Sep.); 1000-1615 Mon.-Sat. (Oct.-April); after 1330 Sun. Guided tours Tue.-Fri. ● Donation.
Built in 1320 by the Anglo-Normans, enlarged in 1486, and much altered since. The current church preserves the shell of the medieval parish church and fragments of an earlier chapel. Inside the church are a 16thC font, a 15thC reader's desk (the 'confessional') and a number of gravestones set in the floor which feature symbols of crafts and professions. According to local tradition Christopher Columbus attended Mass here before setting off on his voyage of discovery which led to America. The church is a popular venue for lunchtime and evening musical recitals.

NORA BARNACLE'S HOUSE Bowling Green, tel: 091-64743.
■ 1000-1700 Mon.-Sat. (May-Sep.). ● £1, child 50p.
The home of Nora Barnacle, wife of James Joyce (see **A-Z***). Joyce visited his in-laws here and spent a three-week family holiday in the house in 1912. The house is re-furnished in the style of that time and has become a museum to the life and work of Nora and her husband.*

SPANISH ARCH
Built in 1594 as one of four arches to protect the quays where Spanish ships unloaded their cargoes. On the west bank of the Corrib estuary is The Claddagh. For many centuries this fishing village retained its own identity outside the city walls, even electing a king to lead the fishing fleet (see **Claddagh Ring***).*

GALWAY CITY MUSEUM Spanish Arch, tel: 091-68151.
■ 1000-1300, 1430-1700 summer. ● 50p.
Photographs and artefacts of the old city.

GALWAY CATHEDRAL University Rd, tel: 091-63577.
■ Daily. ● Donation.
The Cathedral of Our Lady Assumed into Heaven and St. Nicholas beside the salmon weir was built on the site of the old Galway Jail and dominates the city's skyline. The cut limestone building has Connemara marble floors. It was officially dedicated in 1965.

UNIVERSITY COLLEGE GALWAY University Rd, tel: 091-24411. ■ Grounds open daily.
Founded in 1845 as Queen's College. The original Tudor-style building (the 'Quad') was designed by Joseph B. Keane in the style of Oxford and Cambridge universities. The library contains the city's municipal records and many rare books but call first if you want to gain access.

ROYAL TARA CHINA Tara Hall, Mervue, tel: 091-51301.
■ Factory shop & visitor centre 0900-1800 Sep.-June; 0900-2100 July & Aug. Guided tours 1100 & 1500 Mon.-Fri. ● Free.
Exhibits of the 300-year-old craft of china making and decorating.

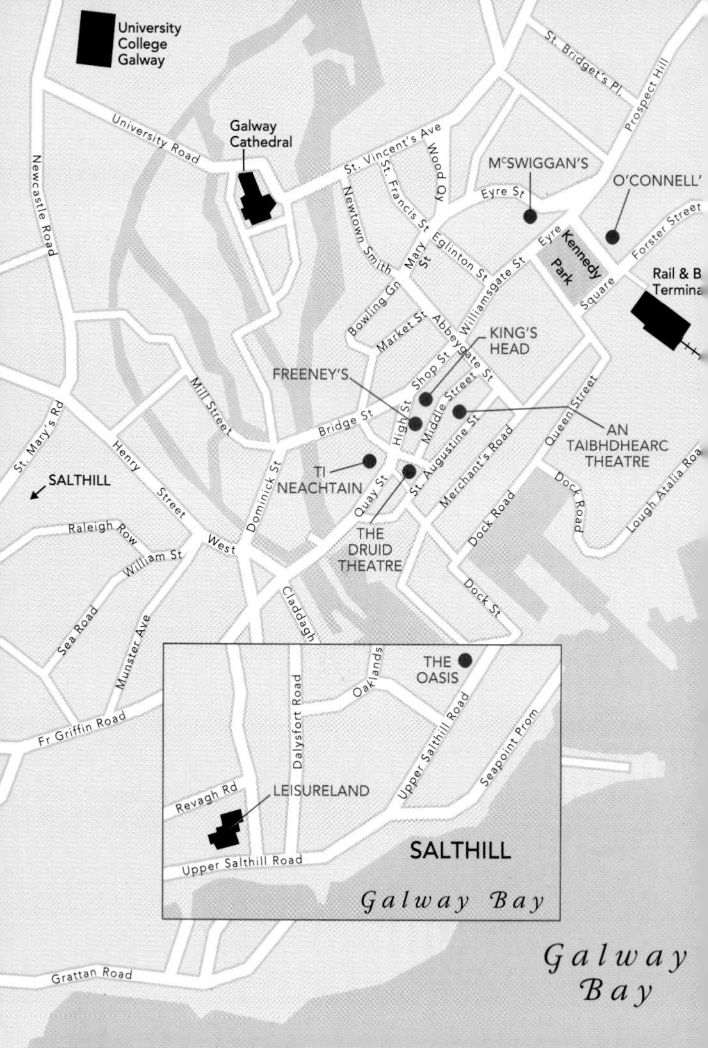
University College Galway
Galway Cathedral
University Road
Newcastle Road
St. Vincent's Ave
Wood Qy
St. Francis St
Newtown Smith
Mary St
Eglinton St
St. Bridget's Pl.
Prospect Hill
McSWIGGAN'S
Eyre St
O'CONNELL'
Eyre
Kennedy Park
Square
Forster Street
Rail & B
Termina
Williamsgate St
Bowling Gn
Market St
Abbeygate St
KING'S HEAD
Shop St
FREENEY'S
Middle Street
High St
Bridge St
Mill Street
AN TAIBHDHEARC THEATRE
Queen Street
St. Mary's Rd
SALTHILL
Henry Street
Dominick St
TI NEACHTAIN
Quay St
St. Augustine St
Merchant's Road
Dock Road
Dock Road
Lough Atalia Roa
THE DRUID THEATRE
Raleigh Row
William St
West
Sea Road
Munster Ave
Claddagh
Dock St
Fr Griffin Road
THE OASIS
Oaklands
Dalysfort Road
Upper Salthill Road
Seapoint Prom
Revagh Rd
LEISURELAND
SALTHILL
Upper Salthill Road
Galway Bay
Galway Bay
Grattan Road

AN TAIBHDHEARC THEATRE Middle St, tel: 091-62024.
The national Irish-language theatre, founded in 1928. Taibhdhearc na Gaillmhe produces and hosts shows throughout the year, including a special bilingual show for foreign visitors during the summer.

THE DRUID THEATRE Chapel Lane, tel: 091-68617.
This company has won international acclaim for its revivals of Anglo-Irish classics. The productions are predominantly by Irish playwrights.

LEISURELAND Salthill, tel: 091-21455.
Concert and drama venue in tacky amusement centre.

THE OASIS Salthill, tel: 091-22715.
Just one of the nightclubs and discos which abound in Salthill. Popular with students. Casual, so a definite no-no for the pinstripe suit!

TI NEACHTAIN Quay St, tel: 091-66172.
You can hear occasional informal music, enjoy cheap and wholesome hot and cold lunches, and perhaps spot a famous face or two in this traditional bar. There's also an excellent, though expensive, restaurant.

O'CONNELL'S 8 Eyre Sq., tel: 091-63634.
One of the city's oldest and most traditional pubs, and just the spot for a quiet pint. Renovated in 1929, it retains many of its original features.

McSWIGGAN'S 3 Eyre St, tel: 091-61972.
Large traditional-style pub with plenty of atmosphere. Regular folk, blues and traditional music. Great bar lunches. Restaurant upstairs.

KING'S HEAD Shop St, tel: 091-66630.
A gift to a Galway soldier from the British parliament in 1649, in gratitude for his role in Charles I's execution. Sun. morning jazz is a 'must'.

FREENEY'S High St, tel: 091-62609.
Traditional long bar; feels like you're drinking in someone's kitchen. It's also a sports shop, which explains the fishing tackle in the window!

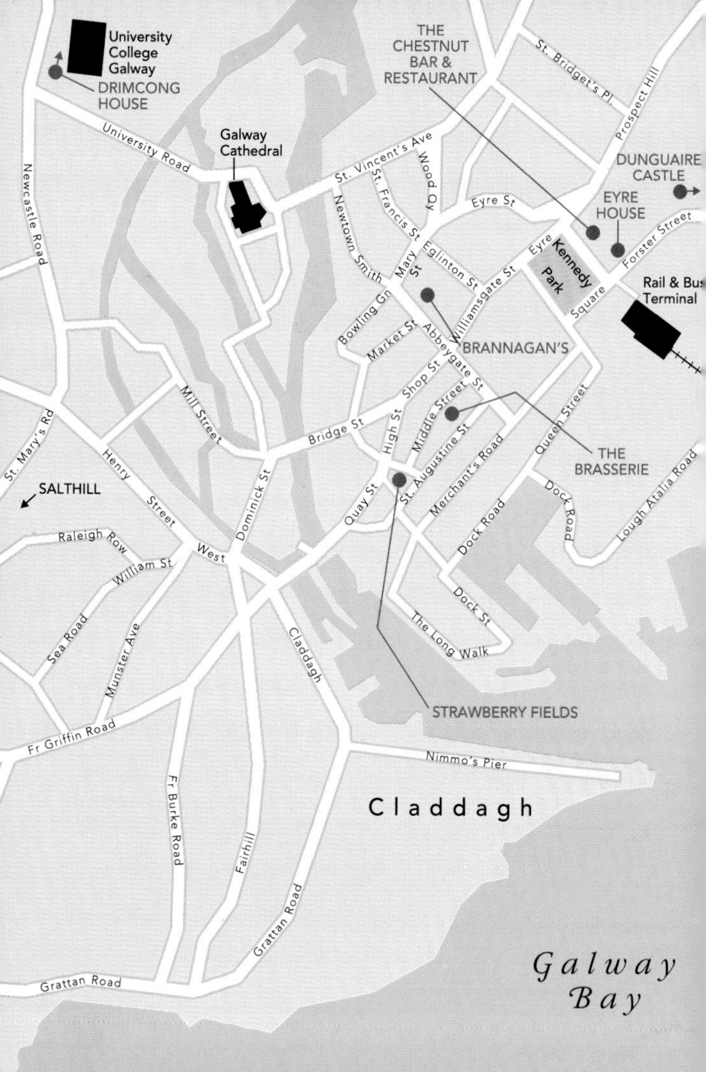

University College Galway
DRIMCONG HOUSE
THE CHESTNUT BAR & RESTAURANT
St. Bridget's Pl.
Prospect Hill
Galway Cathedral
University Road
St. Vincent's Ave
Wood Qy
DUNGUAIRE CASTLE
EYRE HOUSE
Eyre St
St. Francis St
Newtown Smith
Newcastle Road
Forster Street
Eyre
Kennedy Park
Square
Rail & Bus Terminal
Mary St
Eglinton St
Williamsgate St
Bowling Gn
Market St
Abbeygate St
BRANNAGAN'S
Shop St
Middle Street
Mill Street
St. Mary's Rd
Bridge St
High St
St. Augustine St
Queen Street
THE BRASSERIE
Henry
Merchant's Road
Lough Atalia Road
SALTHILL
Dominick St
Quay St
Street
Dock Road
Dock Road
Raleigh Row
West
William St
Dock St
Sea Road
The Long Walk
Munster Ave
Claddagh
STRAWBERRY FIELDS
Fr Griffin Road
Nimmo's Pier
Claddagh
Fr Burke Road
Fairhill
Grattan Road
Galway Bay
Grattan Road

DUNGUAIRE CASTLE Kinvara, 17 miles on the N 67, tel: 061-61788. ■ 1745 & 2100 May-Sep. ● Expensive.
Medieval banquets followed by light-hearted recitals from the works of J. M. Synge (see **A-Z***), W. B. Yeats (see* **A-Z***) and Oliver St. John Gogarty.*

DRIMCONG HOUSE Moycullen, 8 miles on the N 59, tel: 091-85115. ■ 1900-2230 Tue.-Sat. (Mar.-Dec.). Reservation recommended. ● Moderate-expensive.
Well worth the trip from town. Exciting five-course set menu for both carnivores and vegetarians. Home-grown vegetables and home-baked bread (try the onion variety). The cheese board offers a chance to sample the best of Irish.

THE CHESTNUT BAR & RESTAURANT 3 Eyre Sq., tel: 091-65800. ■ 1230-1430, 1830-2200. Bar food 1200-2130. ● Moderate-expensive.
The best of seafood and home-cooking.

EYRE HOUSE Forster St, tel: 091-64924. ■ 1230-1500, 1730-2200 Mon.-Sat., 1230-2130 Sun. ● Moderate-expensive.
Set lunches. Extensive à la carte menu featuring steaks, seafood, fresh salmon, veal and chicken.

BRANNAGAN'S 39 Upper Abbeygate St, tel: 091-65974. ■ 1230-2130 Mon.-Wed. ● Moderate.
A varied menu with pizzas, pastas, seafood and even shark and alligator steaks!

THE BRASSERIE Middle St, tel: 091-61610. ■ 1200-2100 Mon.-Sat. ● Moderate.
Pizzas and ribs, and barbeques in summer.

STRAWBERRY FIELDS Lower Cross St, tel: 091-62202. ■ 0930-1730 Mon.-Sat. ● Inexpensive.
American-look diner with hot sandwich and ice-cream specialities.

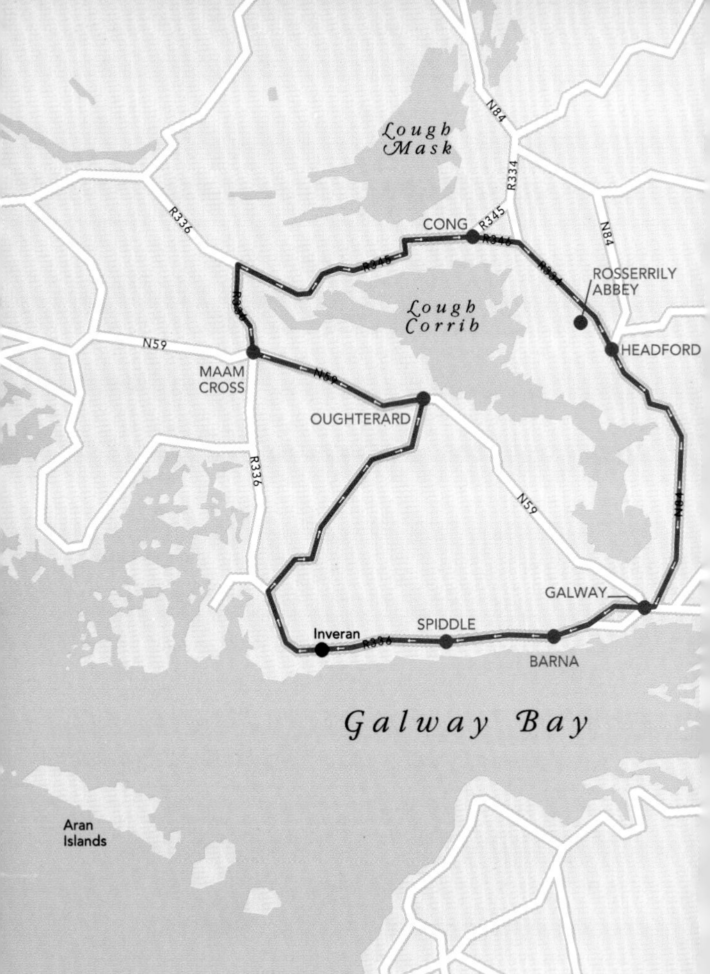

Lough Mask
N84
R334
R345
CONG
R346
R336
R345
R334
ROSSERRILY ABBEY
N84
Lough Corrib
N59
HEADFORD
MAAM CROSS
N59
OUGHTERARD
R336
N59
N84
GALWAY
SPIDDLE
Inveran
R336
BARNA
Galway Bay
Aran Islands

Lough Corrib

Galway city–Oughterard–Cong–Galway city. Duration: 1 day.

From Galway (see **GALWAY CITY**, **A-Z**) take the R 336 through the suburb of Salthill, a long-established, somewhat shabby seaside resort. Drive along the promenade; the hills of Clare can be seen across the bay and the Aran Islands (see **A-Z**) to the southwest.

DETOUR: A left turn after 3 miles leads to Silver Strand, a popular bathing spot.
Enter Barna, where Donnelly's and The Twelve Pins Pub are popular with city residents. Continue along the coast via Furbo.
12 miles – Spiddle. Just before entering the village the picturesque Spiddle Craft Centre is on the right, opposite the beach. Open all year round, its cottages house a collection of workshops showing ceramics, sculpture, weaving and jewellery. Bol Uisce, on the right of the street, is a renowned seafood eatery. Two hundred yards outside the village is the turn for the main pier, where a boat leaves for the Aran Islands three times a day. Continue via Knock and Inveran. After the derelict garage turn right, signposted Casla.
ALTERNATIVE: Keep left for Rossaveel, a fishing harbour and embarkation point for the Aran Islands, and the coastal route to Clifden (see **A-Z**). From Casla the latter goes through Gortmore, Kilkieran, Carna (see **A-Z**), Glinsk, Cashel and Roundstone (see **A-Z**), and a desolate but often spectacular landscape. Mannin Bay, on the last stretch into Clifden, has many beautiful beaches, including a coral strand.
About 2.5 miles from the garage turn right onto an unclassified road, signposted Uachtar Ard. This road should be driven with caution but the journey across mountainous bogland offers some splendid views of the numerous small lakes which dot the landscape, and of Lough Corrib as you descend into Oughterard.

Galway

38 miles – Oughterard. At the edge of Lough Corrib, this is a renowned angling centre. Turn left onto the N 59, then immediately right over the Owenriff River. The road leads into Connemara (see **A-Z**).
ALTERNATIVE: By turning right in Oughterard it is possible to travel back into Galway city, a distance of 17 miles, with a stop at Aughnanure Castle (see **A-Z**).
The landscape becomes bleaker after a few miles.
49 miles – Maam Cross. The crossroads of the West. Turn right onto the R 336.
ALTERNATIVE: Continue straight on for a spectacular drive to Clifden, passing in the shadow of the Maumturks and The Twelve Pins.
The R 336 traverses desolate, open countryside before crossing over higher land, and Leckavrea mountain (2012 ft) looms to the left. Continue in the shadow of the Maumturk range to Maam Bridge and cross the Bealanabrack River, turning right onto the R 345. The view of Lough Corrib on the right includes the island ruins of Hen's Castle or Castle Kirke. According to legend this stronghold was built by a witch and her magical hen in a night and a day, and given to O'Flaherty, husband of Grace O'Malley (see **A-Z**). His life, the witch told him, depended on the hen because if the castle was ever besieged it would lay

Riverside, Galway

enough eggs to feed him and his troops. But O'Flaherty was either too sceptical or sick of eating omelettes, for when the castle came under siege he killed and cooked the hen, and was shortly forced to surrender due to starvation. Continue through barren landscape and the village of Cornamona, keeping alongside the lake for almost 3 miles before the route turns inland again. Turn right, signposted Cong, after the road rises steeply and follow the unclassified route through Cong Woods.

65 miles – Cong (see **A-Z**). Leave the village on the R 346. About 3 miles on in Cross turn right onto the R 334. The road passes the ruins of Moyne Castle on the right, and the ruins of Kinlough Castle and a 13thC church on the left. About 6 miles along are the ruins of Ross, or Rosserrily, Abbey, founded in 1351 and re-founded by a group of Franciscans in 1498. It was finally abandoned in 1765. Some small cloisters in the church are well preserved, as are the abbey's kitchen and other domestic buildings.

75 miles – Headford. A market town and angling centre. The surrounding countryside is rich in ancient remains, particularly ring forts. For the last, and most uninteresting, 17 mile stretch of the trip, join the N 84, passing the ruins of Ballindooly Castle on the right after about 14 miles, into Galway city (92 miles).

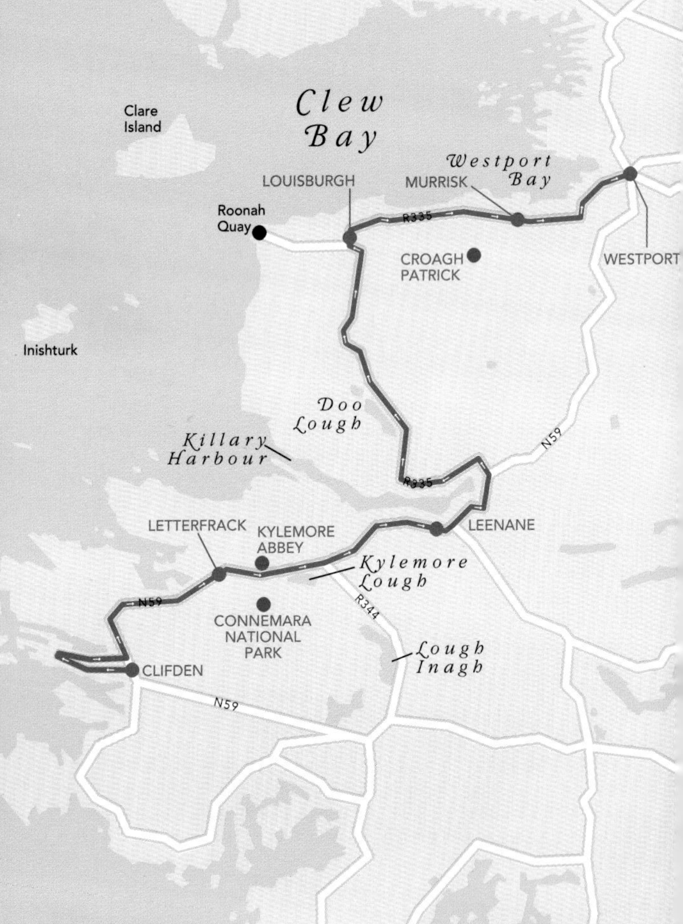
Clew Bay
Clare Island
Westport Bay
LOUISBURGH
MURRISK
Roonah Quay
R335
CROAGH PATRICK
WESTPORT
Inishturk
Doo Lough
Killary Harbour
N59
R335
LEENANE
LETTERFRACK
KYLEMORE ABBEY
Kylemore Lough
N59
R344
CONNEMARA NATIONAL PARK
Lough Inagh
CLIFDEN
N59

Connemara

Clifden–Westport. Duration: 1 day. See **Connemara**.

Leave Clifden (see **A-Z**) on the unclassified but signposted Sky road. The road first follows the line of Clifden Bay, rising to cliff-top level and providing spectacular views of the Atlantic and the bay islands. After 4 miles keep right to follow the shore of Streamstown Bay. The mountains ahead in the distance are the Twelve Pins. After another 3.75 miles veer left onto the N 59 towards Letterfrack, leaving behind the breathtaking coastal scenery for barren countryside.

DETOUR: In Streamstown turn left for Cleggan, where ferries run to lovely Inishbofin (see **A-Z**); and Claddaghduff, where you can walk out to picturesque and peaceful Omey Island, tides permitting.

The route offers views of the Twelve Pins to the right, and then Ballynakill Harbour on returning to the coast. Near Letterfrack watch out for a right turn, signposted National Park.

17.5 miles – Connemara National Park. The park is controlled by the Office of Public Works to conserve the bogs, mountains, flora and fauna in this beautiful area. It covers 5000 acres of countryside, including part of the Twelve Pins range, and offers both challenging and relaxing walks. The visitor centre, about 400 yd into the park, contains exhibitions, an audiovisual show and details of nature trails (1000-1630 June-Sep.; £1, child 40p). The staff can usually suggest safe hiking routes for experienced and inexperienced walkers. The centre also includes free kitchen facilities and an indoor eating area for hikers. Return to the main road and turn right.

18 miles – Letterfrack. This tiny village on the corner of Barnaderg Bay was founded by a 19thC Quaker as one of a series of mission settlements along the north Connemara coast.

DETOUR: A byroad on the left in the village leads to Tully Cross and a series of sandy beaches. Nearby, what is now the Renvyle House Hotel was once the residence of Oliver St. John Gogarty, writer, surgeon and wit. A mile west of the house is a ruined castle, and beyond that a dolmen and ruined church.

Leaving Letterfrack the road traverses the Pass of Kylemore, bounded to the left by Doughruagh mountain and the Pins to the south.

20 miles – Kylemore Abbey. Nestled in a rhododendron-filled hollow,

Killary Harbour

this mock-Tudor building was constructed for British shipping magnate and Irish politician Mitchell Henry. Since 1920 it has been a convent of the Benedictine Dames Irlandaise, and a girls' boarding school now also occupies the house. A coffee shop and pottery showrooms are open to visitors but the house remains private. It is possible, however, to walk through the wooded grounds to the Gothic chapel, which has a Connemara marble interior. Near the church is Taghallai, a pre-Christian tomb. Continue along the N 59 as it skirts the shoreline of Kylemore Lough. To the right, beyond the lake, a 'famine road', built to give work during the famine (see **A-Z**) of the 1840s, ascends the valley to Lough Inagh and Recess. Past the lake the Maumturk mountains appear on the right and the road descends to the shores of Killary Harbour, a picturesque 10 mile-long fjord. Across the harbour are the Mweelrea mountains. The range is dominated by its namesake, which at 2688 ft is the highest peak in Connacht.

30 miles – Leenane. The location for the film *The Field.* This hamlet is a popular angling centre and a base for hikers. Drop into Hamilton's or Gaynor's for a jar. Turn left in the village on the N 59 for Westport, following the south shores of Killary Harbour, with the peak of Devilsmother to the right. After 2 miles, at Aasleagh church, take a left turn on the R 335 for Louisburgh. Cross the Erriff River, with the beautiful Aasleagh Falls to the right, and continue along the harbour shores for about 4 miles, before turning inland along the Bundorragha River valley. At Delphi Bridge (named by Lord Sligo who thought it comparable to the Delphi in Greece!), follow the shores of lovely but sometimes sombre Doo Lough through the Doo Lough Pass, which was constructed in 1806. Continue out of the valley, flanked by the Sheeffry hills to the right.

48 miles – Louisburgh. According to one story, this 18thC village was named after Louisa Browne whose family founded the settlement; according to another after Louisburgh, Nova Scotia in honour of Henry Browne (uncle of the 1st Marquess of Sligo) who was present at its capture in 1758. The Grainne Mhaol Interpretative Centre is on Chapel St (1000-1800 Sun.-Fri., 1000-1600 Sat., June-mid Oct.; £1, child 50p). This provides a fascinating insight into the life of the famous pirate queen (see **O'Malley**) and the area's history and archaeological monuments. Clare Island (see **A-Z**), O'Malley's stronghold, can be reached by boat from Roonah Quay, 5 miles northwest of the village. Sailings are twice daily. Follow the R 335 for lovely views while skirting Clew Bay, with its many sandy beaches, via Leckanvey.

56 miles – Murrisk. This tiny village lies at the foot of Croagh Patrick (see **A-Z**) and a footpath leads to the top. Continue along the R 335 around the shores of Westport Bay.

60 miles – Westport House (1400-1700 May-Sep.; £2, child £1). The seat of the Marquess of Sligo, also known as Lord Altamount, it was designed in 1730 by Richard Cassels around an earlier building, with later additions by Thomas Ivory and James Myatt. The majority of the mahogany in the house was brought from Jamaica by the 1st Marquess, who served as governor there. A zoo and some tacky commercial ventures sit uncomfortably alongside the splendour of the house and garden but the revenue they bring in has probably been the house's salvation.

61 miles – Westport. Tourist Information, The Mall, tel: 098-25711. The town was laid out by an unknown architect in 1780 for the 2nd Earl of Altamount, who had married a sugar heiress. Even today some of its former elegance is preserved, particularly around The Octagon, its tree-lined mall, and the canalized river. During its heyday in the 18thC it was a prosperous town, trading in linen and yarn. It boasts many lively pubs, with music most nights, and a good choice of places to eat.

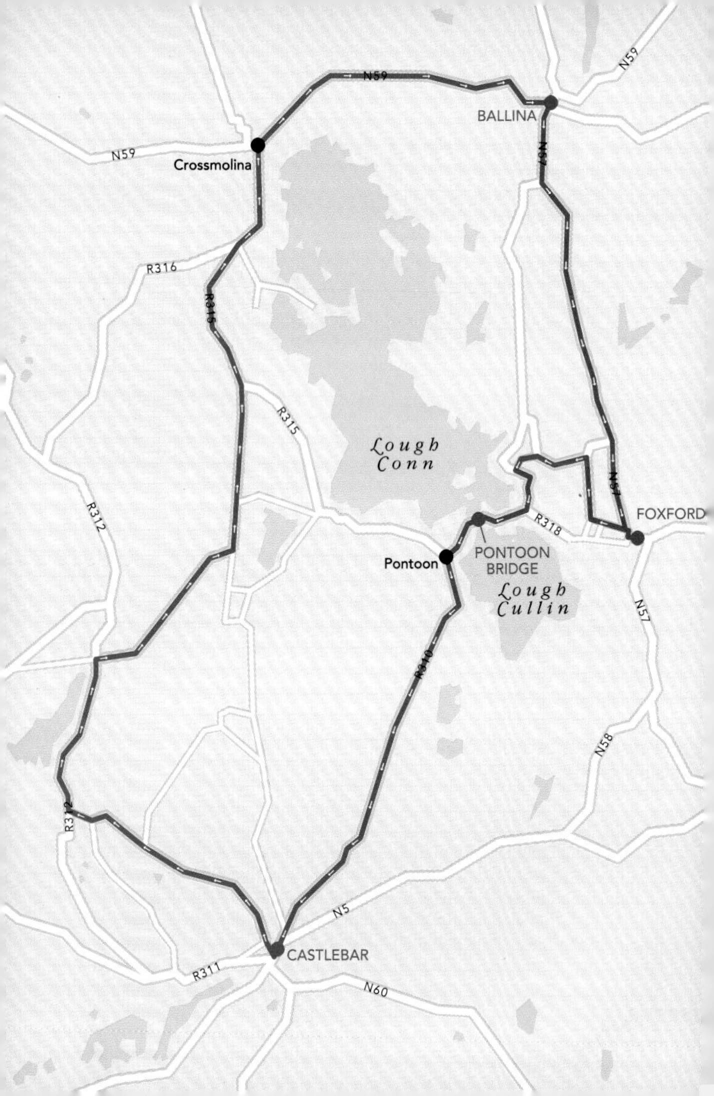
N59
N59
N59
BALLINA
Crossmolina
N57
R316
R315
R315
Lough Conn
R312
N57
FOXFORD
R318
PONTOON BRIDGE
Pontoon
Lough Cullin
N57
R310
N58
R312
N5
CASTLEBAR
R311
N60

Lough Conn

Castlebar–Ballina–Foxford–Castlebar. Duration: 1 day.

Leave Castlebar (see **A-Z**) via the Rathbawn road. Follow the narrow country road which passes through forestry plantations and bogland. To the right the highest peak, with a TV transmitter near its summit, is Croaghmoyle. After 3 miles there are outstanding views of the approaching Nephin Beg mountains. The highest of the range visible is Birreencorragh (2295 ft). A mile further there are views of Beltra Lough at the foot of the mountains, and about 1.5 miles on, just past a church, the road meets the R 312. Keep straight on. A little further on are the shores of Lough Beltra. Birreencorragh is to the right, and the range's namesake rises up ahead. At the lake-end watch out for a right turn before a converted schoolhouse, signposted Lahardaun. This route goes through Glen Nephin, where expansive boglands stretch to the Nephin Beg mountains to the left, and to the hills sloping to the right and ahead. After almost 4 miles take a left turn at a T-junction signposted Crossmolina. Two miles on there are glimpses of Lough Conn to the right, before Lahardaun. Keep straight on along the stone-walled road, veering right after 3 miles, signposted Rake Street.
DETOUR: About a mile further on is a right turn for ruined Errew Abbey, founded in 1413. It is on a slender peninsula jutting out into the lough.
Continue into Crossmolina. Take the N 59, signposted Ballina.
DETOUR: Take the R 315 north to Downpatrick Head (a bracing 5 mile walk from the road), Killala (see **A-Z**), and 15thC Rosserk and Moyne abbeys, just two of the religious settlements burned by Richard Bingham, English governor of Connacht, in the 16thC.
ALTERNATIVE: Turn left for the Mullet peninsula (see **A-Z**).
Follow the road through agricultural land and woodland into Ballina.
29 miles – Ballina (see **A-Z**). Take the N 57 south, signposted Foxford, following the River Moy upstream.
39 miles – Foxford (see **A-Z**). Leave on the R 318, signposted Pontoon. After less than a mile drive over a level crossing and veer right immediately, signposted Scenic Road. This narrow road rises with the Ox mountains to the right and some of the Nephin Begs to the left. After half a mile take a sharp left turn at a schoolhouse. The road continues to climb into the hills for almost a mile before reaching its highest point

under Stoneparkbrogan Hill. The views before you take in Lough Conn and the Nephins ahead, and Lough Cullin. Continue on with views of Lough Cullin to the left and forest plantations on the right. After about half a mile turn left and then take the next right fork. This bad road leads past small farmhouses to a car park with wonderful views overlooking Lough Conn, its many islets and the Nephins behind. Follow the road which falls steeply to the lake shore and turn left on the R 310. Cross over Pontoon Bridge, which divides Lough Cullin and Lough Conn, and skirt Lough Cullin's shores into the hamlet of Pontoon. Turn left, signposted Castlebar. After a short distance the road veers inland into bogland and then into slightly more hospitable agricultural land before entering Ross West. From here the route passes through bogland and poorer pastures, with views ahead to the Partry mountains, back into Castlebar (53 miles).

Castlebar

The Midlands

COUNTIES

Longford, Westmeath, Offaly & Laois

Fore Abbey

LONGFORD
N5
Lisryan
N55
CASTLEPOLLARD
COOLE
R395
EDGEWORTHSTOWN
R393
ARDAGH
TULLYNALLY
CASTLE
FORE
Collinstown
MOYDOW
R398
Lough
Derravaragh
N4
CROOKEDWOOD
R392
NEWTOWN
CASHEL
Lough
Owel
N55
BALLYMAHON
R392
R393
N52
MULLINGAR
N4
Lough
Ree
Lough
Ennell
R400
R390
GLASSAN
N55
BELVEDERE
HOUSE &
GARDENS
N52
N61
ATHLONE
N6
MOATE
HORSELEAP
N6
N6
N62
KILBEGGAN
N6

The Midlands

Athlone–Longford–Mullingar–Athlone. Duration: 1-2 days.

Leave Athlone (see **A-Z**) at the exit for the N 55 on the northern bypass, signposted Ballymahon, passing after a few miles through the village of Ballykeeran. It is possible to park and enjoy the marvellous views of Lough Ree to the left before arriving in Glassan, where there is a lovely craft shop and the excellent Village Restaurant in an old schoolhouse. Three miles outside the village is the start of Oliver Goldsmith (1728-74) country. Much of his writings and poetry are based around this area where he was born and went to school, and an annual summer school is held in Ballymahon. The places which inspired his poems are sign-posted.

11.5 miles – Ballymahon. Built on the Inny River, which offers good fishing. If you decide to stay here the Bog Lane Theatre Company is a vibrant amateur group. Leave the town heading for Lanesborough, taking a left turn, signposted Elfeet Bay and Newtown Cashel, after 3.5 miles. This is a narrow road with sharp turns. At a T-junction after just over 5 miles take a left for Newtown Cashel, a picturesque spot which has won the national Tidy Towns competition. Note the extensive use of stone walls. Barley Harbour on the shores of Lough Ree, 3 miles from the village, offers an opportunity to enjoy extensive lake views. While there call on Michael Casey, an expert wood sculptor, who specializes in producing pieces from bog oak. Return to Newtown Cashel and follow signposts for Lanesborough, turning right after about a mile, signposted Longford. After 3.5 miles turn right, and then immediately left at the staggered crossroads. The road leads through extensive boglands. Ask locally about the ancient roadway uncovered by archaeologists some years ago in Corlea Bog, between here and the village of Keenagh. Reputed to be one of the oldest known roadways in Ireland, it was preserved by the boggy soil and is a major archaeological find. Continue to a T-junction, following signposts for Moydow. Moydow is just over 1.5 miles on and there is the chance to stop at the Vintage pub and restaurant. Continue on the Longford road, taking a right turn after less than a mile (no signpost) which leads after 3.5 miles to Ardagh, a picturesque village. It has consistently won awards in the Tidy Towns competition. All its old buildings and walls have been beautifully maintained and their stonework preserved. Follow signposts for Longford, entering the town past the golf club after about 7 miles.

42.5 miles – Longford. Pop: 5000. Though there is not a huge amount to see, this busy market town is one of the Midlands' liveliest spots, especially for discos and live bands. The imposing limestone Cathedral of St. Mel was built in 1856. For quick, high-quality bar food, day or evening, try the Market Bar on Market Sq. The best evening meals are served at the Companion Restaurant, Killashee St.

DETOUR: Three miles away on the Ballinalee road is Carrigglas Manor (1330-1730 Mon. & Thu.-Sat., 1400-1800 Sun., mid June-Sep.; £3, child £2). This Gothic revival-style manor was built in 1857 and still contains its original furniture. The magnificent stables were designed by James Gandon, and are the only surviving example of his agricultural architecture. There is also a costume and lace museum.

Leave Longford on the main Dublin road, a long straight stretch into Edgeworthstown, named after the Edgeworth family, of which early-19thC author Maria Edgeworth (*Castle Rackrent*) was a member. Turn left onto the Granard road, and then right for Castlepollard on the R 395. After 5.5 miles turn right at the Crossroads Inn, Lisryan, signposted Castlepollard, passing through the lovely village of Coole after another 5.5 miles. The road leads mainly through bogland and during the summer people will be seen 'saving' the turf for use as fuel. Watch out after another 3 miles for a right turn into Tullynally Castle (beware of the ramps).

65.5 miles – Tullynally Castle (House 1430-1800 mid July-mid Aug. or by appointment, tel: 044-61159. Garden daily. House £2. Garden £1). This is the home of the Pakenhams, earls of Longford since 1655, and the biggest castle in Ireland still lived in as a family home. The impressive castle is set in 30 acres of breathtaking woodland and gardens, and has a good collection of portraits and furniture, and some fascinating 19thC gadgets. Return to the road and turn right into Castlepollard, laid out English-style round a green. Take the Oldcastle road and after 3 miles turn right at the crossroads. The scenery here is unusual for the Midlands, with hills and forests, and after a short distance Fore Abbey can be seen above to the left.

70.5 miles – Fore. This was the site of a monastery founded in AD 630

The Jealous Wall, Belvedere House

by St. Fechin. The remains of St. Fechin's Church, an anchorite's cell and a 13thC Benedictine friary can still be seen. The Seven Wonders Bar has information about the 'Seven Wonders of Fore', which include: the water that won't boil; the tree that won't burn; and the water that flows uphill! Continue past the Ben Breeze Open Farm (daily April-Sep.) after a mile. A mile further on take a right turn for Collinstown. After a short distance Lough Lene is to the right. Continue, crossing a main road, through Collinstown. Yield the right of way after 5 miles and take a left turn on the the main Mullingar road. Pass through Crookedwood after 1.5 miles, where the Kenny family run the lovely Crookedwood House Cellar Restaurant.

86 miles – Mullingar. Tourist Information, Dublin Rd, tel: 044-48650. The market centre for this premier cattle region. Its landmark is the twin-towered Cathedral of Christ the King, built in 1939. There is a handicraft centre in Dominick St and the town museum is nearby. The magnificent fishing waters of loughs Ennell, Owel and Derravaragh are all within a few miles. For a quick stop the Coffee Dock on the Longford road offers good home-cooking. Take the N 52 at the traffic lights in the town centre along the shores of lovely Lough Ennell. Watch out for a right turn for 18thC Belvedere House.

90 miles – Belvedere House & Gardens (1200-1630 Mon.-Fri., 1200-1800 Sat. & Sun., April-Sep.; £1, child 50p). The gardens include woodland and lakeside walks, lake swimming areas, a walled garden and 'The Jealous Wall', an artificial abbey ruin built by the 1st Earl of Belvedere in 1760 to block the view of his brother's home in nearby Rochort House! Return to the road, which continues through agricultural land via neat Ballynagore on the River Brosna.

100.5 miles – Kilbeggan. Locke's Distillery is a 'must' (1000-1800 April-Oct., 1000-1630 Mon.-Sat., 1400-1800 Sun., Nov.-Mar.; £2, child £1). This refurbished distillery was in business from 1757 until 1957 but now a mini-village has been built up within the complex, combining a museum, antique shop, art gallery, cooper's workshop and the distillery kitchen which serves excellent home-cooked food.

ALTERNATIVES: The N 6 leads east to Dublin city (see **DUBLIN CITY**, **A-Z**). A second option is to go south on the N 52 to Tullamore (see **A-Z**), Portlaoise or Birr (see **A-Z**).

Return to Athlone on the N 6 through Horseleap. This town derives its name from the time Hugh De Lacy lived nearby during the 12thC. It is said that when pursued by a group of Irish, De Lacy's horse made a huge jump, taking his master into the safety of his own domain. Continue through Moate, where cattle fairs are still held in the wide main street and a small local museum is open during the summer, back into Athlone (118 miles).

The Northwest

COUNTIES

Monaghan, Cavan, Leitrim, Sligo & Donegal

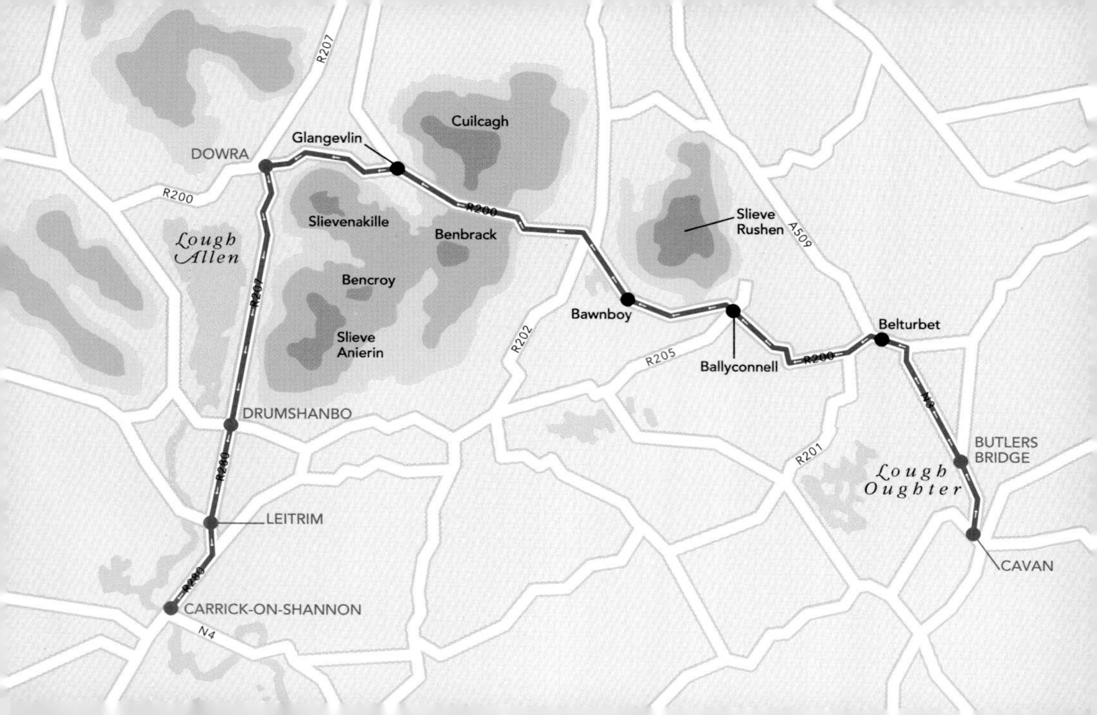

DOWRA
Glangevlin
Cuilcagh
R207
R200
Slievenakille
Benbrack
Lough Allen
Bencroy
Slieve Anierin
Slieve Rushen
A509
Bawnboy
R202
R205
Ballyconnell
Belturbet
DRUMSHANBO
R201
BUTLERS BRIDGE
Lough Oughter
N3
R280
LEITRIM
CAVAN
CARRICK-ON-SHANNON
N4

Iron Mountains

Cavan–Carrick-on-Shannon. Duration: 1 day.

Cavan. Pop: 4000. The county town was originally the seat of the O'Reilly chiefs of East Breifne. The town grew up around a Franciscan friary founded in 1300 but nothing remains of it today, following the town's destruction after the defeat of Jacobite forces in 1690. The Cavan Crystal factory lies on the town's outskirts on the N 3. A factory shop is open daily and there are guided tours during the summer (1030, 1130, 1430 & 1530 Mon.-Fri.). Leave Cavan to the north via the N 3. In Butlers Bridge the Derragara Inn serves reasonably-priced hot food all day, and there is a vast miscellany of curios and antiques to examine. Take the left fork in the village, signposted Belturbet. Pass through Belturbet, on the banks of the River Erne, after about 5 miles.
DETOUR: Six miles south on the R 201 is a left turn for Killykeen Forest Park (access daily; £1, or £3 per car Sat. & Sun.). In Irish Killykeen is *Coill Chaoin*, which means 'the delightful wood' – an apt description. This beautiful area around Lough Oughter has been populated for thousands of years and crannogs (see **A-Z**) have been found on the lake's islands. Thirteenth-century Cloughoughter Castle, a circular tower, sits on one of them. Built over a crannog, it was an O'Reilly fort.
About a mile further on take a left turn for Ballyconnell. Drive through Ballyconnell, following signposts for Glangevlin. The road ascends gradually with Slieve Rushen on the right. Continue through Bawnboy. After a mile the road begins to skirt Brackley Lough on the left. Ahead is Cuilcagh, rising to 2188 ft. Benbrack, Bencroy and Slieve Anierin are to the left. Two miles further is a layby with picnic tables and public toilets. A mile on keep left, signposted Dowra and Glangevlin, and then right after 200 yd.
The road begins to rise steadily through an impressive rugged landscape of bogland dotted with forest plantations. At the 1100 ft summit there are views of the Oranmore River valley. Bin Beg is on the right. Begin to descend. On leaving Glangevlin Slievenakille is on the left. Tiltibane, the extreme west summit (1949 ft) of the Cuilcagh range, is to the right. On its lower slopes is the Shannon Pot, source of the River Shannon (see **A-Z**). The wide mountain gap on the right opens into Northern Ireland.

40 miles – Dowra. Between the east bank of the Shannon and the foot of Slievenakille is a 3 mile stretch of the Worm Ditch or Black Pig's Race, an ancient earthwork which runs to the head of Lough Allen. It is believed that this marked a prehistoric Ulster frontier.

WALK: The Cavan Way, a 16 mile path, begins either here or north in Blacklion, where it links with the Ulster Way.

Keep left, following signposts for Lough Allen Scenic Tour. Descend this winding road which follows part of the lake shore into Co. Leitrim.

DETOUR: A signpost on the left after 6 miles points to St. Aodh's Well and Sweat House, a holy well and ancient sauna!

51 miles – Drumshanbo. Literally translated from the Irish this means 'the back of the old cow'. The village is on the southern tip of Lough Allen and a good coarse angling centre; the lough is noted as the best pike fishery in Europe. Veer left in the square, then right. A mile outside the town on the right is an amenity area on Acres Lake with a picnic area, children's playground and small jetty. Continue through Leitrim village, the county's namesake. Its one street has a lovely situation on the canal.

60 miles – Carrick-on-Shannon. The perfect place to begin a Shannon cruise, hire a boat for a day trip, go fishing or just relax and enjoy the crack (see **A-Z**) in one of the town's lively pubs. Among the best are Burke's Bar, Sean's Bar and The Anchorage Bar, all on Bridge St. The tiny Costello Chapel at the top of Bridge St is reputed to be the second-smallest chapel in the world. Built in 1877 by businessman Edward Costello as a memorial to his wife who died at a young age, it now houses both their coffins laid on either side of the tiled aisle.

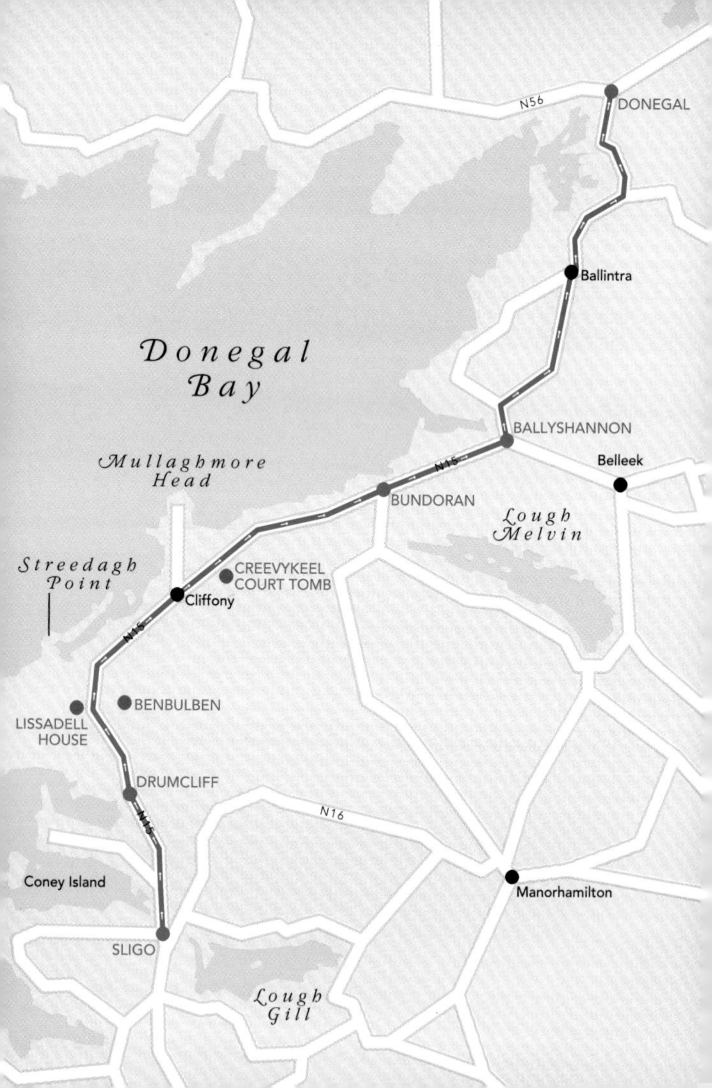
N56
DONEGAL
Ballintra
Donegal Bay
BALLYSHANNON
Belleek
Mullaghmore Head
N15
BUNDORAN
Lough Melvin
Streedagh Point
CREEVYKEEL COURT TOMB
Cliffony
N15
LISSADELL HOUSE
BENBULBEN
DRUMCLIFF
N16
N15
Coney Island
Manorhamilton
SLIGO
Lough Gill

Donegal Bay

Sligo town–Donegal town. Duration: 1 day.

Leave Sligo town (see **A-Z**) on the N 15, with views out to Sligo Bay, Strandhill and Coney Island, which inspired the naming of New York's Coney Island when the captain of a Sligo ship noticed that both islands swarmed with rabbits. Spectacular Benbulben (see **A-Z**) and its fellow peaks in the Dartry mountains rise ahead. After 4.5 miles is Drumcliff, site of a 6thC monastery (see **Battle of the Books**). Poet W. B. Yeats (see **A-Z**) is buried here in the grounds of the Protestant church. His simple gravestone bears the epitaph 'Cast a cold eye/On life, on death./Horseman, pass by!' Watch out for a sharp left turn, signposted Lissadell House. About 1.5 miles further on cross over a bridge and then turn left again.

8 miles – Lissadell House (House 1000-1600 Mon.-Sat., June-Sep. Grounds daily; £2, child 50p). Built in 1830, this was the birthplace of arctic explorer Sir Henry Gore-Booth, and his daughters Eva, the poet, and Constance, who became Countess Markievicz (see **A-Z**), both friends of W. B. Yeats, who stayed here frequently. Return to the N 15. Pass through Cashelgarran, Grange and Moneygold. There are views of Streedagh Point to the left and Mullaghmore Head straight ahead.

DETOUR: At the Cliffony crossroads take a left turn to Mullaghmore Head (2.5 miles) and village, and Classiebawn Castle, built by Viscount Palmerston, the 19thC British prime minister. It became the home of Lord Mountbatten shortly before he was killed in 1979, when his boat was blown up by the IRA, off the coast at Mullaghmore. It is possible to hire boats at Mullaghmore Harbour for the 4 mile trip out to Inishmurray. Uninhabited since 1947, the island contains one of the country's oldest churches among the monastic remains. Try to count the 'speckled' or 'cursing' stones. Legend claims that nobody has counted these stones correctly, twice in succession.

Pull in to the right almost 2 miles past Cliffony.

20 miles – Creevykeel Court Tomb. Creevykeel is an extensive Neolithic court tomb. A passageway on the east side of the cairn leads to a court which opens into a two-chamber gallery grave. Excavations during the 1930s uncovered four cremated burials, Neolithic pottery, stone axes and flints. Continue on the N 15, passing over the River Duff

Enniskillen

and into Co. Leitrim after 3 miles. The landscape becomes hilly, with stone-walled fields and an abundance of yellow gorse. Two miles further on, after crossing the River Drowes, is Co. Donegal.

26 miles – Bundoran. A seaside resort popular with holidaymakers from both sides of the border. There is a promenade along the 300 yd strand in the town centre, and the golf course is spectacularly situated at Aughrus Head to the east. A walk along the cliffs of the head, past the rock formations of the Fairy Bridge (a 24 ft arch), the Wishing Chair and the Puffing Hole, leads to lovely 1.5 mile-long Tullan Strand. Ruined Finner Church is also on the route. The town offers an abundance of bars, hotels, souvenir shops and amusement arcades. Follow the N 15, signposted Ballyshannon, past an army camp on the left.

30 miles – Ballyshannon. The town is situated at the head of the Erne estuary at a strategically important crossing point near the lovely Assaroe Falls. A major hydroelectric station has now been built on the steep river banks. According to legend it was at the Inis Saimer islet in the estuary that the first colonization of Ireland took place, when Partholan landed from Scythia in 1500 BC. Nineteenth-century poet William Allingham lived and worked here, and schoolchildren still recite his compositions. Probably one of the best traditional music festivals is held here every Aug. bank holiday. Continue on the N 15.

ALTERNATIVE: Take the R 230 south to the Celtic Weave basket workshop, where Patricia Daly handpaints china floral baskets, then continue to Belleek (see **A-Z**), Enniskillen (see **A-Z**) and the Fermanagh Lakeland (see **A-Z**).

DETOUR: Follow signposts for Rossnowlagh and visit this magnificent 'heavenly cove' (a literal translation). The third turn on the left leads to an old abbey mill where the wheels and part of the building are being restored. Also try to see the small museum in the nearby Franciscan friary, and Glasbolie Fort, an ancient earthwork said to be the burial place of a high king. Rejoin the main route near Ballintra.

This is one of the best stretches of road in the Republic. It passes through undramatic but pleasant agricultural land.

ALTERNATIVE: Turn right after 11 miles for The Black Gap, Pettigoe, Lough Derg (see **A-Z**) and Lough Erne (see **A-Z**).

Enter Donegal town (see **A-Z**) past the Donegal Craft Village (43 miles).

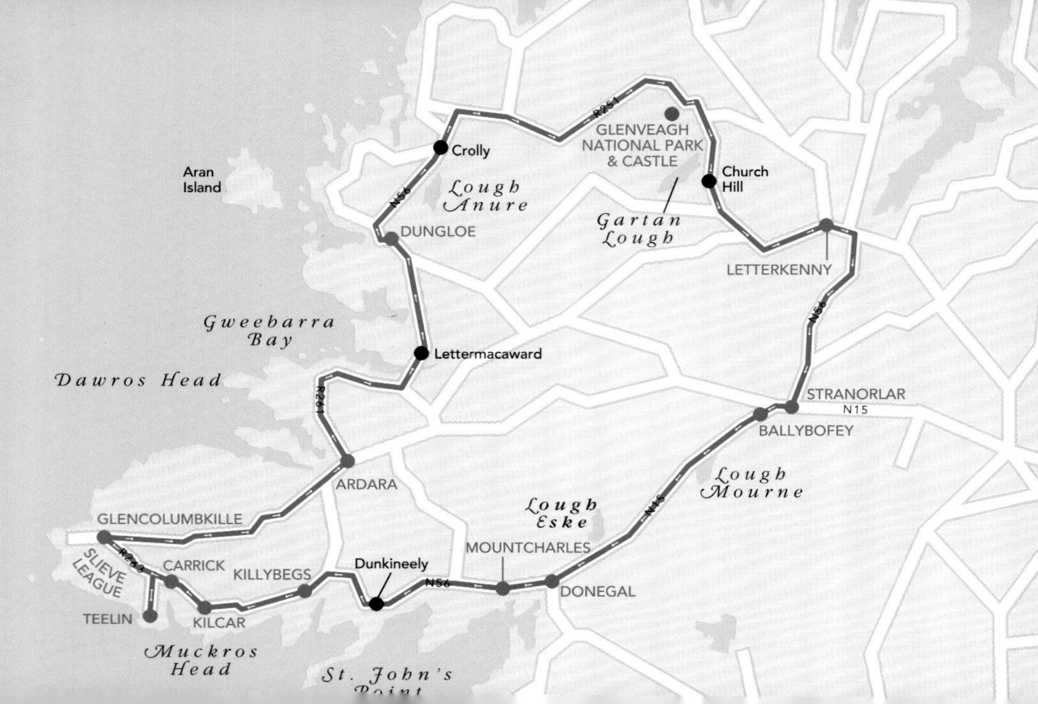

Aran Island
Crolly
Lough Anure
N56
DUNGLOE
R251
GLENVEAGH NATIONAL PARK & CASTLE
Church Hill
Gartan Lough
LETTERKENNY
N56
Gweebarra Bay
Lettermacaward
Dawros Head
R261
STRANORLAR
N15
BALLYBOFEY
ARDARA
Lough Mourne
Lough Eske
N15
GLENCOLUMBKILLE
R263
SLIEVE LEAGUE
CARRICK
KILLYBEGS
Dunkineely
N56
MOUNTCHARLES
DONEGAL
TEELIN
KILCAR
Muckros Head
St. John's Point

Northwest Coast

Donegal town–Glencolumbkille–Dungloe–Letterkenny–Donegal town. Duration: 2 days.

Leave Donegal town (see **A-Z**) on the N 56 for Killybegs, skirting the inlets of the bay before veering inland into the steep-streeted village of Mountcharles. Four miles on, cross the River Eany, with glimpses of the sea on the left, and continue into Dunkineely.

DETOUR: Half a mile on is a left turn for St. John's Point. A road leads along the narrow peninsula which separates Inver and MacSwyne's bays, with a walking track to the point.

A little further, on skirting round an inlet into the village of Bruckless, the seaweed-covered poles in the lagoon below (tides permitting) are for rearing clams. The road ascends inland into dark, wooded hills and lush green fields, returning to the coast after about 3 miles.

17 miles – Killybegs (see **A-Z**). Follow signposts for Glencolumbkille and Scenic Road. After a mile the road begins to descend to the coast, and Crownarad rises steeply to the right. The vegetation is lush and green and dozens of sheltered beaches can be found down sideroads on the left. Two miles on, Muckros Head juts out into the sea and stone-walled pastures roll down to the coast. Just past the Blue Haven Bar, take a left turn signposted Scenic Route to Kilcar. This narrow winding road (be cautious) leads to panoramic views of the hills, cliffs, fields and sea. The perfect accompaniment to this incredible scenery is some rousing traditional Irish music, so tune in the radio or stick a tape in the stereo! After a mile the road begins to descend.

DETOUR: A mile on is a left turn for Muckros Head and White Strand.

On entering Kilcar look below to the idyllically sited Gaelic games pitch. Past the Studio Donegal crafts shop turn left signposted Coast Road. This winding route rises steeply, veering inland occasionally. After 2 miles, round a dangerous bend, panoramic views open up in front, extending across Teelin Bay to spectacular Slieve League (see **A-Z**). The road veers inland again to meet the R 263. Turn left into Carrick, where whiskey lovers should visit the Slieve League pub.

DETOUR: A 'must' for walkers. Turn left in the village for Teelin, a Gaeltacht (see **A-Z**) village, and Slieve League.

Follow signposts for Glencolumbkille, passing through the Owenree

valley with expanses of lake-dotted bogland stretching out on both sides. After 5 miles Glen Head looms ahead, crowned by a Martello tower (see **A-Z**). Descend into Glencolumbkille.

36 miles – Glencolumbkille (see **A-Z**). Retrace the route to the village outskirts, turning left, following signposts for Ard an Rath (Ardara) and Glengesh. The road leads over a river and ascends between Croaghnaleaba and Croaghloughdivna before descending into a valley through a desolate landscape. The Glen River is on the right on entering Min na Aoire. Turn left for Ardara. The scenery is flatter at first but then the road begins to rise and fall through bogland and occasional fertile fields. Climb to 900 ft below Croaghavehy past a small forest plantation at the head of the Glengesh Pass, with the Blue Stack mountains in the distance ahead. At a T-junction turn left into Ardara, a good place for craft shopping.

DETOUR: Half a mile on turn left for beautifully sited Maghera, with its intriguing collection of coastal caves and Essaranka Waterfall.

Follow signposts left for Dungloe.

Killybegs

ALTERNATIVE: Follow signposts for Glenties (see **A-Z**).
The road goes through hilly and agricultural land with small farms and houses. Dawros Head is to the left. The Blue Stack mountains are in the distance to the right, and the Derryveagh mountains in the distance ahead. The road continues through hilly countryside. Turn left after Kilclooney church, signposted Naran, but a mile on veer right at a fork in the road, signposted Dungloe. Aghla Mountain rises ahead. Continue through Clooney, turning left after about a mile for Dungloe, following the winding inlet of Gweebarra Bay and veering inland occasionally. After 3 miles cross over the Gweebarra Bridge into Lettermacaward. Follow signposts for An Clochan Liath (Dungloe), skirting an inlet of Trawenagh Bay and then passing through bogland. Slieve Snaght is the highest peak on the right.
74 miles – Dungloe. This bustling town is the metropolis of the Rosses region, a rocky, lake-sprinkled Gaeltacht (see **A-Z**) area which stretches to the coast and up to Crolly. The town is liveliest during the annual Mary of Dungloe festival in June. It has a small fishing port and is popular with anglers. Take the N 56 to Crolly. The Derryveagh mountains rise up to the right and after 5 miles, just outside Loughanure, there is a chance to stop and enjoy the views over Lough Anure itself. In Crolly keep on the N 56 to the edges of the Gweedore region, before veering east on the R 251. Passing through this desolate but lovely land, Errigal mountain rises up ahead and spectacular Lough Nacung opens up to the right. After about 4 miles take a right fork, signposted Dunlewy. The road continues along the lake shore under the shadow of imposing Errigal.

DETOUR: Watch out for signposts marking a left turn to Ionad Cois Locha (1130-1800 Wed.-Mon., 1200-1900 Sun., June-Sep.; £2, child £1), a farm museum and visitor centre with craft exhibits and a historical audiovisual presentation.

After a few miles the height of the road becomes apparent with the valley far below. The route continues with Cloghaneely Mountain rising up to the side of Errigal, and marvellous views left and right across the bogland. Muckish Mountain then looms up on the left, and a tributary of the Owencarrow River winds along beside the road.

89 miles – Glenveagh National Park & Castle (1030-1830 April-Oct.). Turn left into the park. Its 10,000 hectares are never crowded, and while walking here the only other creatures visitors may meet are the park's red deer. The park is centred on a 19thC castle built by the Adair family and includes a visitor centre, ornate gardens and an expanse of mountains, lakes and glens. Return to the road and turn right, passing through more desolate expanses and following signposts for Glee Gallery at each junction. After 5 miles follow signposts for Church Hill with Lough Akibbon and beautiful Gartan Lough below on the right. Pass through wood- and hedgerow-lined roads for a couple of miles before turning right, signposted Glebe Gallery.

DETOUR: St. Columbcille (see **A-Z**) was born nearby. Enquire locally for directions to the spot in Lackanoo which is marked by a large cross and a stone. This is known as the Flagstone of Loneliness because it is said that the saint, who used to sleep on it, gave it the power to cure sorrow. Many local people, preparing to emigrate, would come here the night before they left in the hope of banishing homesickness. A mile away is the tiny Oratory of St. Columbcille and the Natal Stone, where the baby Columba is said to have been laid after his birth. The stone is still visited by pregnant women who pray for a safe delivery.

97 miles – St. Columb's & Glebe Gallery (1100-1830 Sat. & Mon.-Thu., 1300-1830 Sun., May-Sep.; £1, child 70p). St. Columb's was the home for 30 years of painter Derek Hill. Its remarkable contents include a vast collection of art works, Victorian furniture, textiles and wallpapers by William Morris, Oriental prints, Islamic ceramics and carpets, and a large array of 19thC pottery and glass. The house is sited on the shores of Gartan Lough and its gardens contain many rare plant species. Adjacent is the Glebe Gallery with paintings by Derek Hill, Jack Yeats (see **A-Z**), Annigoni Pasmore and many others. Return to the road and follow signposts for Church Hill. DETOUR: After a mile take a right turn for the Columbcille Centre (1000-1830 Mon.-Sat., 1300-1830 Sun., June-mid Oct.; £1, child 50p). Built overlooking the lough, its exhibitions trace the saint's life, his links with Iona and the spread of Christianity throughout Europe.

Donegal

Pass through Church Hill, following signposts for Letterkenny, with Brown Mountain on the right, and a little further Croaghmore and Gregory Hill on the left. The road continues via hilly pastures and woodland.

110 miles – Letterkenny. This is the county's major commerical centre and boasts one of Ireland's longest main streets. Leave on the N 13. After a mile veer right, signposted Sligo and Ballybofey.

ALTERNATIVE: Turn left for Derry city (see **DERRY CITY**, **A-Z**) and the Inishowen peninsula (see **A-Z**).

The road leads through agricultural land, passing occasional forest plantations, into Stranorlar. Here an arched bridge spanning the River Finn leads into the market town of Ballybofey, where the founder of the 19thC Irish Home Rule movement, Issac Butt, is buried in the graveyard beside the Protestant church. Continue on the N 15, signposted Donegal. After 5 miles skirt Lough Mourne with the Blue Stack mountains ahead and to the right. A little further pass Croaghnageer (1793 ft) on the right. Ascend through the scenic Barnesmore Gap, with Barnesmore mountain (1491 ft) on the left and Croaghconnellagh (1724 ft) on the right. Continue past lovely Lough Eske back to Donegal town (140 miles).

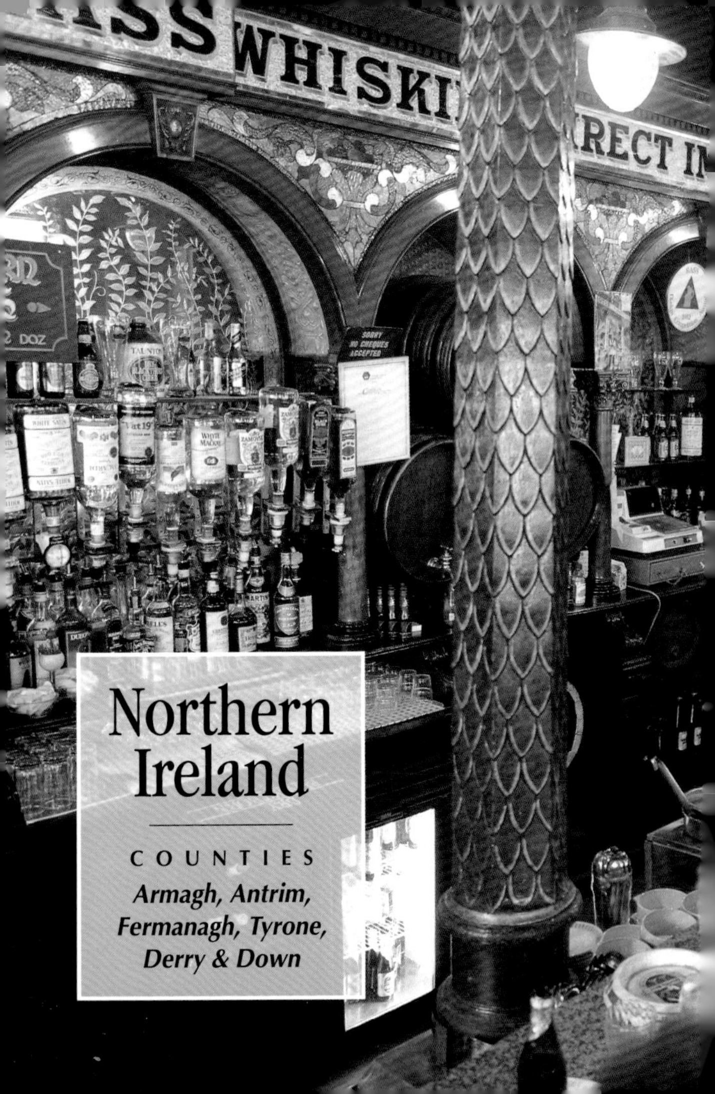

Northern Ireland

COUNTIES

Armagh, Antrim, Fermanagh, Tyrone, Derry & Down

Crown Liquor Saloon, Belfast

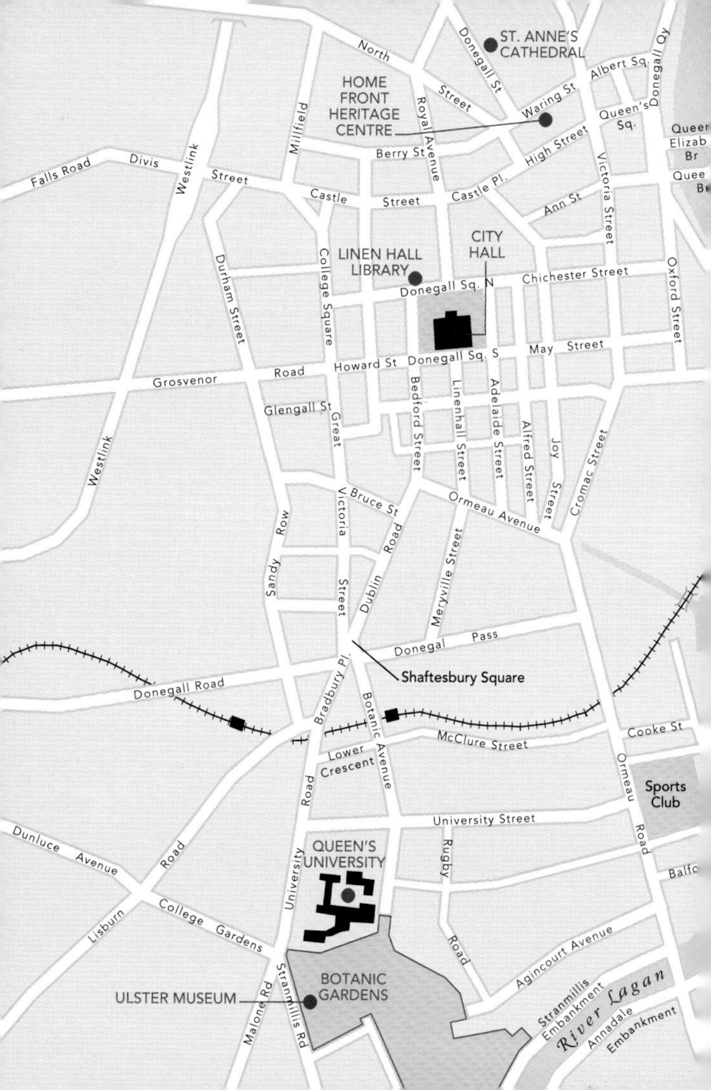
ST. ANNE'S CATHEDRAL
HOME FRONT HERITAGE CENTRE
LINEN HALL LIBRARY
CITY HALL
Shaftesbury Square
QUEEN'S UNIVERSITY
BOTANIC GARDENS
ULSTER MUSEUM
Sports Club
River Lagan
North Street
Donegall St
Albert Sq.
Donegall Qy
Waring St
Queen's Sq.
High Street
Royal Avenue
Millfield
Berry St
Castle Pl.
Castle Street
Divis Street
Falls Road
Westlink
Ann St
Victoria Street
Durham Street
College Square
Donegall Sq. N
Chichester Street
Oxford Street
May Street
Donegall Sq. S
Howard St
Grosvenor Road
Glengall St
Great Victoria Street
Bedford Street
Linenhall Street
Adelaide Street
Alfred Street
Joy Street
Cromac Street
Bruce St
Ormeau Avenue
Dublin Road
Sandy Row
Meryville Street
Donegal Pass
Donegall Road
Bradbury Pl.
Botanic Avenue
McClure Street
Cooke St
Lower Crescent
University Road
University Street
Ormeau Road
Rugby Road
Dunluce Avenue
Lisburn Road
College Gardens
University Sq.
Agincourt Avenue
Malone Rd
Stranmillis Rd
Stranmillis Embankment
Annadale Embankment

CITY HALL Donegall Sq., tel: 0232-320202, ext.227. ■ Guided tours 1030 Wed., twice-daily summer. Book in advance. ● Free.
Built 1898-1906 in Portland stone in classical Renaissance style. There are impressive carved oak interiors, stained glass and Italian marble.

LINEN HALL LIBRARY 17 Donegall Sq. North, tel: 0232-321707.
■ 0930-1800 Mon.-Fri. (until 2030 Thu.), 0930-1600 Sat. ● Donation.
Founded in 1788 to 'improve the mind', its contents include a Robert Burns collection and over 20,000 important Irish volumes.

QUEEN'S UNIVERSITY University Rd, tel: 0232-245133.
The celebrated architect Charles Lanyon modelled the main Tudor-style college building on Oxford's Magdalen College. It is now the centre of a thriving university quarter. See the entrance hall and gallery in the tower.

BOTANIC GARDENS Stranmillis Rd, tel: 0232-324902.
■ Gardens daily. Palm House & Tropical Ravine 1000-1200, 1300-1700 Mon.-Fri., 1400-1700 Sat. & Sun. (April-Sep.); 1000-1200, 1400-1600 Mon.-Fri., 1400-1600 Sat. & Sun. (Oct.-Mar.). ● Free.
The rose garden and herbaceous borders are probably the gardens' best features. Coffee, banana and cotton plants grow in the Victorian Palm House, which is older than the Great Palm House at Kew.

ULSTER MUSEUM Stranmillis Rd, tel: 0232-381251.
■ 1000-1700 Mon.-Fri., 1300-1700 Sat., 1400-1700 Sun. ● Free.
Irish and international art collections, and jewellery recovered from the Armada treasure ship Girona, *wrecked off Giant's Causeway in 1588.*

HOME FRONT HERITAGE CENTRE War Memorial Building, Waring St, tel: 0232-320392. ■ 1000-1600 Mon.-Fri.
Exhibits from World War II, including an incendiary bomb dropped on Belfast in 1941. Building also houses the Royal Ulster Rifles Museum.

ST. ANNE'S CATHEDRAL Donegall St, tel: 0232-328322.
Begun in 1899. A mosaic commemorates St. Patrick's landing at Saul in AD 432. It houses the tomb of Unionist leader Lord Carson (see **A-Z***).*

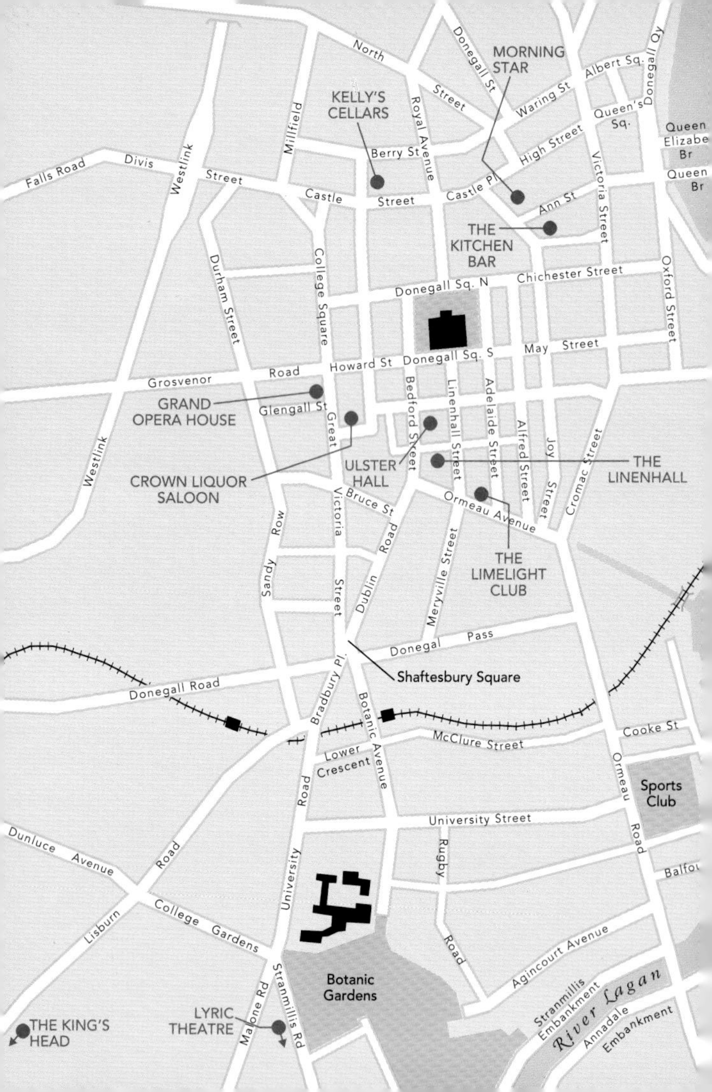
MORNING STAR
KELLY'S CELLARS
THE KITCHEN BAR
GRAND OPERA HOUSE
CROWN LIQUOR SALOON
ULSTER HALL
THE LINENHALL
THE LIMELIGHT CLUB
Shaftesbury Square
Sports Club
Botanic Gardens
LYRIC THEATRE
THE KING'S HEAD
River Lagan
North Street
Donegall St
Albert Sq.
Donegall Qy
Waring St
Queen's Sq.
Queen Elizabeth Br
Queen Br
Royal Avenue
Millfield
Berry St
High Street
Falls Road
Divis Street
Westlink
Castle Street
Castle Pl
Ann St
Victoria Street
Durham Street
College Square
Donegall Sq. N
Chichester Street
Oxford Street
May Street
Howard St
Donegall Sq. S
Grosvenor Road
Glengall St
Great Victoria Street
Bedford Street
Linenhall Street
Adelaide Street
Alfred Street
Joy Street
Cromac Street
Bruce St
Ormeau Avenue
Sandy Row
Dublin Road
Meryville Street
Donegal Pass
Donegall Road
Bradbury Pl.
Botanic Avenue
McClure Street
Cooke St
Lower Crescent
Ormeau Road
University Road
University Street
Rugby Road
Balfour
Dunluce Avenue
Lisburn Road
College Gardens
Agincourt Avenue
Stranmillis Embankment
Annadale Embankment
Malone Rd
Stranmillis Rd

GRAND OPERA HOUSE Great Victoria St, tel: 0232-241919.
Shows ranging from drama, opera and concerts to pantomime.

ULSTER HALL Bedford St, tel: 0232-323900.
Musicals, rock gigs, recitals, and concerts by the Ulster Orchestra.

LYRIC THEATRE Ridgeway St, tel: 0232-381081.
Irish plays, international theatre and new productions.

THE LIMELIGHT CLUB 17 Ormeau Ave, tel: 0232-248948.
Nightclub with live bands, cabaret and comedy.

CROWN LIQUOR SALOON 46 Great Victoria St, tel: 0232-249476.
Spectacular Victorian pub complete with gaslights, carved woodwork, ornate glass and tiles, and snugs. In the care of the National Trust. Bar lunches and oysters in season. A 'must'.

THE KITCHEN BAR Telfair St, across from the William St entrance to the Victoria Centre, tel: 0232-324901.
Founded in 1859. Formerly a famous theatrical haunt. Two long rooms, the Kitchen and Parlour bars, adjoin. Great bar lunches.

MORNING STAR Pottinger's Entry, between Ann St and High St, tel: 0232-323976.
A traceable history back to at least 1810. The original mahogany counter is still intact. A lovely spot. Bar lunches.

THE LINENHALL 9 Clarence St, tel: 0232-248458.
Adventurous bar food. Live music in the back lounge, usually jazz.

KELLY'S CELLARS 30 Bank St, tel: 0232-324835.
Ancient interior. Bar lunches and oysters. Traditional music.

THE KING'S HEAD 829 Lisburn Rd, opposite King's Hall, Balmoral, tel: 0232-667805.
Very lively pub. Popular with students, professionals and locals.

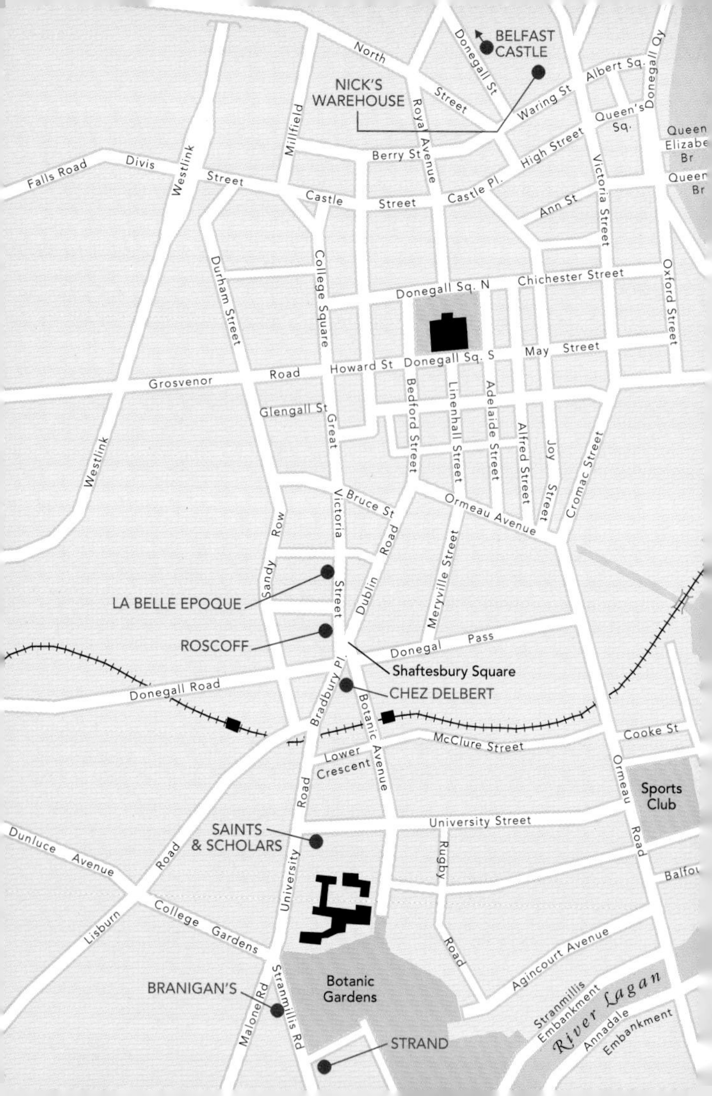
BELFAST CASTLE
NICK'S WAREHOUSE
North Street
Donegall St
Royal Avenue
Millfield
Westlink
Falls Road
Divis Street
Berry St
Waring St
Albert Sq.
Donegall Qy
Queen's Sq.
High Street
Queen Elizabe Br
Queen Br
Castle Street
Castle Pl.
Ann St
Victoria Street
Durham Street
College Square
Chichester Street
Oxford Street
Donegall Sq. N
Donegall Sq. S
May Street
Grosvenor Road
Howard St
Glengall St
Great Victoria Street
Bedford Street
Linenhall Street
Adelaide Street
Alfred Street
Joy Street
Cromac Street
Bruce St
Ormeau Avenue
Sandy Row
Dublin Road
Meryville Street
LA BELLE EPOQUE
ROSCOFF
Donegal Pass
Shaftesbury Square
Donegall Road
Bradbury Pl.
CHEZ DELBERT
Botanic Avenue
McClure Street
Cooke St
Lower Crescent
Ormeau Road
Sports Club
University Road
University Street
SAINTS & SCHOLARS
Dunluce Avenue
Lisburn Road
Rugby Road
Balfou
College Gardens
Agincourt Avenue
BRANIGAN'S
Malone Rd
Stranmillis Rd
Botanic Gardens
STRAND
Stranmillis Embankment
River Lagan
Annadale Embankment

ROSCOFF 7 Lesley House, Shaftesbury Sq., tel: 0232-331532.
■ 1215-1400 Mon.-Fri., 1830-2230 Mon.-Sat. ● Expensive.
Wonderfully varied menu featuring Eastern, European and Ulster cuisine.

BELFAST CASTLE Antrim Rd, tel: 0232-776925.
■ Ben Madigan Restaurant 1900-2130 Thu.-Sat. Bistro 1100-2300.
● Ben Madigan Restaurant: Expensive. Bistro: Moderate.
Increasingly popular with locals. Buffet and carvery lunches in bistro. Impressive à la carte in restaurant has won 'Taste of Ulster' approval.

NICK'S WAREHOUSE 35-39 Hill St, tel: 0232-439690.
■ 1200-1500, 1800-2100. ● Moderate.
Wine bar menu and restaurant in converted warehouse. Dips, fish, meat, unusual sauces. Vegetarian dishes. Awarded 'Taste of Ulster' approval.

STRAND 12 Stranmillis Rd, tel: 0232-682266.
■ 1200-2330 Mon.-Sat., 1200-1430, 1730-2200 Sun. ● Moderate.
Informal restaurant with wide-ranging menu, including crab, goulash, chilli con carne, chicken tikka, vegetarian meals and salmon.

BRANIGAN'S 11a Stranmillis Rd, tel: 0232-666845.
■ 1800-2330 Mon.-Sat. ● Moderate.
Charcoal-grilled steaks, seafood and moussaka.

LA BELLE EPOQUE 103 Great Victoria St, tel: 0232-323244.
■ 1800-2330 Mon.-Sat. ● Moderate.
French-style cuisine. Fish, steaks and game in season.

SAINTS & SCHOLARS 3 University St, tel: 0232-325137.
■ 1200-2300 Mon.-Sat., 1200-1430, 1730-2200 Sun. ● Inexpensive-moderate.
Casseroles, deep-fried brie and stir fries. Very popular.

CHEZ DELBERT 10 Bradbury Pl., tel: 0232-238020.
■ 1600-0100. ● Inexpensive-moderate.
Also known as Frogties. Crepes, seafood, steak au poivre, *baked oysters.*

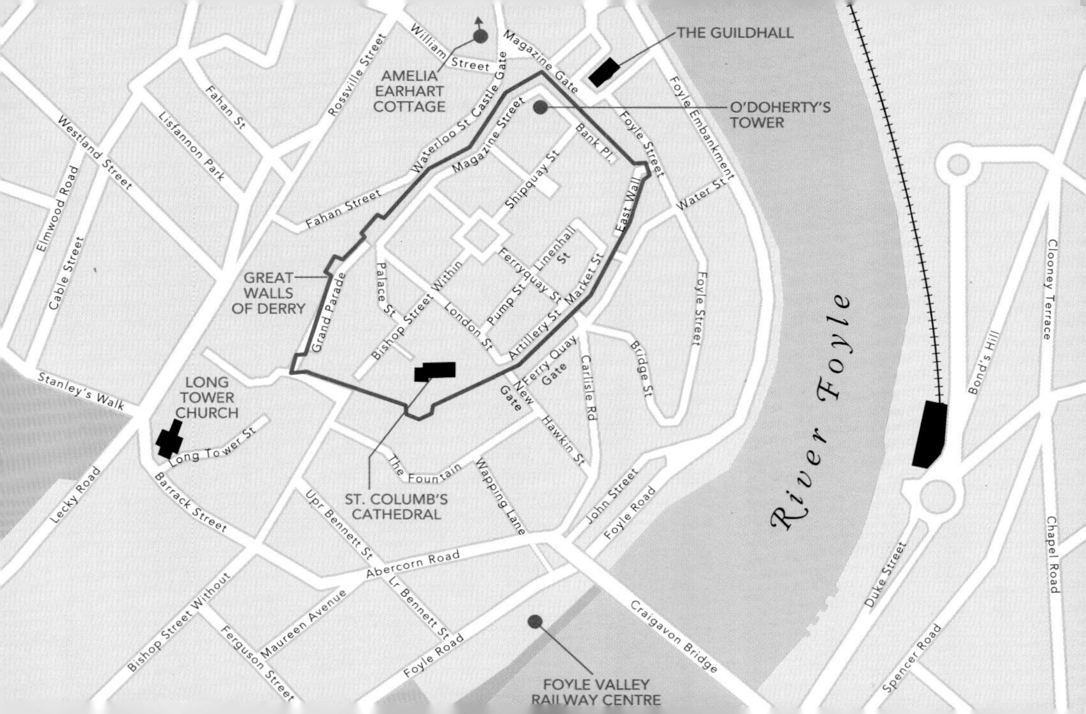

THE GUILDHALL
AMELIA EARHART COTTAGE
O'DOHERTY'S TOWER
William Street
Magazine Gate
Rossville Street
Fahan St
Castle Gate
Waterloo St
Magazine Street
Bank Pl.
Foyle Street
Foyle Embankment
Westland Street
Lisfannon Park
Shipquay St
Water St
Elmwood Road
Cable Street
Fahan Street
East Wall
Linenhall St
Ferryquay St
Market St
Foyle Street
GREAT WALLS OF DERRY
Grand Parade
Palace St
Bishop Street Within
Pump St
London St
Artillery St
Ferry Quay Gate
New Gate
Carlisle Rd
Bridge St
Bond's Hill
Clooney Terrace
River Foyle
Stanley's Walk
LONG TOWER CHURCH
Long Tower St
Hawkin St
The Fountain
Wapping Lane
John Street
Foyle Road
Lecky Road
Barrack Street
ST. COLUMB'S CATHEDRAL
Upr Bennett St
Abercorn Road
Chapel Road
Duke Street
Bishop Street Without
Lr Bennett St
Maureen Avenue
Ferguson Street
Foyle Road
Craigavon Bridge
Spencer Road
FOYLE VALLEY RAILWAY CENTRE

GREAT WALLS OF DERRY
Barbed wire and barricades make it impossible to walk a full circuit of these incredible mile-long walls, completed in 1618. Originally there were four gates and nine bastions; today there are seven arch gates and six bastions. The walls are up to 24 ft high. See **Siege of Derry**.

THE GUILDHALL Foyle St, tel: 0504-365151.
■ 0900-1600 Mon.-Fri. Ring to book guided tours. ● Free.
Dozens of stained-glass windows illustrate the city's history and former trades. Also used as a venue for concerts and theatrical productions.

ST. COLUMB'S CATHEDRAL Off London St and St. Columb's Court, tel: 0504-262746. ■ 0900-1300 Mon.-Sat., 1400-1700 Mon.-Fri., 1400-1600 Sat. ● Donation.
Consecrated in 1633 and named after the city's founder. The chancel, chapterhouse (1910) and spire are later additions. The chapterhouse has the locks of the original four city gates, and relics of the 1689 siege.

O'DOHERTY'S TOWER Union Hall Pl., tel: 0504-265238.
■ 1000-1700 Tue.-Sat. (June-Sep.). ● 50p, child 25p.
A modern replica of the 16thC O'Doherty castle which stood nearby in Magazine St. There are views of the city from the roof platform.

LONG TOWER CHURCH (St. Columba's), Bishop St.
Built in 1784 on the site of the medieval church of Tempeall Mor ('great church') and later enlarged, it has a magnificent interior.

FOYLE VALLEY RAILWAY CENTRE Foyle Rd, tel: 0504-265234. ■ 1000-1700 Tue.-Sat.; 1400-1700 Sun. (April-Sep.); narrow-gauge railway Sat. & Sun. pm (May-Sep.). ● £1.50, child 75p.
Over a mile of working railway runs through the Foyle Riverside Park.

AMELIA EARHART COTTAGE Ballyarnett, off the B 194, tel: 0504-353379. ■ 1400-1700 Tue.-Sun. (June-Sep.). ● Free.
Commemorates Amelia Earhart, the first woman to fly the Atlantic solo. She landed in a field near the cottage in 1932.

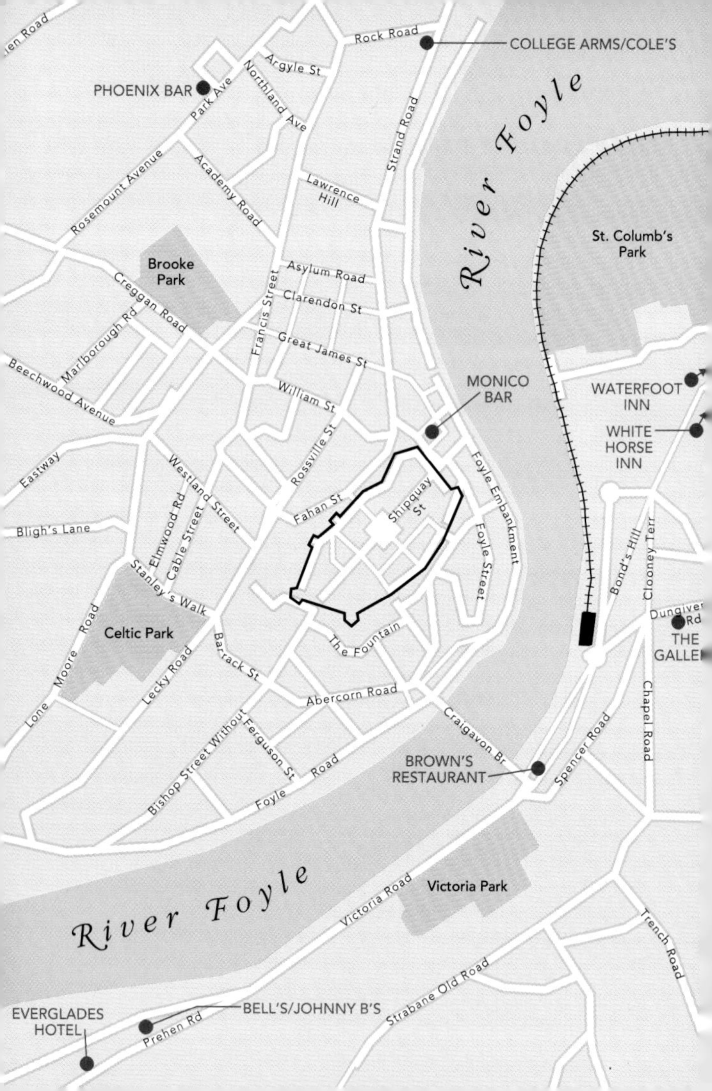
Rock Road
COLLEGE ARMS/COLE'S
Argyle St
PHOENIX BAR
Park Ave
Northland Ave
Strand Road
River Foyle
Lawrence Hill
Rosemount Avenue
Academy Road
St. Columb's Park
Brooke Park
Asylum Road
Creggan Road
Clarendon St
Francis Street
Marlborough Rd
Great James St
Beechwood Avenue
William St
MONICO BAR
WATERFOOT INN
WHITE HORSE INN
Rossville St
Eastway
Westland Street
Foyle Embankment
Fahan St
Shipquay St
Elmwood Rd
Bligh's Lane
Cable Street
Foyle Street
Bond's Hill
Clooney Terr
Stanley's Walk
Dungiven Rd
Celtic Park
Lone Moore Road
The Fountain
THE GALLE
Lecky Road
Barrack St
Abercorn Road
Chapel Road
Craigavon Br
Bishop Street Without
Ferguson St
Spencer Road
BROWN'S RESTAURANT
Foyle Road
River Foyle
Victoria Road
Victoria Park
Trench Road
Strabane Old Road
EVERGLADES HOTEL
BELL'S/JOHNNY B'S
Prehen Rd

EVERGLADES HOTEL Prehen Rd, tel: 0504-46722.
■ Last orders 2145 Mon.-Sat., 2130 Sun. ● Moderate-expensive.
A la carte only. Steaks and fish. Approved by 'Taste of Ulster'.

WATERFOOT INN Caw Roundabout, Clooney, tel: 0504-45500.
■ 1230-2230. ● Moderate.
A favourite with locals. Seafood specialities. Carvery.

BELL'S/JOHNNY B'S 59 Victoria Rd, tel: 0504-41078.
■ 1230-1430 Mon.-Fri. & Sun., 1830-2200 Mon.-Sat., 1500-2100 Sun.
● Moderate.
Restricted but enjoyable menu in Johnny B's basement wine bar. More expensive à la carte upstairs.

WHITE HORSE INN 68 Clooney Rd, Campsie, tel: 0504-860606.
■ Last orders 2115 Mon.-Sat., 2100 Sun. ● Moderate.
A grill restaurant with a friendly bar, as well as live music and karaoke.

BROWN'S RESTAURANT 1 Victoria Rd, tel: 0504-45180.
■ 1130-2300 Tue.-Sat., 1230-1430, 1730-2300 Sun. ● Inexpensive-moderate.
Housed in an old railway terminus. Serves spare ribs, Caesar salads, vegetarian dishes, etc. Popular.

MONICO BAR Custom House St, tel: 0504-263121.
Popular spot. Serves stews, quiches, bar lunches and snacks.

COLLEGE ARMS/COLE'S Junction of Rock Rd & Strand Rd.
Cole's, downstairs, is a pleasant and busy bar, and a little more sedate than the College Arms upstairs, a favourite with local students.

PHOENIX BAR 10-14 Park Ave, tel: 0504-268978.
Regular traditional music sessions. Very popular.

THE GALLERY 18 Dungiven Rd, tel: 0504-43698.
Lively establishment with good pub food lunchtime and evening.

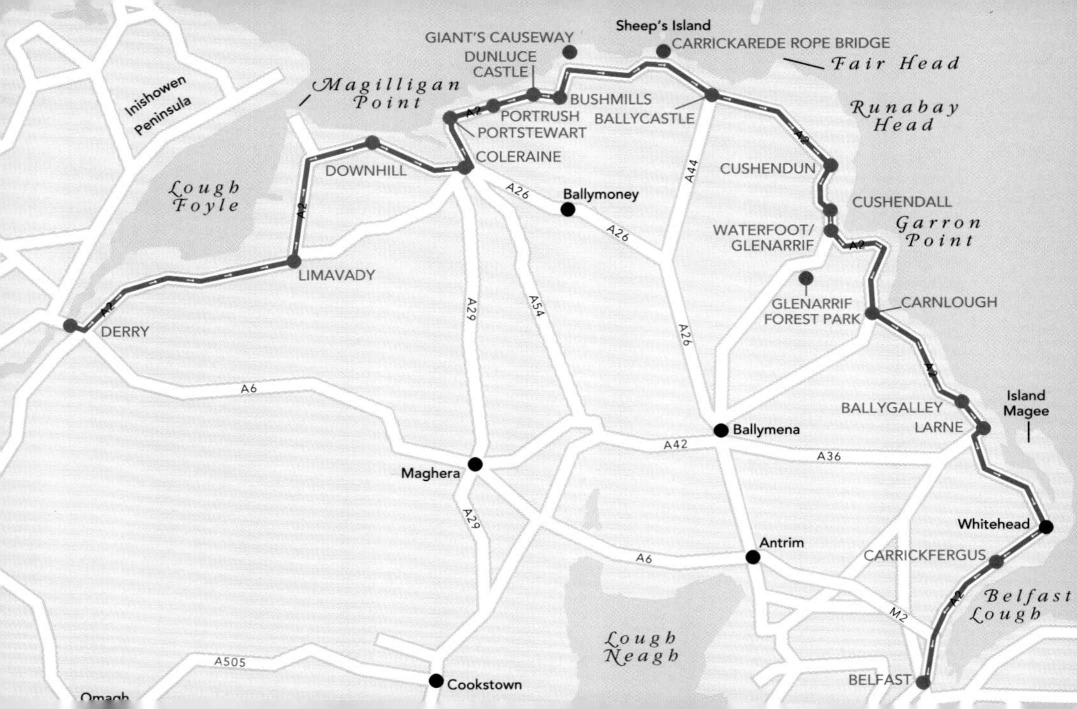
Sheep's Island
GIANT'S CAUSEWAY
CARRICKAREDE ROPE BRIDGE
DUNLUCE CASTLE
Fair Head
Magilligan Point
Inishowen Peninsula
BUSHMILLS
PORTRUSH
BALLYCASTLE
PORTSTEWART
Runabay Head
COLERAINE
DOWNHILL
CUSHENDUN
Lough Foyle
Ballymoney
CUSHENDALL
WATERFOOT/ GLENARRIF
Garron Point
LIMAVADY
GLENARRIF FOREST PARK
CARNLOUGH
DERRY
BALLYGALLEY
Island Magee
LARNE
Ballymena
Maghera
Whitehead
Antrim
CARRICKFERGUS
Belfast Lough
Lough Neagh
BELFAST
Cookstown
Omagh
A2
A26
A44
A29
A54
A6
A42
A36
M2
A505

Antrim Coast

Derry city–Belfast city. Duration: 1-2 days.

Leave Derry city (see **DERRY CITY**, **A-Z**) on the A 2 for Coleraine. After a few miles Lough Foyle can be seen on the left. Across the water is the Inishowen peninsula (see **A-Z**). Binevenagh (1270 ft) rises ahead. Pass through Ballykelly Forest and Ballykelly village. It was in Limavady that Jane Ross noted down the *Londonderry Air* (*Danny Boy*) in 1851, when she heard it played by a travelling fiddler. Turn left for Bellarena and pass through after about 5 miles. Binevenagh continues to loom overhead.

DETOUR: About 3 miles on is a left turn to Magilligan Point and its Martello tower (see **A-Z**). The point is very popular with hang-gliders.

Continue through the seaside village of Downhill.

30 miles – Mussenden Temple (1200-1800 July & Aug., 1200-1800 Sat. & Sun., April-June & Sep.). A little outside Downhill, on the left, is the Lion's Gate, and the Mussenden Temple (park car inside gate and walk). A mile further is Bishop's Gate, a more ornate entrance, where you can walk for a mile along the glen past Downhill Castle, the ruined bishop's palace built by John Adam in 1780, to the temple. This domed building, perched precariously on a cliff over Downhill Strand, is almost all that remains of the great estate built in the 18thC by Frederick Hervey, 4th Earl of Bristol and Anglican Bishop of Derry. The temple was built in honour of his cousin, Mrs Frideswide Mussenden, who died before it was completed. The bishop then used it as his summer library and even allowed locals to celebrate Mass there as there was no Catholic church in the area.

DETOURS: A little further on is a left turn for lovely Castlerock, overlooked by the temple and castle; and a right for Hezlett House (1400-1800 Easter, July & Aug.; Sat. & Sun., April-June & Sep.; £1, child 50p), a thatched 17thC rectory.

Continue through Articlave with views across to Portstewart.

36 miles – Coleraine. Built on land granted to the London Company by James I of England during the Plantations (see **A-Z**). Follow signposts across the River Bann into the bustling town centre. There is a boating marina on the river and children will love the Jet Centre, which includes an ice rink, bowling alley and adventure playground. A mile southeast is Mountsandel Fort, a 200 ft oval mound. Archaeologists say that wooden houses stood alongside the mound up to 9000 years ago. Leave on the A 2 for Portstewart, passing the ugly University of Ulster.

42 miles – Portstewart. Tourist Information, Town Hall, The Crescent, tel: 265-832286. Parts of this popular resort town look shabby but its huge stretch of beach is a dream and surfers usually find the waves perfect. As in just about every northern coastal town there is a golf links and there are plenty of pubs and restaurants. Keep on the A 2 along the seafront past the caravan parks.

45 miles – Portrush. Tourist Information, Town Hall, tel: 265-823333. Similar to Portstewart. Beautiful strands flank both sides of the town. The Waterworld complex at the harbour includes a water cannon, giant water slides and a kiddies' pool, while adults can opt for a sauna or steam bath. Golfers will enjoy the challenge of the Royal Portrush Club's Dunluce course. For a culinary treat the Ramore on the harbour serves lunches in the wine bar while the restaurant upstairs opens for dinner. Continue on the A 2 for Bushmills. A couple of miles outside the town the beautiful White Rocks beach is to the left. A mile on, the ruins of Dunluce Castle (1000-1900 Mon.-Sat., 1400-1800 Sun., April-Sep.; 1000-1600 Mon.-Sat., 1400-1600 Sun., Oct.-Mar.; 75p, child 35p) perch precariously on the cliffs. This 16thC stronghold, built above a cave, was the home of Sorley Boy MacDonnell, whose clan ruled north-eastern Ulster. It withstood sieges but during a storm in 1639 its kitchen, with the cooks and dinner, fell into the sea! The road veers inland but the coastal village of Portballintrae can be seen to the left.

51 miles – Bushmills. Tourist Information, 44 Causeway Rd, tel: 2657-31855. Turn right into the town, famous for its whiskey distillery, which is reputed to be the oldest legal distillery in the world, having received a licence in 1608. There is a visitor centre on Distillery Rd and guided tours are available (0900-1200, 1330-1530 Mon.-Thu., 0900-1145 Fri.; free). The River Bush, from which the town takes its name, once supported flour and paper mills and also generated power for the world's first hydroelectric tramway, which operated from the town to the Giant's Causeway from 1883 until 1949. Take the A 2 left, signposted Ballycastle Scenic Route, veering left for the Giant's Causeway after a mile. Enjoy the expansive sea views to the left and ahead.

53 miles – Giant's Causeway (see **A-Z**). The visitor centre's tearooms serve hot lunches, home-made soups, cakes and biscuits. The adjacent schoolhouse museum is open daily July & Aug., offering a glimpse back at education and schoolyard games in the 1920s. It is a 15 min walk down to the columns of the 'little', 'middle' and 'grand' causeways but a minibus (with wheelchair hoist) is also laid on from the centre. If you really want to stretch your legs, however, and see a lot more of the causeway, try the following walk.

WALK: A 5 mile walk around the causeway to Hamilton's Seat. From the visitor centre walk along the cliff tops past the viewpoint at Weir's Snout, where the causeway juts out to the sea below. In the distance the columns of the Chimney Tops stand out clearly. A little further is Aird Snout. Here the 40 ft-high columns of The Organ become visible. At the Shepherd's Path descend the 149 steps, walking back to examine the honeycomb formations. Turn again and take the lower path into Port Noffer, which is regarded as one of the best-developed causeway amphitheatres, and on to Port Reostan, where The Harp's curving columns can be seen. The Chimney Tops are high in the cliffs overhead. Port an Spaniagh is the next stop. It was here that the Spanish treasure ship, *Girona*, was wrecked in 1588 and discovered by divers in 1968.

The path continues into Port na Callian, with views of the gap-riddled Horse Back headland. This rock formation is replicated all the way to lovely Horseshoe Bay which flanks Port na Plaiskin. Ascend the steps to Benbane Head, which rises to 350 ft, and continue to Hamilton's Seat for spectacular views across to the Inishowen peninsula. Return to the visitor centre on the upper cliff path.

Drive back to the main road and turn left, signposted Ballycastle. After about 2 miles the views stretch out to Rathlin Island (see **A-Z**). Pass the remains of a castle at Dunseverick, turning left to Ballintoy after a mile. Follow signposts for the Coastal Route skirting the seafront.

Keep straight on in Ballintoy, taking a left turn signposted Larrybane after a mile.

61 miles – Larrybane & Carrickarede Rope Bridge (spring-mid Sep.). There is a National Trust information centre beside the car park, where there is a £1 charge per day. Larrybane is a huge white limestone headland, most of which has been quarried away. Walk to the bridge and cross its bouncing planks 80 ft above the water to Sheep's Island – if you

dare! The bridge is erected across the chasm to the island every year to allow the local salmon fishermen access to their fisheries. Return to the road and turn left. On a clear day views from here stretch across to Scotland. The road ascends along the cliff edges and after a couple of miles Fair Head can be seen jutting out ahead, while the Antrim mountains rise up in the distance.

68 miles – Ballycastle. Tourist Information, 7 Mary St, tel: 2657-62024. Beautifully sited facing Rathlin Island, with the ancient landmark of Fair Head to the east. Enquire locally about ferry services to the island. This bustling town is best known for the Old Lammas Fair held in The Diamond or market square during the Aug. bank holiday. Fair-goers are expected to buy and eat dulse, an edible dried seaweed, and 'yellowman', sticky slabs of yellow toffee. Turn left for Cushendall and follow signposts for Coastal Route out by the golf links, passing through pleasant countryside into Ballyvoy. Here follow Scenic Route signposts.

DETOUR: Take the other fork for Watertop Open Farm (1000-1730 July & Aug.; 80p, child 50p), where there are sheep-shearing demonstrations, boating, game birds and a tearoom.

DETOUR: A mile on is a left turn for Fair Head car park. This is a good place for a bracing walk and some panoramic views.

The road stays inland for about 4 miles, passing through forest-covered hills, before the sea reappears. The road ascends and descends sharply. If possible park and take in the panoramic views. While winding round Runabay Head small fields are marked out along the cliffs below and Garron Point juts out ahead. Veer inland again for a short distance, then back out to the sea.

82 miles – Cushendun. Tourist Information, 1 Main St, tel: 26674-506. Sited at the foot of Glendun, the first of the nine glens of Antrim. The Cornish-style cottages in the heart of the village were built by Lord Cushendun in memory of his wife Maud who came from Cornwall. The cottages and the beach are preserved by the National Trust. There is an

information centre beside the bridge, which crosses the Glendun River. Leave the village following signposts for Cushendall. The road moves inland again with the peaks of Trostan (1815 ft) and Slieveanorra ahead.
88 miles – Cushendall. Tourist Information, Chapel Rd, tel: 2657-71180. The Capital of the Glens is sited at the junction of Glenaan and Glenballyemon at the mouth of the River Dall, and is regarded as the best base for exploring the glens. Its four main streets meet at the 'curfew' or Turnley's Tower, a red sandstone tower built in 1809 by landlord Francis Turnley as a 'place of confinement for idlers and rioters'. Follow the A 2 into Waterfoot, skirting Red Bay. After a mile pass under ruined Red Bay Castle and a number of caves which were once inhabited and used for a series of activities, including a school during penal times (see **Penal Laws**). The largest of the caves is Nanny's Cave, which is 40 ft long. Ann Murray, a famous distiller of poitin (see **A-Z**), lived here and it appears that her life style proved good for her health – she died in 1847 aged 100!
90 miles – Waterfoot/Glenarrif. At the entrance to Glenarrif, considered to be the most beautiful of the nine Antrim glens. Lurigethan dominates the landscape, with Trostan and Croaghlough behind. Glenarrif Forest Park, which is a few miles up the glen, contains a number of waterfalls. Keep on the A 2 round impressive Garron Point.
99 miles – Carnlough. This village at the head of Glencloy has a picture-book stone harbour. Keep on the A 2 to pleasant Glenarm, at the tip of the southernmost of the glens, and turn left. The road continues under towering cliff faces but the coastal landscape becomes more austere. After about 3 miles, in front is Ballygalley Head.
109 miles – Ballygalley. The 17thC castle in this neat town, built around a wide bay and sandy beach, is now a three-star restaurant serving good carvery lunches. Behind are the Sallagh Braes, which offer some of the most scenic walks in Ulster. Continue on the A 2 round the head and travel alongside Drains Bay.
113 miles – Larne. Tourist Information, Victoria Rd, tel: 574-72313. Known as The Gateway to Ulster. Ferries from the port to Cairnryan and Stranraer offer the shortest route to Scotland and Britain. It's rather a dismal spot, though there are some good shops, and golf, tennis and fishing facilities. The A 2 passes through an industrial area into Glynn, then

St. Anne's Cathedral, Belfast

runs alongside Larne Lough, with the peninsula of Island Magee across the water, and through Magheramorne. Just before the A 2 begins to skirt Belfast Lough, the coastal town of Whitehead can be seen below. Continue through Eden.

DETOUR: Turn left in Eden for the Andrew Jackson Centre, a commemorative centre based in a reconstructed 18thC thatched cottage, in honour of the 7th American president, whose parents emigrated from Carrickfergus (1000-1300, 1400-1600 Mon.-Fri., 1400-1600 Sat. & Sun., until 1800 June-Sep.).

128 miles – Carrickfergus (see **A-Z**). Keep on the A 2 into Belfast via Newtownabbey. Cave Hill, on top of which are five ancient caves and a flat-topped stronghold named McArt's Fort, is ahead. Follow the M 2 or A 2 into the city centre (see **BELFAST CITY**, **A-Z**) (138 miles).

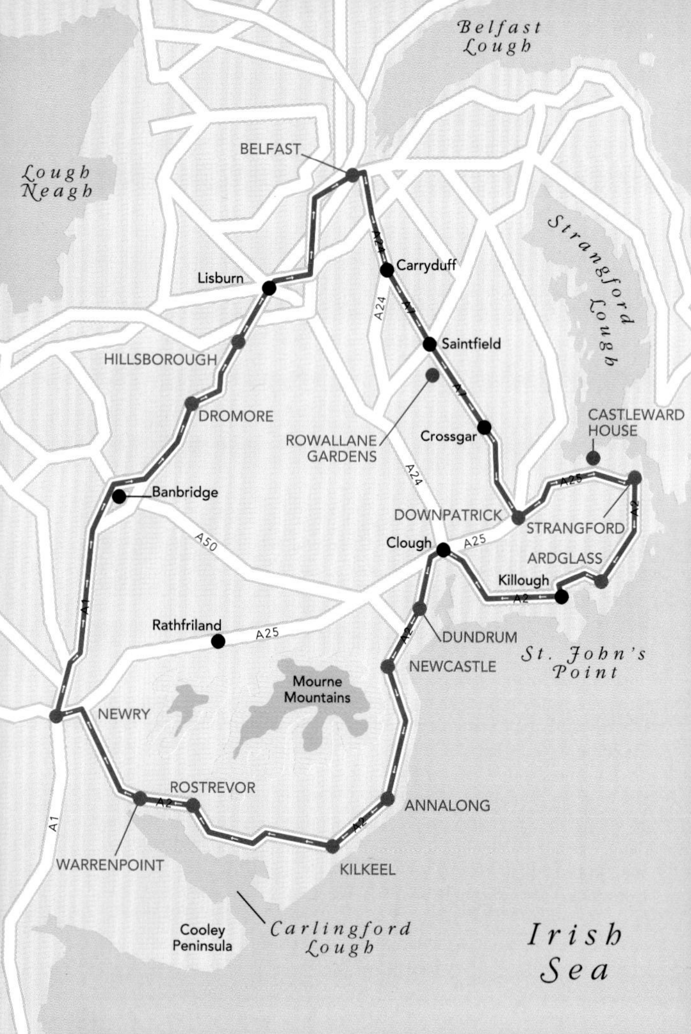
Belfast Lough
Lough Neagh
BELFAST
Lisburn
Carryduff
A24
A7
Saintfield
HILLSBOROUGH
DROMORE
Strangford Lough
ROWALLANE GARDENS
Crossgar
CASTLEWARD HOUSE
Banbridge
A24
A25
A2
DOWNPATRICK
STRANGFORD
A50
Clough
A25
ARDGLASS
Killough
A2
A1
Rathfriland
A25
DUNDRUM
A2
St. John's Point
NEWCASTLE
Mourne Mountains
NEWRY
ROSTREVOR
A2
ANNALONG
A2
A1
WARRENPOINT
KILKEEL
Cooley Peninsula
Carlingford Lough
Irish Sea

EXCURSION 15

Belfast city–Ardglass–Newcastle–Newry–Belfast city. Duration: 1-2 days.

Leave Belfast city (see **BELFAST CITY**, **A-Z**) via Ormeau Rd, taking the A 24 in Newtownbreda and then the A 7, signposted Downpatrick, in Carryduff, finally entering the hilly countryside after 7 miles. Pass through Saintfield and take a right turn into Rowallane Gardens.

11 miles – Rowallane Gardens (daily except winter weekends; £2, child £1). The gardens are noted for their magnificent rhododendrons, azaleas, rare trees and shrubs. Continue on the A 7, with the Mournes in the distance to the right after 3 or 4 miles, through Crossgar.

DETOUR: Four miles outside Crossgar is a right turn for ruined Inch Abbey (1000-1900 Tue.-Sat., 1400-1900 Sun., Easter-Sep.; 1000-1600 Tue.-Sat., 1400-1600 Sun., Oct.-Easter; 50p, child 25p), founded in 1180 by John de Courcy, who also built Carrickfergus Castle, and reached by a causeway through the Quoile marshes. Cross over the Quoile River into Downpatrick.

21 miles – Downpatrick (see **A-Z**). Leave on the A 25 for Strangford. This quiet hedgerow-lined road passes through gently undulating land that is emblazoned with gorse. There are glimpses of Strangford Lough on the left after a few miles.

DETOUR: Two miles further on is a left turn for ruined Audley's Castle. It is 2 miles to the castle, perched on the lough edge.

A left turn leads to Castleward House (grounds daily dawn-dusk; house 1300-1800 Fri.-Wed., April-Aug.; Sat., Sun. & hols, Sep. & Oct.; grounds £3 per car, house £2.30, child £1.15), the 18thC residence of Lord and Lady Bangor, who agreed to differ and had one side of the house built in the classical Palladian style and the other in a neo-Gothic fashion.There is a Victorian laundry, a children's centre and a variety of walks through the mansion's 900 acre estate. Return to the A 25 and cross the lough.

29 miles – Strangford. This tiny but picturesque village looks across to Portaferry on the Ards peninsula (see **A-Z**) and ferries commute regularly between the two. The Lobster Pot in The Square is a good option for a break and a bite to eat. Leave on the road to Ardglass. Ballyquintin Point is the furthest tip of land on the left as the mouth of the lough opens into the sea. The road veers inland again and the Mournes loom up to the right and ahead. Pass through Chapeltown.

39 miles – Ardglass. A lively fishing village. Jordan's Castle, a four-storey tower house on Low Rd beside the Anchor pub, is the only one of the town's seven small castles open to the public. It now houses the local museum (1000-1300, 1330-1900 Tue.-Sat., 1400-1900 Sun., June-Sep.; 50p, child 25p). The solitary turret on the hilltop is Isabella's Tower, built in the 19thC by Aubrey de Vere Beauclerc as a gazebo for his invalid daughter. Take the road through nearby Coney Island, which circuits an extremely tidal bay into Killough. Here take the A 2 for Clough, veering inland again. For a couple of miles it is easy to forget that the sea is so near until suddenly there's a panoramic view of Dundrum Bay, backed by the Mournes 'sweeping down to the sea'. The highest peak is Slieve Donard (2796 ft). Skirt the bay with rolling pastures to the right. Follow signposts for Clough through the hamlets of Rossglass, Minerstown and Tyrella, veering inland occasionally. The mountains ahead are constantly changing colour. When the road meets the A 24 turn left signposted Newcastle and continue into Dundrum.
DETOUR: Half-way through the village is a right turn for the Norman-built Dundrum Castle which towers spectacularly over the village.
Keep on the A 2 with Slieve Donard, Slieve Commedagh, Slieve Meelmore and Chimney Rock Mountain ahead.
58 miles – Newcastle (see **A-Z**). Take the A 2 for Kilkeel along the coast. St. John's Point is to the left across the bay. Up close the mountains look black and forbidding. Pass through Glasdrumman, Mullartown, Annalong (which has an old working cornmill with a water wheel) and Ballymartin.
DETOUR: Watch out for a right turn to the peaceful Silent Valley, to the left of Slieve Binnian.
72 miles – Kilkeel. Tourist Information, Mourne Esplanade, tel: 6937-64666. In ancient times this was the capital of the kingdom of Mourne. Nowadays it is the base of the area's fishing fleet. A ruined 14thC church stands in a rath (a circular enclosure) at the town centre. Continue straight on for Lisnacree. The road goes alongside Carlingford Lough with views across to the Cooley peninsula and hills.
84 miles – Rostrevor (see **A-Z**). Continue on the A 2.
86 miles – Warrenpoint. Tourist Information, Boating Pool, tel: 6937-72256. As late as 1780 the settlement here consisted of only two houses

and a scatter of fishermen's huts but in the early 19thC it became a packet station with a service to Liverpool and began to grow. Now a popular seaside resort and port, its large square and tree-lined promenade make it particularly attractive. Facilities include a marina and golf course. Enquire locally about boat trips to Omeath in the Republic, across Carlingford Lough. The Diplomat Inn and restaurant near the quay serves good seafood. Rejoin the A 2. Two miles outside the town is Narrow Water Castle, built by the Magennises of Iveagh in the 16thC to guard the entrance to the lough.

91 miles – Newry. Tourist Information, Bank Parade, tel: 693-66232. On the border of counties Down and Armagh, the town hall straddles the Clanrye River and is actually halved between them. The town is the area's largest commercial centre. Its development was accelerated in 1741 by the opening of the Newry Canal linking Lough Neagh with Carlingford Lough but little of the old town remains today. Ships no longer use the canal but it's a top coarse fishing location. Newry is much frequented by day-trippers from the Republic in search of shopping bargains. Take the A 1 north to Belfast, bypassing Banbridge after about 13 miles. After another 6.5 miles turn right.

111 miles – Dromore. Built on the Lagan, this is the ancient ecclesiastical capital of Down and is believed to have been the site of a 6thC abbey founded by St. Colman. The present cathedral, built in 1661, replaced an earlier medieval church. It contains a 17thC font and a poor-man's box. A stone inscribed with a cross in the south wall is

probably a relic of the original monastery. The old parish stocks can be seen in Market Sq., while a 12thC fortified motte stands on the right bank of the river. Return to the A 1, turning right for Hillsborough after about 4.5 miles.

116 miles – Hillsborough. Tourist Information, The Square, tel: 846-682477. This Georgian town is centred on Hillsborough Castle, formerly the governor's residence but now used only for State occasions and for visiting royalty. The town's massive fort, which was remodelled in the 18thC, can be visited (1000-1900 Tue.-Sat., 1400-1900 Sun., closes 1600 Oct.-Mar.). Go back onto the A 1 into the outskirts of Lisburn, and follow signposts for the M 1 and Belfast (129 miles).

Achill Island: Co. Mayo. 8 miles northwest of Mulrany on the R 319. The largest island off the Irish coast has been connected to the mainland by bridge since 1888. The seaside resort of Doogort is at the base of the island's highest point, Slievemore (2204 ft). There is a 2 mile sandy beach at Keel, bordered to the east by the spectacular Cathedral Rocks. Nearby Dooagh and Keem strands are sheltered by Moyteoge Head, a good spot to begin an ascent of Croaghaun (2195 ft).

Act of Union (1800): Under the Act, which came into effect on 1 Jan. 1801, the parliaments of Ireland and Great Britain were again joined together, in what was called the 'United Kingdom'. Until 1921 Irish representatives met in Westminster. Unlike Scotland and Wales, the Crown was represented in Ireland by a viceroy and chief secretary.

Adare: Co. Limerick. 10 miles southwest of Limerick city on the N 21. Situated on the River Maigue, Adare is regarded as one of Ireland's prettiest villages. The picturesque thatched cottages, which were built in the 19thC as tenant dwellings by the 3rd Earl of Dunraven, have a distinct English character. The 12thC Augustinian and 13thC Trinitarian abbeys were partly restored by the Dunravens and serve as the local Church of Ireland and Catholic churches. The village boasts a selection of antique and craft shops but probably the best known is Micheline and George Stacpoole's outlet. The Inn Between, the more pricey Mustard Seed, and the Maigue Restaurant in the Dunraven Arms Hotel are all good choices for food.

Aherlow, Glen of: Co. Tipperary. Turn left at Bansha on the N 24 between Cahir and Tipperary town. This beautiful remote glen lies between the Galty mountains and Slievenamuck. Historically this was an important pass between the Golden Vale of Co. Tipperary and Limerick, and many battles were fought here between the O'Briens and rival clans. At the head of the valley near Galbally is the ruined Franciscan Moor Abbey, used as a fortress during the Elizabethan Wars.

Anglo-Irish Treaty (1921): This compromise treaty was negotiated over two months following the truce which ended the War of

Independence, and reluctantly signed by the Irish representatives. It made Ireland a Free State but with the exception of northeast Ulster and with the stipulation that all Irishmen should swear allegiance to the Crown of England. Its signing began the Civil War (see **A-Z**).

Antrim: Co. Antrim. Northwest of Belfast city on the A 6. Tourist Information, Pogue's Entry, Church St, tel: 8494-64131. A busy but somewhat shabby spot. Pogues Entry, an 18thC cottage on Church St, was the childhood home of Alexander Irvine, author of *My Lady of the Chimney Corner* (0900-1700 Mon.-Fri., June-Aug.; free. Key from Antrim Forum). A mile north in Steeple Park is a 10thC 93 ft tapered round tower. It marks the site of a monastery which thrived here between the 6th and 12thC. Shane's Castle is nearby on Lough Neagh (see **A-Z**) and has a deer park, narrow-gauge railway and nature trails.

Aran Island: Co. Donegal. Less than a mile from Burtonport, this Gaeltacht (see **A-Z**) island buzzes during the summer, even outside the Aug. festival. The hilly landscape stretches back to the rugged western cliffs but sheltered sandy beaches dot the island's opposite end. There's an hourly ferry service from Burtonport.

Aran Islands: Co. Clare. Inishmore (7635 acres), Inishmaan (2253 acres) and Inisheer (1400 acres) lie about 30 miles off the Galway coast and even today remain relatively isolated. Fishing is done from *currachs*, fragile-looking boats covered in tarred canvas, and the islanders have cultivated small pockets of soil using seaweed and sand. Kilronan on Inishmore is the islands' capital and the liveliest spot, with plenty of music in the pub. Dun Aengus, on Inishmore, a semicircular fort perched over 300 ft cliffs, is the most important of the islands' antiquities. Others include the tiny ancient church of Teampall Bheanain at Killeany, Inishmore and Doonconor on Inishmaan. Inishmaan, which is the least visited of the islands, is also the most colourful and the most solitary. It was here that J. M. Synge (see **A-Z**) stayed, to study the life and language of the people, and where he based his play *Riders to the Sea*. Inisheer, the smallest of the islands, is dominated by a huge rock formation, topped by the ruins of a 15thC O'Brien castle. The ancient

Church of St. Kevin, who is the islands' patron saint, is near the beach. Aer Arann operates a regular air service to Inishmore from Carnmore airport near Galway, tel: 091-55437/55448, while daily ferries run from Galway, Spiddle, Rossaveel and Doolin, and between the islands (weather permitting). See **EXCURSIONS 6 & 7**.

Aran Sweaters: The intricate stitches were originally designed on the Aran Islands (see **A-Z**), where fishermen's wives knitted the spun fleece with goose quills. The stitches were passed from mother to daughter, and it is said that the different patterns helped island families identify bodies long lost at sea. The cable stitch recalls the fisherman's rope and the diamonds the net. The trellis stitch represents the stone-walled fields of the West.

Ardglass: Co. Down. See **EXCURSION 15**.

Ardmore: Co. Waterford. Southwest of Waterford city on the R 673. This lovely resort has the remains of a 7thC monastic settlement founded by St. Declan. The 97 ft round tower which dominates the area was one of the last to be built in Ireland. Inside, ugly carved stone heads protrude from the walls. There are pleasant walks along the cliffs.

Ards Peninsula: Co. Down. This scenic peninsula flanks the east side of Strangford Lough. Attractions include: Mount Stewart House and Gardens, formerly the Irish seat of the Londonderry family; 12thC Grey Abbey; the fishing villages of Kearney and Portavogie; Ballycopeland windmill near Millisle; and Bangor (see **A-Z**). See **EXCURSION 15**.

Arklow: Co. Wicklow. 41 miles south of Dublin city on the N 11. An old port town formerly famed for its shipbuilding. *Gipsy Moth IV*, the yacht in which Sir Francis Chichester sailed solo around the world, was built here. The Wexford Rebellion led by Fr John Murphy in 1798 ended here. Today the town is best known for its pottery.

Armagh: Co. Armagh. Pop: 13,000. 38 miles southwest of Belfast city on the A 3. Tourist Information, Market House, Market St, tel: 861-524072. This small city is probably one of the country's oldest settlements, and is sited on the Moyry Pass, an ancient roadway which stretched from the south of Ireland, through Tara, to the north. It was here that St. Patrick (see **A-Z**) built his first stone church in Ireland, and today it remains the ecclesiastical capital of Ireland. The spartan Church of Ireland cathedral, on St. Patrick's original site, is predominantly a 19thC building. A tablet marks the grave of High King of Ireland, Brian Boru (see **A-Z**). The elaborate and airy Catholic cathedral on another hill is more recent. The Armagh Planetarium and Observatory on College Hill is a 'must'. The hall of astronomy contains displays of astronomical instruments, mock-ups of spacecraft and hands-on computer demonstrations (1400-1645 Mon.-Sat.; free). Star shows are held in the theatre under the huge dome of the Planetarium (1400 & 1500 Sat. all year, Mon.-Sat., July & Aug.; £2, child £1.50). The County Museum is on the east side of the elegant tree-lined Mall (1000-1300, 1400-1700 Mon.-Sat.; free). Beside the courthouse is the Royal Irish Fusiliers Museum, which tells the story of the regiment from 1793 to 1968. Navan Fort, 2 miles west of the city off the A 28, is an 18 acre hill fort that was the chief stronghold of the kings of Ulster from about 600 BC until its destruction in AD 332. Its summit was crowned by Eamhain Macha, the palace of Macha, the queen c. 300 BC, from which Armagh takes its name. The city is at the centre of an area so fertile that it is known as 'The Garden of Ireland'. Co. Armagh is also the Orchard County, and in May and June there is an orchard drive.

Ashford: Co. Wicklow. 17 miles south of Dublin city on the N 11. The town is beautifully situated on the Vartry River. Close by are Mount Usher Gardens, with collections of rhododendrons, azaleas, camellias and plants from across the globe (1030-1800 Mon.-Sat., 1100-1800 Sun., Mar.-mid Oct.; £2, child £1.30). A mile away is the renowned Hunter's Hotel, a lovely spot for lunch.

Athlone: Tourist Information, 17 Church St, tel: 902-94630. The River Shannon here divides the counties of Westmeath and Roscommon and the provinces of Leinster and Connacht. As it was a strategic crossing point there were frequent battles in the town, first between the Irish tribes and then with the Anglo-Normans. Bishop John de Gray, the English justiciar, built a castle in 1210 to guard the bridge into Connacht. In 1691 the Williamite forces laid siege to and later defeated the Jacobite troops here. The museum in the remains of Athlone Castle has exhibits dating from the Stone Age, artefacts from the Siege of Athlone and memorabilia of one of Ireland's most famous singers, John McCormack (1130-1300, 1400-1700 Mon.-Sat., June-Sep.). The town is one of the best-known river cruiser bases. The Prince of Wales Hotel has a good restaurant. See **EXCURSION 10**.

Aughnanure Castle: Oughterard, Co. Galway. Built in the 15thC by the O'Flahertys, during the Cromwellian (see **A-Z**) era this was one of the outposts guarding Galway and proved to be among the strongest fortresses in Ireland. The remains include a six-storey tower which stands on a rock island. One of the 'duties' of the chief who ruled here, it appears, was to sleep with each woman from the surrounding settlement on her wedding night! 0930-1830 mid June-mid Sep.; 80p, child/student 30p. See **EXCURSION 7**.

Avoca: Co. Wicklow. 41 miles south of Dublin city on the R 752. Made famous by the Thomas Moore song *The Meeting of the Waters*, which refers to the picturesque joining of the Avonmore and Avonbeg rivers north of the village, and which is now home to Avoca Handweavers and Handcrafts. There is a series of good forest walks in the steep hills surrounding the village.

Ballina: Co. Mayo. The county's largest town, and also a popular base with anglers eager to fish the waters of Lough Conn, nearby Killala Bay or the River Moy, which is famous for its salmon. The town was captured by Gen. Humbert during the 1798 Rebellion (see **A-Z**). As the Franco-Irish troops skirmished with the English on the town's outskirts, local people lit straw to guide them in. The road is still referred to as Bothar na Sop ('Road of the Straw'). Near the station is the Dolmen of the Four Maols, though one of the four uprights has fallen. Beneath lie four foster-brothers who murdered a local bishop, Ceallach. His brother had them killed and they were buried here. See **EXCURSION 9**.

Ballinasloe: Co. Galway. 42 miles east of Galway city on the N 6. Sited at the crossing of the River Suck, the town straddles the border of counties Galway and Roscommon. It is famous for its Oct. Horse Fair, though other animals are also bought and sold.

Ballinrobe: Co. Mayo. 30 miles north of Galway city on the N 84. The town, on the Robe River, and near both Lough Mask and Lough Carra, is a popular angling base. On its outskirts are the remains of a 14thC Augustinian friary. About 4 miles southwest is Lough Mask House. This was the residence of Capt. Charles Boycott, the agent of Lord Erne, who because of his treatment of tenants was – on the recommendation of Parnell (see **A-Z**) – totally ostracized by tenants, workers and tradesmen, adding a new word to the English language – 'boycott'.

Ballinskelligs: Co. Kerry. A scenic Gaeltacht (see **A-Z**) village boasting a 4 mile beach. The area is thronged with schoolchildren learning Irish in summer. West of the village, on Ballinskelligs Point, are the remains of a MacCarthy castle, and an Augustinian monastery founded by the monks from Skellig Michael who moved here in the 12thC. Enquire locally about boat trips to The Skelligs (see **A-Z**) and Puffin Island. See EXCURSION 5.

Ballintubber: Ballintober. Co. Mayo. North of Galway city on the N 84. This little village is famous for its abbey, which has the only church in the English-speaking world where Mass has been continuously celebrated for over 750 years, despite the suppression of religious communities by Henry VIII, its unroofing by Cromwellian (see **A-Z**) troops, and the Penal Laws (see **A-Z**). Excavations have unearthed the papal seal bestowed on the abbey by Pope Pius II in 1463, portions of the cloister arcade which has been re-erected, and a hospice for pilgrims on their way to Croagh Patrick (see **A-Z**).

Ballybunion: Co. Kerry. 52 miles west of Limerick city on the R 551. The glorious beach at this seaside village makes it one of Ireland's most popular resorts, and therefore not the place to seek solitude. There are dramatic cliff walks and a championship golf course.

Ballycastle: Co. Antrim. See EXCURSION 14.

Ballynahinch: Co. Galway. Situated off the Recess–Clifden road, signposted Toombeola, is Ballynahinch Castle, a much-modified 18thC mansion, home to the Martin family who ruled Connemara from 1700 until the time of the Great Famine (see **A-Z**). It is now a hotel. Probably the best known of this family was Richard Martin, known as 'Hairtrigger Dick' because of his love for duelling, and rechristened 'Humanity Dick' for his part in founding the RSPCA. Beautiful Ballynahinch Lake is the most southerly of a chain enclosing the Twelve Pins to the south and east. One of the lake's islands has a ruined castle which once belonged to the Martins and was possibly used as a prison for their enemies.

Ballyshannon: Co. Donegal. See **EXCURSION 12**.

Baltimore: Co. Cork. A small fishing port and good sea-angling and sailing base, which serves as a port for ferries to Sherkin Island (see **A-Z**) and Cape Clear (see **A-Z**). The remains of the castle, owned by the seafaring O'Driscoll clan, overlook the harbour. The village was raided by pirates in 1631 and 200 of its inhabitants were captured. See **EXCURSION 4**.

Baltinglass: Co. Wicklow. 36 miles southwest of Dublin city on the N 81. This little town stands at the foot of Baltinglass Hill. On its summit, which affords lovely views of the Wicklow mountains, there are substantial remains of a cairn and passage grave. On the banks of the River Slaney are the ruins of the 12thC Cistercian abbey of Vallis Salutis, founded by Dermot MacMurrough, 12thC King of Leinster.

Bandon: Co. Cork. 19 miles southwest of Cork city on the N 71. This market town, which straddles the River Bandon, is a popular angling centre. It was established by the Earl of Cork, Richard Boyle, in 1608. Boyle, who arrived from England with only £20, a diamond ring, a gold bracelet and his clothes, acquired huge tracts of land in Munster. In Bandon he ousted the local Catholic clans from the surrounding lands and built a town wall to keep them out.

Bangor: Co. Down. 11 miles northeast of Belfast city on the A 2. Tourist Information, 34 Quay St, tel: 247-270069. In the 6thC this was the site of a monastery, founded by St. Comgall, which became home to 3000 monks. A reconstruction can be seen in the Heritage Centre at Bangor Castle which is now the Town Hall. Bangor prospered as a Victorian seaside resort and still retains its villas and parks. Today there is a large range of family amenities and leisure facilities on offer.

Bantry: Co. Cork. See **EXCURSION 4**.

Battle of the Books: According to tradition St. Columbcille (see **A-Z**) secretly copied a rare psalter lent to him by St. Finian of Moville.

When Finian discovered this he demanded that the copy be handed over. Columbcille refused and fighting broke out between their followers. The matter was finally brought to the high king Diarmaid, who made the famous copyright ruling, 'To every cow her calf, and to every book its copy.'

Battle of the Boyne: When the British monarchy was restored after Cromwell's reign, Charles II, who was under an obligation to Protestant parliamentarians in Britain and Ireland, failed to restore any rights to Catholics who had been persecuted, and whose lands had been confiscated. James II's succession to the throne was therefore welcomed and he managed to repeal the Act of Settlement (see **Cromwell**). But before it could be implemented William of Orange was called in by the English Establishment to put a stop to James' 'Popish ways', and James fled to France and then Ireland where he raised an army. He was resisted in Enniskillen and in Derry (see **Siege of Derry**), and at the Battle of the Boyne in July 1690 'King Billy's' 36,000-strong force soundly defeated James' smaller army. The victory is still celebrated on 12 July (see **Orange Order**). Another defeat in 1691 at Aughrim, Co. Galway, and finally the surrender of the Jacobites in Limerick, ended the struggle. Measures were then taken to ensure the continued power of the Protestant minority by the introduction of the Penal Laws (see **A-Z**).

Beara Peninsula: This most westerly of the Cork peninsulas is also called Bear Haven peninsula. It stretches for over 30 miles, separating Bantry Bay from the Kenmare River estuary, and is dominated by the Caha and Slieve Miskish mountains. The peninsula is linked to Dursey Island by cable car. The spectacular Healy Pass crosses the Caha mountains from Adrigole to Lauragh. It is named after Tim Healy who was appointed governor general of the new Irish Free State in 1921. See **EXCURSION 4**.

Behan, Brendan (1923-64): Remembered as much for his drinking sprees and 'colourful' wit as for his plays and books, which include *The Borstal Boy* and *The Quare Fellow*. He was born in Mountjoy Sq., Dublin. Recommended reading is *Brendan Behan's Ireland*.

Belfast City Hall

Belfast: Co. Antrim. Pop: 300,000. Tourist Information, River House, 48 High St, tel: 0232-246609. The capital of Northern Ireland since the partition of the country in 1921, and Ireland's greatest seaport. It began as a small settlement around a crossing over the River Farset then gradually grew up around the mouth of the River Lagan, particularly after the 'planting' of Sir Arthur Chichester in the area by James I in 1608 (see **Plantations**), and the granting of a town charter. With the arrival of the French Huguenots at the end of the 17thC, a local linen industry began to thrive, and though the town was destroyed by fire in 1708, the textile and shipbuilding industries continued to grow. Today the skyline to the east is dominated by the two gigantic cranes in the Harland and Wolff shipyard, bearing testimony to the ongoing importance of shipbuilding in the city's economy. By the time it was granted city status by Queen Victoria in 1888, Belfast's population exceeded 208,000, and by the end of the century exceeded even Dublin's. Divisions between Catholic and Protestants are a relatively new phenomenon in the city. During the 18thC it was here that the nationalist society, the United Irishmen, was founded by Presbyterian Ulstermen, and local Protestants contributed generously to the building of a Catholic church. But in the 19thC, spurred on by the achievement of Catholic emancipation, the rise of the Orange Order (see **A-Z**) and an increase in the Catholic population, many Presbyterian ministers began open attacks on Catholicism. As the division grew so did the outbreaks of violence, and Belfast became the centre of Unionist opposition to home rule. The most obvious divide today is in west Belfast, where the Protestant strongholds are the Shankill and Crumlin roads, and the Catholic the Falls and Divis areas. Bombings during World War II destroyed a great deal of the city but major redevelopment began over a decade ago. Today, despite the derelict sites and no-go zones which pervade most urban areas, it remains a beautiful and exciting city, surrounded by lovely countryside. But – despite what the tourist board will have you believe – it is still a city torn by imbedded hatreds nurtured by a small group on both sides of the divide who continue to profit by others' misery. See **BELFAST CITY, EXCURSIONS 14 & 15.**

Belfast City Hall

Belleek: Co. Fermanagh. Northern Ireland's most westerly village is the home of Ireland's oldest handcrafted pottery china, famed worldwide for its creamy lustre and intricate basketwork. The pottery was founded in 1857 by Sir John Caldwell Bloomfield. There are guided tours of the pottery and the visitor complex includes a museum, audiovisual presentation, shop and restaurant (0900-1800, 2000 July & Aug., Mon.-Fri., 1000-1800 Sat., 1400-1800 Sun., Mar.-Sep.; 0900-1700 Mon.-Fri., Oct.-Feb.; guided tours £1). See **EXCURSION 12**.

Benbulben: Dartry Mountains, Co. Sligo. Rising to 1722 ft, the unmistakable 'table-topped' shape of this mountain dominates the countryside around Sligo town. There are panoramic views from its summit, where many alpine plant species can be found. W. B. Yeats (see **A-Z**) was just one of this mountain's fans, and his wish to be buried in its sight was granted when he was interred at Drumcliff. See **EXCURSION 12**.

Bewley's Oriental Cafés: Since their foundation by the Quaker Bewley family over 150 years ago, Bewley's Oriental Cafés have been a Dublin institution, and are one of the city's most popular places to breakfast, sip tea or drink coffee Bewley's-style with whipped milk. Branches are now open in other areas of Dublin and around the country, though the atmosphere of its original Grafton St and Westmoreland St outlets in Dublin is impossible to capture.

Birr: Co. Offaly. This former garrison town still retains some lovely Georgian houses. The rivers Camcor and Little Brosna join here, and there is good trout fishing. Birr Castle was originally an O'Carroll fortress and withstood many sieges. Sir Laurence Parsons rebuilt the castle around a ruined keep in 1620 and his descendants, the Earl and Countess of Rosse, still live here. Its magnificent walled demesne and gardens include the tallest box hedge in the world (0900-1300, 1400-1800, dusk in winter).
There is also an exhibition of the telescope built by the 3rd Earl in 1845, which for 75 years was the world's largest (1430-1730 May-mid Sep.). See EXCURSION 10.

Blarney: Co. Cork. 6 miles northeast of Cork city on the R 617. Although it was noted for its tweed industry in the 18thC, Blarney has become best known for the Blarney Stone, set in the castle's battlements 83 ft above the ground. According to legend kissing the stone – and it is no easy task – bestows the gift of eloquence. Tradition has it that this gift was first used by Cormac McCarthy, Lord of Muskerry and Blarney, to avoid accepting the authority of Elizabeth I. He is said to have been able to talk 'the noose off his head'. The castle itself is an impressive fortification, built in 1446 by Dermot McCarthy, King of Munster. Its walls are 18 ft thick. The Rock Close in the castle grounds is reputedly built on Druidic remains. 0900-1600 Oct.-April, 0900-1830 May & Sep., 0900-2030 June & July, 0900-1930 Aug.; £2.50, student £1.50, child £1.

Blaskets, The: Co. Kerry. Located off the tip of Kerry's Dingle peninsula, these islands are no longer inhabited. Inishtooskert has the remains of a small church dedicated to St. Brendan the Navigator. See EXCURSION 5.

Blarney Castle

The Blaskets

Blessington: Co. Wicklow. 19 miles southwest of Dublin city on the N 81. This one-street village is adjacent to the Blessington lakes, or Poulaphouca reservoir, one of the main sources of Dublin city's water. Nearby Russborough House, designed by Richard Castle, is one of Ireland's finest Palladian houses. The magnificent Beit art collection is housed here and includes works by Rubens, Gainsborough, Guardi and Bellotto. 1430-1730 Sun. & hols, Easter-Oct.; daily June-Aug.; main rooms and buildings £2.50, child £1; upstairs £1.

Bloomsday: On the morning of 16 June 1904, James Joyce's (see **A-Z**) fictional Leopold Bloom set out from Sandycove, a coastal village east of Dublin city. The day he spent wandering through Edwardian Dublin is recorded in *Ulysses*, published in 1922. Many of the locations and pubs Bloom visited remain in existence today, including Davy Byrne's (see **DUBLIN CITY-NIGHTLIFE**) where he ate Gorgonzola sandwiches with a glass of Burgundy, and Olhausen's pork butchery, Talbot St where he bought a *crubeen* (pig's foot) on the way to 'Nighttown' or Monto, Dublin's red-light district. The *crubeens* are still there but Monto is long gone. Joyce aficionados now celebrate Bloomsday with a selection of walks, talks and readings on the Sat. closest to 16 June. These usually begin at the Sandycove tower, now home to the Joyce Museum.

Bodhrán: A circular, wooden-framed, hand-held 'drum' or tambourine which is made with goatskin and beaten with a drumstick or the hand.

Book of Kells: This national treasure is kept on public display in the Long Room at Trinity College (see **DUBLIN CITY-ATTRACTIONS 1**). It is a beautifully illuminated Latin text of the Gospels' account of the life of Christ, and the most ornate of the Middle Age manuscripts to have survived. The exact origins of the book are unknown but it dates from c. AD 800. It was donated to the college by Bishop Henry Jones of Meath in 1661, and the single volume was restored and rebound into four in 1953. It is usual for just one illuminated page and one of text to be on display.

KELLS
COLLEGE DUBLIN
DONATE

Boru, Brian (c. 940-1014): As King of Munster Brian Boru became the first Irish leader to assemble a fleet of ships to defend his territory against the Vikings. His fleet sailed up the Shannon from his seat at Kincora (now Killaloe, Co. Clare). His main rival was Malachy, King of Meath, but in 1002 Malachy conceded the high kingship. Boru was killed in his tent during the Battle of Clontarf on 23 April 1014, when the Vikings, and their supporters the Leinstermen, were finally routed by his army.

Bowls: Road bowls, also known as 'bullets', is now only played in counties Armagh and Cork. The sport consists of hurling a 28 oz iron ball along several miles of winding public roads in the least number of throws. Great skill is displayed in 'lofting' round bends. The All-Ireland Championships are held in west Cork during June.

Boyle: Co. Roscommon. 25 miles south of Sligo town on the N 4. Overlooked by the Curlew hills, Boyle grew up around the county's great estate of Rockingham, which is long disbanded. It took its name, Abbey Boyle, from Mainister na Buaille, the 12thC Cistercian monastery built on the Boyle River. Though greatly vandalized by Cromwellian (see **A-Z**) troops, the remains of the abbey are very well preserved (0930-1830 mid June-mid Sep.; 80p, child 50p). Two miles away is Lough Key Forest Park (see **A-Z**).

Bray: Co. Wicklow. 18 miles south of Dublin city on the N 11. It was the arrival of the railway which turned this seaside town into a prosperous resort and began its popularity with day-trippers. Today it is a satellite town of Dublin city, and the last DART (see **A-Z**) stop. At the south of the mile-long promenade is Bray Head (791 ft). Kilruddery House is only 1.5 miles away on the Greystones road. The house includes some fine plasterwork ceilings and the ornamental gardens feature a lovely Victorian conservatory (1300-1700 May, June & Sep.; house £2.50, child £1.50; gardens only £1, child 50p).

Brontë Country: Co. Down. The quiet Bann valley, from Banbridge to Rathfriland, is where Patrick Brontë, father of novelists Emily,

Charlotte and Anne, was born. A Brontë Homeland route is signposted and includes the ruined cottage at Emdale where he was born and the hill-top school at Drumballyroney where he taught.

Brown's Hill Dolmen: Co. Carlow. 2 miles east of Carlow town on the R 726. Dating from 2000 BC, this is one of Ireland's finest megalithic field monuments. Its capstone, which weighs an estimated 100 tons, is reputed to be Europe's largest.

Buncrana: Co. Donegal. 14 miles northwest of Derry city on the R 238. The beach south of this holiday resort stretches 3 miles down to lovely Fahan, while to its north are a number of other beaches, including golden Stragill Strand. The town is usually besieged in summer by Derry people, and many cross the border just to play the amusements. The tower of a 14thC O'Doherty castle, rebuilt in the 17thC, is at the north end of the town.

Bundoran: Co. Donegal. See **EXCURSION 12**.

Bunratty: Co. Clare. The castle and folk park here are among Ireland's best-known tourist attractions (0930-1700 Sep.-May, 0930-1900 June-Aug.; £3.10, child £1.50). Built by Sioda McNamara in 1425, the castle was an O'Brien stronghold during the 16th and 17thC. It was purchased by Lord Gort in 1954, restored by the Office of Public Works and is now probably the most complete medieval castle in the country. Banquets are held here throughout the year (see **LIMERICK CITY-RESTAURANTS**). The park began when a small traditional farmhouse, which obstructed the proposed path of a runway at Shannon airport, was taken apart and reconstructed at Bunratty. There is now a full range of building replicas from throughout the region (mainly 19thC), including eight different farmhouses, a fisherman's cottage, a watermill, a blacksmith's forge and an entire village street. The Talbot Collection of agricultural machinery is on display at Bunratty House, which overlooks the park. A visit to Bunratty would not be complete without calling into Durty Nelly's pub, though the place is often chock-a-block with passengers from coach tours. There's bar food, music night and day, and generally a good atmosphere. See **EXCURSION 6**.

Burren, The: This incredible area of limestone, extending northwards from Lisdoonvarna in Co. Clare towards Galway Bay, covers 50 sq. miles and is estimated at over 300 million years old. The limestone hills and terraces hide extensive cave systems and shelter rare alpine, Mediterranean and arctic flora whose existence side by side remains somewhat of a mystery. Hundreds of dolmens, gallery graves, ring forts and crosses are scattered through the area. See **EXCURSION 6**.

Bushmills: Co. Antrim. See **EXCURSION 14**.

Cahir Castle: Sited on a rock island in the River Suir, this predominantly 15thC defensive castle is the largest of its period in Ireland. It is built on the site of a 3rdC fort, and King Brian Boru (see **A-Z**) had a residence here during the 10thC. Despite its many defences, the castle was taken in 1599 by the Earl of Essex after a 10-day siege and by Cromwell (see **A-Z**) in 1650. 1000-1800 May-mid June & mid-end Sep.; 0930-1930 mid June-mid Sep.; 1000-1300, 1400-1700 Mon.-Sat., 1400-1700 Sun., Oct.; 1000-1300, 1400-1630 Mon.-Sat., 1400-1630 Sun., Nov.-mid Mar.; 1000-1700 Mon.-Sat., 1400-1700 Sun., mid Mar.-April; £1, child 70p, family £3. See **EXCURSION 3**.

Cahirciveen: See **EXCURSION 5**.

Cape Clear: Clear Island. Co. Cork. Ireland's most southerly island is at the entrance to Roaringwater Bay. Its wild and precipitous southern coast contrasts with the pastoral quality of the interior landscape and sheltered northern coastline. The 150 or so 'Capers' are Gaelic speakers and in summer are vastly outnumbered by Irish language students. The island is reputed to be the birthplace of St. Ciaran, an earlier saint than even St. Patrick (see **A-Z**). There is a bird observatory at the North Harbour which has extensive records of rare songbird migrants. A Hallowe'en festival, Feile Shamhna Chleire, is usually held but there are regular informal music sessions year-round. Ferries run from Baltimore (see **A-Z**), May-Sep. and Skull, June-Sep. See **EXCURSION 4**.

Cappoquin: Co. Waterford. This market town is beautifully sited in wooded countryside where the Glenshelan river meets the Blackwater at the foot of the Knockmealdown slopes. Nearby is the Cistercian monastery of Mount Melleray, founded by monks in 1832 after their expulsion from France. There is still no charge at the abbey guesthouse, but donations are usually made, and are always welcome. See **EXCURSION 3**.

Carlingford: Co. Louth. At the foot of Slieve Foye, this is a perfect base for walkers who wish to explore the surrounding hills and countryside and savour this land of legends, which featured most notably in the *Tain Bo Culainge* (*Cattle Raid of Cooley*). The *Tain* recounts how Connacht's Queen Maeve, in a bid to own a bull better that her husband Ailill's white bull, tried to capture the brown bull of Cooley from Ulster and started a bloody war. The hero of the piece is Ulster's Cuchulainn, who single-handed holds off the men of the West until the men of Ulster recover from a curse. The peaceful and somewhat unreal beauty of the views across Carlingford Lough is only interrupted by the sound of British Army helicopters patrolling the border which divides the lough. The oldest visible remains in this ancient settlement is King John's Castle, built by Hugh de Lacy in the 12thC, which traverses the main road at the water's edge. The narrow village streets also house a 15thC mint, and a *tholsel* (tollhouse), originally one of the town gates which served as a meeting place for the town leaders, and later in the 18thC as a jail. Taafe's Castle, near the main road, is a fortified 16thC town house. Ask directions to the nearby 'magnetic hill' to witness your car defy gravity! You can enjoy oysters at P. J.'s and O'Hare's in Tholsel

St. The latter pub's yard contains murals depicting the area's most popular walks. And don't forget to ask about the leprechaun suit in the bar! See **EXCURSION 1**.

Carlow: Co. Carlow. Pop: 11,000. 24 miles northeast of Kilkenny city on the N 9. The county town has a lovely situation on the bank of the River Barrow and is a bustling market and manufacturing centre. Because of its strategic location it served as an important Norman and English stronghold during the Middle Ages, and was a vital frontier town of the Pale until the 17thC. It was here that the first clash of the 1798 Rebellion (see **A-Z**) took place, and over 600 rebels were slaughtered. Only a wall remains of a 13thC castle. It was destroyed when a doctor leased it in 1814 for use as a mental hospital. The doctor, who wanted an open-plan ward system, set explosives to remove the inner walls and managed to blow up most of the building!

Carna: Co. Galway. A small fishing and holiday village. South of Carna wander out to Mweenish Island and look out to St. MacDara's Island where the ruins of his monastery remain. Some fishermen still dip their sails in reverence as they pass. See **EXCURSION 7**.

Carrantouhill: MacGillicuddy's Reeks, Co. Kerry. Ireland's highest mountain, at 3414 ft. It stands west of the Lakes of Killarney. For breathtaking views take the road by Beaufort Bridge to Gortbue School at the entrance of the Hag's Glen. Walk through the glen and up the Devil's Ladder to reach the summit. Enquire locally about safety measures and suitable cliff faces for rock climbing.

Carrickfergus: Co. Antrim. Tourist Information, Castle Green, tel: 9603-63604. The 12thC castle (1000-1800 Mon.-Sat., 1400-1800 Sun., April-Sep.; 1000-1600 Mon.-Sat., 1400-1600 Sun., Oct.-Mar.; 75p, child 35p) dominates the town. Built in 1180 by John de Courcy, it remained in continuous use until 1928, serving mainly as the seat of English power in the North. Carrickfergus also has many literary connections: Jonathan Swift (see **A-Z**) was a Church of England incumbent based in nearby Boneybefore, while poet Louis MacNeice spent his

childhood here. The lively Lughnasa Fair in late July or early Aug. is a good excuse to spend a few days here. See **EXCURSION 14**.

Carrickmacross: Co. Monaghan. 26 miles south of Monaghan town on the N 2. This market town, which still retains some impressive Georgian houses and old shop fronts, is famous for its lace-making, established by the nuns of the St. Louis Convent in 1820. A display can be seen at the Carrickmacross Lace Co-op. There are some lovely walks in the Lough Fean estate, just outside the town.

Carrick-on-Shannon: Co. Leitrim. See **EXCURSION 11**.

Carrick-on-Suir: Co. Tipperary. 17 miles northwest of Waterford city on the N 24. It was the Butlers, earls of Carrick and Ormond, who created this town in an idyllic setting on the River Suir. Margaret Butler, daughter of the 7th Earl, was the mother of Ann Boleyn (who is reputed to have been born in the castle) and grandmother of Elizabeth I. The manor house (0930-1830 mid June-mid Sep.; 80p, child 30p) was built by 'Black Tom' in anticipation of a visit from Elizabeth I.

Carrowmore Megalithic Tombs: Co. Sligo. See **Sligo Town**.

Carson, Lord Edward (1854-1935): A Dublin barrister who was elected Liberal Unionist MP for Trinity College and became one of the most vigorous critics of the Home Rule Bill. He was the first Irish QC to 'take silk' in England, and became renowned for his cross-examination of Oscar Wilde. Knighted in 1910, he agreed to lead the Irish Unionist Parliamentary Party and with James Craig (see **A-Z**) headed the mass Ulster Day campaign which obtained 471,414 signatures on a covenant to defeat home rule in 1912. The Ulster Volunteer Force was founded in 1913, and when Carson committed its men to fight in the British Army during World War I all home rule legislation was suspended. Carson finally realized that home rule was inevitable outside Ulster and became a Belfast MP in 1918.

Cashel: Co. Tipperary. See **EXCURSION 3**, **Rock of Cashel**.

Castlebar: Co. Mayo. A tree-bordered green is the focal point of this busy county town. It has been a town of stature since the 16thC, receiving a royal charter from James I in 1613. A variety of wars, however, has meant that little of the old settlement remains. Historically it is best known for its role in the 1798 Rebellion (see **A-Z**), when the numerically inferior Franco-Irish forced the retreat of Gen. Lake's troops from the town to as far as Tuam and Athlone. The retreat of the British cavalry was so fast that it became known as 'The Races of Castlebar'! See **EXCURSION 9**.

Castleisland: Co. Kerry. The town takes its name from a 13thC castle built by Geoffrey de Marisco, of which there are some remains. Nearby is Crag Cave, an ancient fossil cave system, with some spectacular limestone formations (1000-1800 April-Nov.; £2.50, child £1.50, under 6 free). See **EXCURSION 5**.

Castle Matrix: Rathkeale, Co. Limerick. 27 miles southwest of Limerick city on the N 21. This tower house was built in 1440 by the 7th Earl of Desmond. In 1580 two of the era's then unknown poets met

here for the first time – Edmund Spenser and Walter Raleigh. The castle has been wonderfully restored by Col. Sean O'Driscoll and contains documents referring to the Wild Geese (see **A-Z**). The castle's name derives from the ancient Celtic sanctuary of Matres, goddess of love and poetry, on which it was built. It is the HQ of the Heraldry Society of Ireland. 1300-1700 Sat.-Tue., mid May-mid Sep.; £2, child £1.

Cavan: Co. Cavan. See **EXCURSION 11**.

Civil War, The (1922-23): The refusal of Republican leader Eamon de Valera (see **A-Z**), among others, to accept the compromise 1921 treaty (see **Anglo-Irish Treaty**), brought about a bitter division in southern Ireland, culminating in a bitter and bloody civil war. Men who had fought side by side to earn Ireland's freedom, and even families, were now divided into the 'Free Staters', who supported the treaty, and the Republicans, who did not. The war began in Dublin on 28 June 1922, when the Republicans seized control of the Four Courts and other buildings, and continued until 24 May 1923, when de Valera called for peace. The divisions of the war were continued by the founding of two rival political parties, Fianna Fail (de Valera) and Fine Gael, and even today an element of 'Civil War Politics' remains in their dealings with each other. In Northern Ireland one of the main effects of the war was the founding of the Ulster Special Constabulary, including the notorious B-Specials. Following a series of raids by Republicans across the border, the B-Specials retaliated with raids into the South. See **Collins**.

Claddagh Ring, The: According to legend the ring was the creation of Richard Joyce who was captured as a slave from the fishing village of Claddagh, Co. Galway in the 16thC. In captivity he trained as a goldsmith and proved so good he was given his freedom. On his return home he designed the symbol of two hands cradling a crowned heart. Worn on the right hand, heart inwards, it shows the heart is unoccupied. On the same hand, turned out, it shows a romantic tie is being considered. On the left hand, heart inwards, it announces that you and your lover are inseparable.

Clare Island: Co. Mayo. Located at the entrance to Clew Bay, this former stronghold of Grace O'Malley (see **A-Z**) is now frequented by sea anglers and divers. O'Malley is buried in the ruined Carmelite friary here, and her castle is at the eastern end of the island. Enquire at Roonagh Quay, near Louisburgh for boat services. See **EXCURSION 8**.

Clifden: Co. Galway. A popular base for touring Connemara (see **A-Z**), with a selection of lively pubs and good restaurants in summer. Sited at the northern end of Clifden Bay, the Twelve Pins provide a spectacular scenic backdrop to the town. There is a choice of strands and sheltered coves for bathing within walking distance. Four miles from the town, on the Ballyconneely road, a 14 ft monument in the shape of an aircraft's tail fin juts out from the bog. This marks the spot where John Alcock and Arthur Whitten Brown crash-landed at the end of their first transatlantic flight in 1919. See **EXCURSIONS 7 & 8**.

Clonalis House: Castlerea, Co. Roscommon. 18 miles northwest of Roscommon town on the N 60. The ancestral home of the O'Conor clan, Europe's oldest family. The 45-room mansion, built in 1878, contains an incredible collection of archive material. There are also exhibitions of antique lace and costumes, and 19thC horse-drawn machinery.

Clonmacnoise: Clonfanlough, Co. Offaly. 15 miles south of Athlone off the N 62 at Ballinahowen. This is one of Ireland's most important monastic and historical sites. Founded in AD 548 by St. Ciaran, it was once a great city and medieval university. The remains include a cathedral, seven church buildings, two round towers, three high crosses and two holy wells. Ireland's last high king, Rory O'Connor, was buried here in 1198. 1000-1700 Nov.-mid Mar., 1000-1800 mid Mar.-May, Sep. & Oct., 0900-1900 June-mid Sep.; £1, child 40p.

Clonmel: Co. Tipperary. 30 miles west of Waterford city on the N 24. This handsome market town is in a lovely situation on the River Suir, while the Comeragh and Knockmealdown mountains loom in the distance. The remains of its 14thC town walls, including the West Gate, and Old St. Mary's Church are just two of its historical attractions. It is

regarded as the capital of Ireland's greyhound industry and the controversial blood sport of coursing.

Cobh: Co. Cork. Pop: 8000. 9 miles east of Cork city on the R 624. Pronounced 'cove'. This popular resort town is dominated by St. Colman's Cathedral, designed by Pugin and Ashlin and built of blue Dalkey granite. The harbour's deep-water anchorage was used as an assembly point for ships during the Napoleonic wars, and a departure point for emigrant ships. It was also a stopping place for transatlantic liners, including the *Titanic* on her first and only voyage. A monument to the victims of the *Lusitania*, hundreds of whom are buried in the town, stands in Casement Sq., and the local maritime museum includes a display about the disaster. Fota Island, on which Cobh sits, also has a restored early-19thC house with an extensive collection of paintings, an arboretum and a 70 acre wildlife park (house 1100-1800 Mon.-Sat., 1400-1800 Sun., May-Oct.; estate & wildlife park 1000-1715 Mon.-Sat., 1100-1715 Sun., April-Sep.; house £2, child 50p.; estate & wildlife park £2.20, child £1.10).

Collins, Michael (1890-1922): Born near Clonakilty, Co. Cork, he was a major revolutionary leader. A member of the Irish Republican Brotherhood and the Irish Volunteers, he fought at the GPO during the Easter Rising (see **A-Z**). A reluctant signatory of the Anglo-Irish Treaty (see **A-Z**), he became chairman of Ireland's provisional government and was one of the leaders of the 'Free Staters' during the Civil War (see **A-Z**). He was ambushed and killed during the war at Beal na mBlath in Cork.

Cong: Co. Mayo. Nestling between Lough Corrib and Lough Mask, this picturesque village was one of the locations for the film *The Quiet Man*, and is popular with tourists for angling and shooting. A dry canal, built during the famine (see **A-Z**) to connect the two lakes, has become a local curiosity. The village is on the site of a 6thC monastery, rebuilt as an Augustinian abbey by King Turloch O'Connor early in the 12thC. At one stage 3000 people lived within its walls. The base of a medieval cross in the village street and some impressive monastic ruins are reminders of the abbey. Ashford Castle, built for the Guinness family in 1870 but now a luxury hotel, is along the river behind the abbey ruins. See **EXCURSION 7**.

Connemara: Co. Galway. Dominated by the Twelve Pins and the Maumturk mountains, this is considered one of the most spectacular, unspoilt and most barren areas of Ireland. While emigration is rife, many people still remain to eke out a living between the inhospitable land and the sea. It is a predominantly Gaeltacht (see **A-Z**) region. See **EXCURSIONS 7 & 8**.

Connolly, James (1870-1916): Born in Edinburgh, Scotland of Irish parents, Connolly came to Ireland in 1896 and founded the Irish Socialist Republican Party. He served as chief organizer of the Irish Transport and General Workers Union in Belfast between 1910 and 1913, and led the 100 members of the Irish Citizen Army who marched on the GPO during the Easter Rising (see **A-Z**). He was wounded in the fighting, and was executed for his role in the uprising, facing the firing squad seated in a chair.

Coole Park: Co. Galway. 21 miles southeast of Galway city on the N 18. Now a lovely forest park, this was the former home of Lady Augusta Gregory (see **A-Z**) and served as a favourite retreat for many of the leading writers of the 19th-20thC literary and dramatic revival in Ireland, including W. B. Yeats (see **A-Z**), who preserved its beauties forever in his poetry. The autograph tree is where many of Lady Gregory's guests carved their names. Initials still legible include JBY and WBY (Jack and William B. Yeats) and GBS (George Bernard Shaw).

Cork City: Co. Cork. Pop: 130,000. Tourist Information, Tourist House, Grand Parade, tel: 21-23251. Ireland's third city after Dublin and Belfast, though Corkonians would say otherwise. The settlement began as a monastery, founded by St. Finbarr in the 7thC, on an island in the swampy Lee estuary; its Irish name Corcaigh means 'marsh'. It was raided by the Vikings, who later returned to settle, and invaded by the Anglo-Normans who forced the local chiefs to submit to Henry II. Formerly one of Europe's principal ports, many of the main streets, including Patrick St, were built over boat channels. See **CORK CITY**.

Craggaunowen Bronze Age Project: Co. Clare. Northwest of Limerick city on the N 18 and R 462. The project is centred on Craggaunowen Castle, which has been restored and now contains a selection of medieval exhibits. The grounds also contain replicas of a crannog (see **A-Z**), a ring fort and a farmer's house dating from the 4th or 5thC. Also on show is *The Brendan*, the hide boat in which Tim Severin sailed from Ireland to the USA in 1976, re-enacting the voyage of St. Brendan, who is reputed to have discovered America centuries before Columbus. 1000-1800 Mar.-Oct.; £2.50.

Craig, James (Viscount Craigavon) (1871-1940): Son of a wealthy Presbyterian whiskey distiller, and a Boer War veteran, who turned to politics and became one of the leaders of Ulster's Unionist movement. He became Northern Ireland's first prime minister following the Anglo-Irish Treaty (see **A-Z**) and partition. See **Carson**.

Crom Old Castle

Crannog: A fortified island, often artificial, for dwellings in a lake or marsh. Access to the mainland was usually by submerged causeway.

Cratloe Woods House: Co. Clare. The ghost of red-haired Maire Rua O'Brien, who agreed to marry an English army officer to prevent the family lands being given to English settlers, is said to guard the driveway. The house is one of the few roofed examples of an Irish long house, and the only one still used as a home. In the yard are displays of horse-drawn farm machinery, and a Pets Corner for children. 1400-1800 Mon.-Sat., June-mid Sep.; £1.75, child £1. See **EXCURSION 6**.

Cresslough: Co. Donegal. 16 miles northeast of Letterkenny on the N 56. A little village which overlooks the inlet of Sheep Haven, this is an ideal base for climbing Slieve·Muckish. Doe Castle, a former MacSweeney fortress much altered since the 15thC, is on a nearby peninsula.

Croagh Patrick: Co. Mayo. This 2510 ft reek between Westport and Louisburgh is where St. Patrick (see **A-Z**) spent 40 days and nights in AD 441, and according to legend it was here he banished snakes from Ireland. Every year, on the last Sun. in July, thousands of people take part in a pilgrimage to the oratory on the summit. The wonderful view from the top takes in the Twelve Pins to the south, and the expanse of Clew Bay. See **EXCURSION 8**.

Crom Estate: Co. Fermanagh. 3 miles west of Newtownbutler. This is one of Northern Ireland's most important conservation areas, with 1350 acres of woodland, parkland and wetlands. Walks around the estate take in the ruins of Crom Old Castle and Crichton Tower. Day tickets for coarse fishing are available, tel: 036573-8825. 1400-1800 Easter-Sep.; parking £1.50.

Cromwell, Oliver (1599-1658): When Cromwell and his 'Ironsides' arrived in Ireland in 1649 they began one of the most ruthless campaigns in Ireland's history. Sweeping through the country, they slaughtered thousands of men, women and children, selling survivors into slavery in the West Indies. Many towns controlled by Protestant Royalists were forced to surrender. By 1652 about a third of the Catholic Irish population had been butchered, and under the Act of Settlement their lands confiscated and given to soldiers or other Protestants. The Catholics were ordered west of the Shannon – 'to Hell or to Connaught'.

Curragh, The: Co. Kildare. 28 miles southwest of Dublin city on the N 7. Ireland's largest area of arable land is home to hundreds of sheep, horse studs and training centres, and The Curragh racecourse (see **Horse-racing**). Scattered over the grassland are a number of prehistoric earthworks.

Cushendall: Co. Antrim. See **EXCURSION 14**.

Dail Eireann: The lower house of the Oireachtas (parliament) to which Teachta Dail (MPs) are elected by the people. The leader of the government is An Taoiseach (pronounced 'on Tee-shock'). The upper house is called An Seanad (the senate).

Derry City: Londonderry. Co. Londonderry. Pop: 130,000. Tourist Information, Foyle St, tel: 504-267284. The name Derry derives from the Irish word *daire* meaning 'oak-grove'. The area is one of the longest-inhabited in Ireland but it was in the 6thC that, according to legend, St. Columbcille (see **A-Z**) founded a monastery here. During the 12th and 13thC Derry prospered under the Mac Lochlainn clan, before declining in importance during the later Middle Ages. After repeated attempts during the 16thC, it was finally captured by English forces in 1600. In 1613 James I granted a charter to the London Companies to found a new city as part of the Plantations (see **A-Z**). The walled city was laid out, renamed Londonderry, and planted with Protestant settlers. In 1649 the city and its garrison, who were loyal to the 'republican' parliament in London, were besieged by Presbyterian forces loyal to the king. The more famous siege, however, came in 1688 (see **Siege of Derry**). During the 18th and 19thC the city was a major departure point for emigrants to America. Today it is a shabby, and somewhat depressing, skeleton of a beautiful city. See **DERRY CITY, EXCURSIONS 13 & 14.**

de Valera, Eamon (1882-1975): This American-born nationalist led the fighting at Dublin's Boland's Mills during the Easter Rising (see

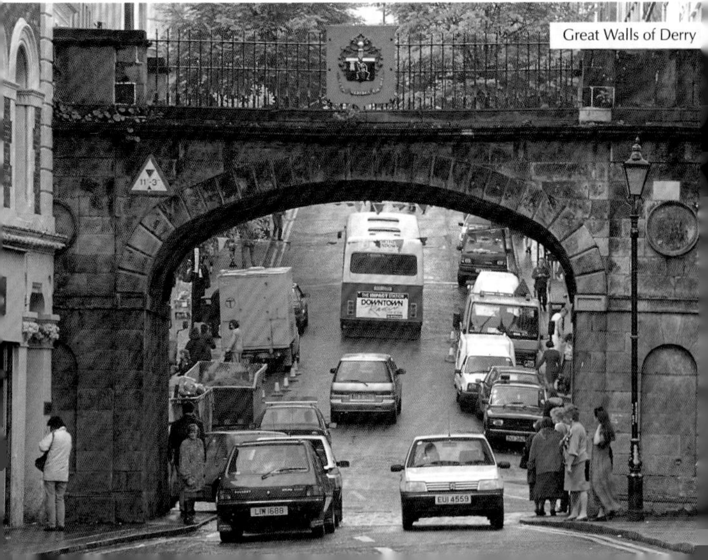

Great Walls of Derry

A-Z) but had his death sentence commuted. Elected MP for East Clare, he succeeded Arthur Griffith as president of Sinn Fein, and though interned in 1918, escaped from Lincoln Jail to be elected president of the separatist Dail Eireann. He rejected the Anglo-Irish Treaty (see **A-Z**) and led the Republican faction during the Civil War (see **A-Z**). In 1926 he broke with Sinn Fein to found Fianna Fail, which held political power from 1932 to 1948, serving as Ireland's prime minister and maintaining Ireland's neutrality during World War II. He was elected president of Ireland in 1959 and served two 7-year terms.

Devinish Island: Lough Erne, Co. Fermanagh. The monastery here was founded by St. Molaise in the 6thC, and the impressive remains include a 12thC church, oratory and tower. Further along the island are the ruins of the later Augustinian Abbey of St. Mary and graveyard. Though founded in the 12thC, most of the remains date from the 15thC. Access is by boat from the Round O Quay in Enniskillen.

Long Tower Church, Derry

Dingle Bay

Dingle: Co. Kerry. The town, which served as a vital port for trade with Spain and was walled during Elizabethan times, has many claims to fame. Among them is its use as a location for the film *Ryan's Daughter*. It was also 'nearly' famous as a safe haven for Marie Antoinette. A Count Rice, who owned a house here, prepared it to receive the former French queen following a bid to rescue her from prison. According to tradition, however, she refused to travel here. From Easter to Oct. there are some good restaurants to choose from in all price ranges. Doyle's Seafood Bar on John St is probably the most renowned but the adjacent Half Door is also a good bet. See **EXCURSION 5.**

Donegal Town: Co. Donegal. From the Middle Ages to the 17thC the town was the seat of the O'Donnells, princes of Tir Chonaill. Following the Flight of the Earls (see **A-Z**) in 1607 the town was 'planted' (see **Plantations**) by Sir Basil Brooke. The ruins of Donegal Castle, near The Diamond, include the square tower of the castle built by Red Hugh O'Donnell in 1505. Brooke added the turret and other Jacobean features, and also built the adjoining mansion. On the seashore south of the town are the remains of a Franciscan abbey founded by Red Hugh O'Donnell and his mother Nuala O'Conor in 1474. Both are buried here. Following the English conquest of Donegal in the early 17thC, the community wandered from one place of refuge to another, before settling at Bundrowes, near Bundoran, where the Four Masters who had collected all known documents of Irish history, compiled their celebrated *Annals* between 1630 and 1636. The first entry recalls a visit by Noah's granddaughter to Ireland! An obelisk commemorating the Four Masters stands in The Diamond. Near the pier is a large anchor, believed to date from the time French troops arrived to aid the 1798 Rebellion (see **A-Z**). The town is a good base for exploring the surrounding Blue Stack mountains. For food try McGroarty's Pub and the Hyland Central Hotel. See **EXCURSIONS 12 & 13.**

Downpatrick: Co. Down. Tourist Information, 24 Strangford Rd, tel: 396-4331. St. Patrick (see **A-Z**) was buried on Cathedral Hill c. AD 461. His grave, marked by a huge block of Mourne granite, in the grounds of Down Cathedral in English St is a place of pilgrimage on St. Patrick's Day (17 Mar.). The bones of St. Brigid, Ireland's second saint, and St. Columba are also reputed to be in the same grave. A church has stood on the cathedral site since the early 6thC. The original building was destroyed almost completely over the centuries but a major restoration project took place in the 18thC. Down County Museum, also on English St, is housed in the former governor's residence and jail. The St. Patrick Heritage Centre (1100-1700 Mon.-Fri., 1400-1800 Sat. & Sun., July-mid Sep.; 1100-1700 Tue.-Fri., 1400-1700 Sat., mid Sep.-June; free) is in the gatehouse. Ireland's first preserved railway, the Downpatrick and Ardglass Railway, is located behind the Ulsterbus station on Market St (1400-1800 Sun., July & Aug.; Easter Mon. & Tue.; St. Patrick's Day; Christmas hols). See **EXCURSION 15**.

Drogheda: Co. Louth. Pop: 20,000. Steeped in history, Drogheda was originally two walled municipalities on either side of the Boyne. It became an important English town in the Middle Ages. The squat turret-shaped building on a hill is Mill Mount, the motte of a Norman castle built in the 12thC over a prehistoric tomb. It now houses the Museum of the Old Drogheda Society on Barrack St, and there are a number of adjacent arts and crafts enterprises. Other town highlights include St. Lawrence's Gate, two linked battlemented towers with a portcullis entry at the junction of Palace St and St. Lawrence St, and St. Peter's Church in West St, where the embalmed head of martyred St. Oliver Plunkett can be seen at a side altar. See **EXCURSION 1**.

Dromahair: Co. Leitrim. Southeast of Sligo town. This pretty village on the River Bonet was once the chief seat of the O'Rourke kings of Breifne. Its major attraction is Parke's Castle, situated on Lough Gill (see **A-Z**) and considered to be Ireland's finest Plantation (see **A-Z**) castle (0930-1830 June-Sep., 1000-1700 May & Oct.; £1, child 40p).

Drumcliff: Co. Sligo. See **EXCURSION 12**.

Dublin Castle: At first sight it may prove disappointing but investigation is well worthwhile. It includes a melange of architectural styles,

from the original castle commissioned in the 13thC by King John, to George Hall, built as a supper room in 1911. Until 1922, when it was handed over to the provisional Irish government, it was the citadel of English authority in Ireland, functioning as a military fort, prison, treasury and courts of law. Today it houses government offices and is used for important State functions. See **DUBLIN CITY-ATTRACTIONS 1**.

Dublin City: Pop: 525,000. Tourist Information, 14 Upper O'Connell St, tel: 1-747733. There was a settlement here as far back as prehistoric times. It was not until the arrival of the Norsemen in AD 840, however, that a town began to develop. About 12 years later the settlement became a Viking stronghold. The Danes then held control until 1014 and their defeat at the Battle of Clontarf (see **Boru**). But it was the half-Danish ruler Sigtrygger (Sitric) Silkbeard, who founded Dublin's first cathedral, Christ Church, and issued Ireland's first coins. Following an appeal by former King of Leinster Dermot McMurrough to Henry II, 'Strongbow' and a group of Norman allies took much of Leinster and stormed Dublin in 1169, taking control. But in 1172 Henry curbed their powers with a large army, and the walled town became a citadel of English power, which ruled over much of Leinster – the Pale. When the power of the English finally became consolidated in the 17thC Dublin began to expand, and the 18thC saw the building of what is now called Georgian Dublin. With the conceding of autonomy to the Irish Parliament in 1783 the city blossomed, but William Pitt, alarmed by the United Irishmen's 1798 Rebellion (see **A-Z**), brought about the reunion of the parliaments in 1801. Dublin then became an increasingly Irish town, and towards the end of the century became the centre for two cultural movements, the Gaelic League (Conradh na Gaeilge) and the Irish literary renaissance, which continued into the 20thC with the foundation of the Abbey Theatre. The early part of the century saw the struggle to establish the trade union movement, which culminated in the Great Lock-out of 1913. Later the Easter Rising (see **A-Z**), the War of Independence and the Civil War (see **A-Z**) scarred much of the city. As

the capital of the Free State, and later the Republic, it grew slowly until the economic upswing of the 1960s, when both the population and development boomed – the latter with some disastrous results. For more extensive information on the capital, see Collins Traveller: *Dublin*. See **DUBLIN CITY, EXCURSIONS 1 & 10**.

Dundalk: Co. Louth. See **EXCURSION 1**.

Dungarvan: Co. Waterford. See **EXCURSION 3**.

Dungloe: Co. Donegal. See **EXCURSION 13**.

Dunmore Caves: Co. Kilkenny. 7 miles north of Kilkenny city on the N 78. The caves are a series of limestone chambers formed over millions of years. They were the site of a Viking massacre in AD 928. 1000-1700 Tue.-Sat., 1400-1700 Sun., mid Mar.-mid June; 1000-1830 mid June-mid Sep.; 1000-1700 Sat., Sun. & hols, mid Sep.-mid Mar.; £1, child 40p, family £3.

Dysert O'Dea: Co. Clare. The area was the site of a 7thC monastery founded by St. Tola. Dysert Castle (1000-1800 May-Sep.; £1.50) was built in 1480 by the O'Dea clan, and though its upper floors and staircases were knocked down by the Cromwellian (see **A-Z**) commissioners, enough remained to allow its restoration in 1986. It now houses an award-winning archaeological centre. Sites include an 11thC round tower, a high cross, holy wells, ring forts, and church ruins which feature ancient 'Sile-na-Gig' sculptures. These exaggerated depictions of the female form may have been fertility symbols, representations of the sin of lust or figures to ward away the devil. A 2 mile archaeological trail, taking in 25 sites of interest in the area, has been mapped out for visitors. See **EXCURSION 6**.

Easter Rising, The: The 1916 Rising was largely a Dublin affair, with only minor incidents involving Volunteers in Galway and Enniscorthy. On Easter Mon. about 2000 armed nationalists seized a number of Dublin's principal buildings. Among their leaders were Padraic Pearse (see **A-Z**), James Connolly (see **A-Z**), Countess Markievicz (see **A-Z**), Eamon de Valera (see **A-Z**) and Michael Mallin. Their HQ was the GPO (see **A-Z**), where the tricolour was hoisted and Pearse read the Proclamation of the Irish Republic.
For six days the British Army shelled the city, until the leaders agreed to unconditional surrender. Over 1000 people had been killed or wounded, and £3m in damage caused to property. Though the rising had been unpopular, opinion swung to the nationalist cause when the British executed 15 of the leaders at Kilmainham Jail (see **DUBLIN CITY-ATTRACTIONS 2**).

Emmet, Robert (1778-1803): Expelled from Trinity College, Dublin for his membership of the United Irishmen, as a wanted man he planned a revolution. On the eve of 23 July 1803 he led a hundred followers to Dublin Castle (see **A-Z**) but on the way the carriage of the Lord Chief Justice was stopped and the rebels killed him and his nephew. Emmet and his troops were scattered but his love for Sarah Curran prevented him leaving the country. He was discovered, tried and hung in Thomas St, Dublin.

Emo Court & Gardens: Co. Laois. 46 miles southwest of Dublin city off the N 7. This lovely house was designed by James Gandon for the 1st Earl of Portarlington in 1760. The portico and magnificent rotunda room are later additions. There are extensive formal gardens. House 1400-1800 Mon., mid Mar.-mid Oct.; gardens 1430-1730. House £2.50; gardens £2, child £1.

Ennis: Co. Clare. Pop: 6000. Tourist Information, Bank Pl., tel: 065-28366. Clare's county town. Its streets were described in the 19thC as 'ill-defined and scattered' but today the narrow thoroughfares add to its character, if not an easy traffic flow. Many of the old shop fronts remain on some of the best Irish crafts and knitwear outlets. The column in the town centre commemorates Daniel O'Connell (see **A-Z**) who was MP for Clare, 1828-31. The ruins of a 13thC Franciscan friary, built by the kings of Thomond, are on Abbey St (1000-1800 mid June-mid Sep.). The friary was originally on an island in the River Fergus, around which the town has grown. The most notable of its 14th and 15thC features are the carvings of Christ's Passion and death on a McMahon tomb. Ennis has always been a great place for traditional music. Considine's, which serves good lunches, and Brogan's, O'Connell St, are just two of the town venues, while Cois na hAbhna, on the Gort road, holds ceilidhs, music sessions and stage shows. See **EXCURSION 6**.

Enniscorthy: Co. Wexford. Home to the Strawberry Fair every July. The County Museum (1000-1800 Mon.-Sat., 1400-1700 Sun., June-Sep.; 1400-1730 Feb.-May & Oct.; 50p, child 30p) is housed in the Norman castle overlooking the River Slaney. It contains some interesting documentation on both the 1916 (see **Easter Rising**) and 1798 rebellions (see **A-Z**). The castle itself, built in 1205, has had many owners, including the poet Edmund Spenser. The castle was given to him by Elizabeth I of England, reputedly in gratitude for his epic poem *The Faerie Queene*. On the far side of the river is Vinegar Hill, the site of the main rebel encampment during 1798. On the west bank of the river is St. Aidan's Cathedral, designed by Augustus Pugin in the 1840s. Walkers should also try the well-maintained path along the banks of the Slaney. See **EXCURSION 2**.

Enniskillen: Co. Fermanagh. Pop: 10,000. Tourist Information, Shore Rd, tel: 365-323110. This lovely county town grew up on the strategic narrow neck between upper and lower Lough Erne (see **A-Z**) and is an ideal spot from which to explore the lakes. The impressive Watergate beside the lough incorporates a 15thC Maguire castle. It was rebuilt and added to by William Cole, who was given the town and environs in 1609 during the Plantations (see **A-Z**). It now houses the county and regimental museum. Just over 1.5 miles away is Castle Coole, purported to be the finest classical mansion in Ireland, completed in 1798 (1400-1800 Fri.-Wed., June-Aug.; Sat. & Sun., April, May & Sep.; £2, child £1). See **EXCURSION 12**, **Florence Court**, **Marble Arch Caves**.

Famine, The Great (1845-48): The failure of the potato crop today because of blight would not be a disaster but in the 19thC it was the subsistence crop of the Irish. Wheat, barley, cattle, sheep and pigs continued to be shipped to England during the Famine but none was returned to the Irish, while British landlords (usually absentee) evicted tenants who could no longer afford the rent. At least one million people died in the most horrendous circumstances, while another million emigrated to America, though many never survived the journey on the 'coffin ships'.

Fenians, The: A 19thC nationalist organization, also known as the Irish Republican Brotherhood. Its aim was to organize a military coup against English rule.

Fermanagh Lakeland: Co. Fermanagh. A waterland paradise. The largest lake, Lough Erne (see **A-Z**), is 50 miles long. Together with fishing and cruising there is an abundance of castles, antiquities and other sights to investigate. 'Musts' include Enniskillen (see **A-Z**), Castle Coole, Devenish Island (see **A-Z**), White Island, Florence Court (see **A-Z**), Belleek (see **A-Z**), the Marble Arch Caves (see **A-Z**) and the Crom Estate (see **A-Z**). See **EXCURSION 12**.

Flight of the Earls: Despite the allegiance many Irish chiefs pledged to the English Crown under Elizabeth I, they continued to be treated with suspicion, and most of their estates were confiscated. Unable to accept this treatment, or the loss of their ancient authority, many chose to go into exile in Continental Europe. This mass exodus in 1607 became known as the Flight of the Earls.

Florence Court: Co. Fermanagh. 8 miles south of Enniskillen on the A 4 and A 32. One of Ulster's most important 18thC houses, with magnificent rococo plasterwork. 1300-1800 Sat. & Sun., April, May & Sep.; Fri.-Wed., June-Aug.; grounds open daily; £2, child £1.

Fore: Co. Westmeath. See **EXCURSION 10**.

Foxford: Co. Mayo. Situated on the River Moy with views of the Ox mountains to the northeast. The Providence Woollen Mills, where the famous Foxford rugs are made, was founded in 1892 by Agnes Morrogh Bernard to stop emigration from the area. Though some of the products have changed the mill still operates today, albeit under a new name. Admiral William Brown, who became leader of the Argentinian Navy, is the town's most famous son. He is commemorated by a bronze bust, completed in 1957 by Argentinian sculptor Vergotinni. See **EXCURSION 9**.

Foynes: Co. Limerick. This village and port on the Shannon estuary was a transatlantic seaplane base from 1939 to 1945. The GPA Foynes Flying Boat Museum includes a 1940s-style cinema and tearoom, and the original terminal building and radio equipment (1000-1800 April-Oct.; £2, child £1). See **EXCURSION 5**.

Gaelic: Irish or An Gaeilge (pronounced 'on gwale-ga'). Officially the first language of the Republic but for a variety of historical reasons, predominantly British rule, English has been the prevalent tongue since as far back as the 16thC. All signposts are bilingual. A stong revivalist movement still exists, particularly in non-Gaeltacht areas. It is a compulsory subject for all school children.
Accents and dialects differ between regions but some useful phrases include: dia duit (dee-a gwit) – hello; dia is muire duit (dee-a iss mura

gwit) – hello (in response); conas ata tu (cunis a-taw too) – how are you?; le do thoill (leh daw hull) – please; go raibh maith agat (guh row mah aw-gut) – thank you; failte romhat (fawl-tcha row-at) – welcome; and slan leat (slawn lat) – goodbye. See **Gaeltacht**.

Gaeltacht: Gaelic-speaking districts which have been given special protection by the Irish government since the 1920s. Areas include: South Connemara, Co. Galway; Geesala, Co. Mayo; Gweedore, Co. Donegal; Ring, Co. Waterford; and Rath Cairn, Co. Meath.

Galway City: Co. Galway. Pop: 27,000. Tourist Information, Eyre Sq., tel: 91-63081. The chief town of Connacht, and a thriving industrial and university town. It has become home to a very lively arts movement, which includes the Druid Theatre, An Taibhdhearc, and Macnas, which stages spectacular street pageants.

The town began with the seizure of an O'Halloran settlement and fort by the de Burgos who built a castle here before 1240. The town was walled and fortified by the close of the century, and when a steady trade grew up with Spain, Richard II of England granted a charter in 1484 which made Galway in effect a city-state, and independent of the de Burgos. It was ruled by a small group of merchants, predominantly from the 14 'tribes'. The dispossessed de Burgos, or Burkes, were a traditional city foe, but the greatest enemies of the city were the O'Flaherties, whose lands had also been seized by the Normans. The Williamite wars at the end of the 17thC brought a lengthy siege, which was followed by a decline in the city. The Great Famine (see **A-Z**) was another disaster, and it was only with the re-establishment of the Irish state that the city began to blossom once again. See **GALWAY CITY, EXCURSIONS 6 & 7**.

Seagan Ua Neactain
CROSS STREET

Galway

Gap of Dunloe: MacGillicuddy's Reeks, Co. Kerry. About 5 miles from Killarney, this famous and spectacular 4 mile gap through the Reeks leads to the Kenmare road and Lord Brandon's Cottage, or deep into the desolate and remote Black Valley. Ponies can be hired but most are trained to stop a short distance up the gap and budge not an inch further. It's best to walk, savouring the views; the nicest time is early evening. Kate Kearney's Cottage – named after a 19thC local beauty who sold poitin (see **A-Z**) to tourists – is a great spot for a jar, particularly after a bracing walk.

Garinish Island: Ilnacullin. Glengarriff, Co. Cork. This barren island, bathed in the warm waters of the Gulf Stream, was transformed into a subtropical garden by the Bryce family at the start of the century. The magnificent Italian Garden is surrounded by a wild garden, and there are a Martello tower (see **A-Z**), Grecian temple and clock tower. Magnolias, camellias, rhododendrons and rare conifers all thrive here. 1000-1600 (last landing) Tue.-Sat., 1300-1700 Sun., Mar. & Oct.; 1000-1830 Mon.-Sat., 1300-1900 Sun., April-June & Sep.; 0930-1830 Mon.-Sat., 1100-1900 Sun., July & Aug. See **EXCURSION 4**.

General Post Office (GPO): Dublin city. Built in 1818, this focal point in O'Connell St is referred to by its initials. The HQ for the Easter Rising (see **A-Z**), it remains the centrepoint for parades and political gatherings. Designed by Francis Johnson, the front features a Greek-Ionic-style portico with six columns, and statues of Fidelity, Hibernia and Mercury. 0800-2000 Mon.-Sat., 1030-1830 Sun.; free.

Giant's Causeway, The: Co. Antrim. The causeway consists of thousands of symmetrical basalt columns which jut out to sea. According to legend it was built by Irish giant Finn MacCool as stepping stones, so he could walk across the sea to Scotland without getting his feet wet. However, the stones are the result of volcanic activity about 60 million years ago. Though not quite as spectacular as pictures may have led you to believe, the entire area is extraordinary. Visitor centre 1000-1900 July & Aug.; earlier closing rest of year. Car park £1.50. Audiovisual exhibition £1, child 50p. See **EXCURSION 14**.

Glencolumbkille: Co. Donegal. St. Columbcille (see **A-Z**) came here to pray during the 6thC and today it still remains a place of pilgrimage. At midnight on 9 June, locals walk barefoot for 3 miles, stopping at each of the penitential cross-inscribed slabs that dot the valley, finishing with Mass at 0300. The Folk Park (1000-1800 Mon.-Sat., 1200-1800 Sun., Easter-Sep.; £1) beside the beach is one of the main attractions for visitors. An archaeological walk through the park takes in a Mass rock, tower, limekiln and many other artefacts. One of the park's latest developments is a 'sweathouse' – a medieval sauna – while you can also visit the old National School replica, and the shebeen house for a taste of seaweed wine! See **EXCURSION 13**.

Glendalough: Co. Wicklow. 30 miles south of Dublin city on the R 576. A monastic settlement founded by St. Kevin in the 6thC flourished around the valley's two lakes for over 600 years. It survived many attacks before being burned and abandoned in 1398. The area became a place of pilgrimage until it was suppressed by Cardinal Cullen of Dublin in 1862. Conservation work on the buildings, which include a 103 ft round tower, a 12thC monastic cemetery and a 7thC cathedral, began in 1873 and has continued since. Among the other religious remains on the site are St. Saviour's, an 11thC church, and the tiny St. Kevin's Church. St. Kevin's Bed, a cave where the saint is said to have begun his solitary life, can be seen in a cliff 30 ft above the water of the upper lake. Visitor centre 1000-1630 Tue.-Sun., Nov.-mid Mar.; 1000-1700 mid Mar.-mid May & Oct.; 1000-1800 mid May-mid June & mid-end Sep.; 1000-1900 mid June-mid Sep.; £1, child 40p.

Glens of Antrim: Co. Antrim. See **EXCURSION 14**.

Glenties: Co. Donegal. North of Donegal town. Set at the foot of two glens, this is a handsome Plantation (see **A-Z**) village, but its visual highlight is probably the lovely modern church of St. Conall, designed by Derry architect Liam McCormack to blend in with its environs. A museum and heritage centre is housed in the courthouse (June-Sep.; £1). Aside from its pubs, nightlife is provided by the Limelight disco, which draws crowds from miles around. See **EXCURSION 13**.

Glin: Co. Limerick. 32 miles west of Limerick city on the N 69. This Shannon-side village adjoins the demesne of Glin Castle, seat of the Fitzgeralds, who have lived in Glin for over 700 years. The present castle was built by the 24th Knight in 1785 as a Georgian house. There is some remarkable plasterwork and contents include an 18thC bookcase with a secret door. The castellations were added in 1820 by his successor. 1000-1200, 1400-1600 May-early June or by appointment, tel: 068-34173; £2, child £1.50.

Gorey: Co. Wexford. 27 miles north of Wexford town on the N 11. This market town played a dominant role in the 1798 Rebellion (see **A-Z**), and the rebels camped on Gorey Hill before marching on Arklow. On the road to Courtown, one of the country's most popular family resorts, is Marlfield House, where nonresidents can enjoy some of the best cuisine on offer along the east coast.

Gougane Barra National Park: Co. Cork. Off the Macroom–Glengarriff road (B 584), 3.5 miles south of Ballingeary. The park encompasses 1000 acres, with spectacular drives, walks and nature trails. Gougane Barra Lake is the source of the River Lee and is surrounded by steep mountains. Streams cascade down their sides to feed the lake, becoming foaming waterfalls after rain. It was on the tiny island here (reached by a causeway) that St. Finbarr founded a monastery before moving down the river to establish the settlement that became Cork city (see **A-Z**). Pilgrimages are still made here annually on the Sun. after 25 Sep., the saint's day, and there are some 18thC remains and a modern oratory on the island. The main road south towards the Bantry–Glengarriff road goes via the craggy-sided Pass of Keimaneigh which climbs to 662 ft, shadowed by the heights of Doughill and Foilastooken. In Irish Keimaneigh means 'the deer's step', and according to legend a pursued deer managed to leap across the pass to safety.

Gregory, Lady Augusta (1852-1932): One of the leaders of the Irish literary revival and founder of the Irish National Theatre, the Abbey Theatre, in 1904. The home of this celebrated folklorist and playwright in Coole Park (see **A-Z**) was the HQ for the literary movement.

Grianan of Aileach: Carrowreagh, Co. Donegal. 4 miles west of Derry city on the N 13. Set on top of 800 ft Greenan hill, this fort, built c. 1700 BC, possibly as a druidic sun temple and occupied until the 12thC, offers views over both loughs Swilly and Foyle. Grianan means 'sun palace' and the kingdom of Aileach consisted of Co. Donegal and most of counties Derry, Tyrone and Armagh, over which the O'Neill clan, the kings of Ulster, ruled. It is thought that the O'Neills built the stone cashel in early Christian times as their royal seat and stronghold. The entire enclosure, including outlying earthen banks, covers 4 acres.

Guinness: The first pint of the 'black stuff' was 'sunk' in 1759 when Arthur Guinness founded his brewery at St. James Gate on the south bank of Dublin's River Liffey. Originally called porter but nowadays known as stout, it has become synonymous with Ireland, though the company is currently British-owned. Though it is now brewed in 16 other countries the discerning Guinness drinker says it tastes best in Dublin, but contrary to popular myth it is not made using Liffey water. The St. James site covers 60 acres and until 1939 was the largest brewery in the world. Drawing a pint of Guinness is regarded as an art, and after ordering expect a wait of a few minutes, while the creamy head is allowed to 'settle'. See DUBLIN CITY-ATTRACTIONS 2.

Hill of Tara: Co. Meath. For over 2000 years this low hill was a place of religious, and later political, importance. Excavations have found remains dating from 2000 BC, though the true story of Tara's origins remains veiled by the mists of time. It reached the height of its fame during the first centuries AD when it became the seat of the high kings of Ireland, and though it declined in power after the advance of Christianity it remained in use until 1022. A circuit of the monuments should include: Adamnan's Cross; the Fort of the Synods, mutilated in

the late 1930s during a search by British Israelites for the Ark of the Covenant; the Fort of the Kings; the Mound of the Hostages; the Royal Seat; and Cormac's House. South of the Fort of the Kings are the remains of Logaire's Fort, a large ring fort. The Banqueting Hall, a rectangular earthwork, may in fact have been the ritual entrance to the hill. See **EXCURSION 1**.

Holy Cross Abbey: Thurles, Co. Tipperary. Northeast of Tipperary town. The church of this 12thC monastery on the banks of the Suir has been meticulously restored and is now used as a parish church. The monastery took its name from a relic of the True Cross, which was contained in a golden shrine here, attracting crowds of pilgrims. Guided tours 0900-2000. Free access to abbey.

Howth: Co. Dublin. 10 miles east of Dublin city. The steep streets of this lovely fishing village are usually thronged in summer with day-trippers from other parts of Dublin. Overlooking the harbour are the remains of a 13thC parish church. The first church on this site was built by King Sigtrygger (Sitric) in 1042. The Abbey Tavern just below has a good restaurant but is best known for its evening music sessions and cabaret. The King Sitric on the pier is more expensive but reputed to be one of Dublin's best seafood restaurants. The grounds of Howth Castle contain a transport museum (1400-1730 Sat. & Sun., Sep.-May; 1100-1700 June-Aug.; £1, child 50p). Howth Head above the village offers wonderful walks and views.

Inishbofin: Co. Galway. The island lies low in the sea off the Galway coast surrounded by reefs and flanked by uninhabited Inishark. The cliffs on its western end are wild and windswept but the eastern end has sheltered beaches. Its turbulent history is recalled by the ruined castle which guards the harbour entrance. Originally a fort built by Spanish pirate Don Bosco, it was later used by woman pirate Grace O'Malley (see **A-Z**). In the mid-1600s it was extended and rebuilt as a castle. It was garrisoned by Cromwellian (see **A-Z**) soldiers who used the island as a transportation centre for priests. A ferry service operates from Cleggan, tel: 095-45806, during the summer. See **EXCURSION 8**.

Inishcealtra: Holy Island. Lough Derg, Co. Clare. Boat trips run from nearby Mountshannon to this little island where St. Caimin founded a monastery in the 7thC. Among the remains are five churches, a round tower, a hermit's cell and the 'Saint's Graveyard', which contains inscribed slabs dating from the 8th to the 12thC. The monastery was repaired and restored by King Brian Boru (see **A-Z**) in 1027, after its almost total destruction by the Vikings.

Inishowen Peninsula: Co. Donegal. Separating the inlets of Lough Foyle and Lough Swilly, this landmass encompasses some of the country's finest scenery. From glorious Fahan beach to Malin Head (see **A-Z**), Ireland's most northerly point, and south to Muff it is largely unspoilt. Its centre is dominated by Slieve Snaght ('mountain of the snows'). The border (see **A-Z**) extends beyond Culmore Point on the eastern side. See **EXCURSION 13**, **Buncrana**.

Inistioge: Co. Kilkenny. 18 miles southeast of Kilkenny city on the R 700. The lovely square is lined with lime trees, and the motte of a Norman fortification stands on a rock overlooking the village and River Nore. The Protestant parish church adjoins the remains of an Augustinian priory built in 1210.

Joyce, James (1882-1941): The writer who constantly maligned his native Dublin, and whose writings were greeted with initial disdain in Ireland, is now predominantly responsible for a thriving literary tourism industry, particularly in the capital. *Ulysses*, his most famous novel, which describes a day in Dublin, is heavy going to say the least but it has enticed thousands of visitors and sparked off Bloomsday (see **A-Z**). Novices may enjoy *Dubliners* and *Portrait of the Artist as a Young Man*. Joyce left Dublin for Trieste in 1904 with his lover Nora Barnacle, returning only a few times before his final visit in 1912. He lived in Zurich and Paris, finally marrying Nora in 1931, and died in Switzerland in 1941. There is a Joyce Museum (1000-1300, 1400-1700 Mon.-Sat., 1430-1800 Sun., April-Oct.; £1.30, child 70p) in the Martello tower (see **A-Z**) at Sandycove, southeast of the city. See **GALWAY CITY-ATTRACTIONS 2**.

Kanturk: Co. Cork. 35 miles northwest of Cork city on the N 20 and N 72. This market town is at the meeting of the Dalua and Allow rivers. A little south of the town is the shell of Kanturk Castle, or MacDonagh's Court. According to tradition MacDonagh MacCarthy, the local Irish chief, began to build the house c. 1609. Jealous English settlers, however, complained about its size and the English Privy Council forbade its completion. An enraged MacCarthy is said to have scattered the blue glass tiles for the roof; the house still stands unfinished.

Kells: Co. Kilkenny. 10 miles south of Kilkenny city on the R 697. Near this ancient village stands the only complete walled medieval town or monastery in Ireland. The Augustinian priory of St. Mary, which dates from around the 14thC, covers 5 acres, surrounded by a curtain wall with dwelling towers.

Kells: Ceanannus Mor. Co. Meath. 39 miles northwest of Dublin city on the N 3. The town occupies the site of a monastery founded by St. Columbcille (see **A-Z**). Remains include five high crosses, a round tower and St. Columbcille's House. Among the artistic treasures which have survived, despite numerous Viking raids, are the famed *Book of Kells* (see **A-Z**) and the Crozier of Kells, which is in the British Museum.

Kenmare: Co. Kerry. The town was founded in 1670 on land given to Sir William Petty by the English government. The colonists fought off local attacks while they established a foundry and set up a fishery but were finally forced to flee when the town was besieged by 3000 men in 1688. The colony was re-established, however, by William III. The Lime Tree on Shelbourne St is an award-winning restaurant in a converted schoolhouse but only opens for dinner Easter-Oct. Pop into the famous, and pricey, Park Hotel for a drink – if you haven't booked in! See **EXCURSIONS 4 & 5**.

Kildare: Co. Kildare. 34 miles southwest of Dublin city on the N 7. Once an important ecclesiastical centre, and a Norman stronghold, but now famed as the centre of the Irish horse-breeding and training industry. St. Brigid founded a convent here in the 5th or 6thC and an adjoining monastery was built a little later. Today's St. Brigid's Cathedral incorporates a 13thC church. The town's 105 ft round tower, believed to date from the 12thC, is usually open to the public. For equine enthusiasts the National Stud is in Tully on the outskirts of the town (1030-1700 Mon.-Fri., 1030-1730 Sat., 1400-1730 Sun., Easter-Oct.; £2, child £1). Adjacent are the tranquil Japanese Gardens, which are landscaped to plot out the life of man.

Kilfenora: Co. Clare. See **EXCURSION 6**.

Kilkee: Co. Clare. 34 miles southwest of Ennis on the N 68. A busy seaside resort at the head of Moore Bay. The town, which boasts a wonderful beach in a dramatic cliff setting, contains the obligatory amusements, souvenir shops and cafés. The local Heritage Gallery in the library has a collection of old household implements and tools which reflect the area's seafaring tradition. Many pubs serve bar food in the summer but you will get heart-warming home-made soup and fresh sandwiches at the Central Bar throughout the year. The area is perfect for bracing walks north or south along the cliffs. One short option is to head for the Duggerna Rocks at the west side of the bay, where the sea spouts up through a puffing hole. There's also a strenuous 16 mile trek to the tip of Loop Head, which flanks the Mouth of the Shannon.

Kilkenny City: Co. Kilkenny. Pop: 13,000. Tourist Information, Rose Inn St, tel: 056-21755. One of Ireland's most attractive towns, where medieval lanes and buildings blend with Georgian elegance – the tourist office itself is housed in a restored Tudor almshouse built in 1582 by Sir Robert Shee for six male and six female paupers. The town initially grew round a monastery founded by St. Canice in the 6thC. The tower built on the same site four hundred years later can be climbed, while the adjoining 13thC St. Canice's Cathedral contains its original baptismal font and St. Kieran's Chair, an ancient stone of enthronement for bishops. After the Anglo-Norman invasion 'Strongbow' built a castle here in 1172, and his heir replaced it with a stone fortress. In 1391 the castle and town were purchased by James Butler, 3rd Earl of Ormond. The castle, which was remodelled in Victorian times, is set in extensive parkland overlooking the River Nore (1030-1245, 1400-1700 Tue.-Sat., 1100-1245, 1400-1700 Sun., Nov.-Mar.; 1000-1700 April & May; 1000-1900 June-Sep.; £1, child 40p, family £3). Kilkenny became a rival to Dublin as the capital in the 14thC and the Anglo-Irish parliament met here regularly. During a famous meeting in 1366 it enacted the Statutes of Kilkenny in a bid to stop the Gaelicization of the Anglo-Normans. The statutes proved unsuccessful. In 1609 James I conferred the status of city on Kilkenny, and from 1642-48 it was the seat of the General Assembly of the Catholic Confederation, a shortlived Irish parliament. In 1650 the city was taken by Cromwell (see **A-Z**) after a five-day siege. Rothe House on Parliament St was built in 1549 for a prosperous Tudor merchant and now contains the museum of the Kilkenny Archaeological Society (1030-1230, 1400-1700 Mon.-Sat., 1500-1700 Sun., April-Oct.; 1500-1700 Sat. & Sun., Nov.-Mar.; £1, child 30p). The Black Abbey on Abbey St is a Dominican friary built in 1225 and now restored. Kilkenny is also the home of Smithwick's beer and guided tours of the brewery off Parliament St, which was built around the 13thC St. Francis' Abbey, start at 1500 Mon.-Fri., June-Aug. For food the award-winning Lacken House on the Dublin road is open to nonresidents, while Edward Langton's pub and restaurant on John St is another favourite. Lively pubs are plentiful and include the Marble City Bar and The Metropole, both on High St. See **EXCURSION 3**.

Kilkenny Castle

Rothe House, Kilkenny

Killala: Co. Mayo. This village on the west shore of lovely Killala Bay takes its name from a church founded by St. Patrick (see **A-Z**), and was a prominent cathedral town. A round tower survives from the early monastic settlement, and a 17thC Protestant cathedral now stands on the site of the medieval church. It was here in Aug. 1798 that 1067 Frenchmen, led by Gen. Humbert, landed to join the United Irishmen's rebellion. See **EXCURSION 9**.

Killaloe: Co. Clare. 14 miles northeast of Limerick city on the R 643. Scenic Killaloe is at the southern tip of Lough Derg, the largest of the Shannon lakes. Its most fascinating building is the 12thC St. Flannan's Cathedral, which was restored in the 18thC. Beside the door is Thogrim's Stone, a cross shaft with a unique bilingual inscription in ogham (see **A-Z**) and Viking runes. The message requests a blessing for Thogrim who carved it. In the churchyard is St. Flannan's Oratory, a well-preserved 12thC church with a traditional stone roof. The 12thC St. Mo-Lua's Oratory, beside the Catholic parish church, was removed from Friar's Island in 1929 when the island was submerged for the Shannon hydroelectric scheme. There are pleasure cruises from the marina on Lough Derg (May-Sep.) and some good walks into the Slieve Bernagh and Arra mountains.

Killarney: Co. Kerry. Pop: 8000. Tourist Information, Town Hall, Main St, tel: 064-31633. This small country town has boomed since the 19thC, when tourists began to arrive to explore its magnificent environs. Its most distinguished building is the 19thC Cathedral of St. Mary, built to a design by Alexander Pugin. The National Museum of Irish Transport (1000-1800; £2, child £1) is a good option on a wet day. Fourteenth-century Ross Castle, the last stronghold in Munster to surrender to Cromwellian (see **A-Z**) forces, on the Ross road is accessible by foot from the town or via the main path of the Knockreer estate (entrance through the gates opposite St. Mary's Cathedral). Boat excursions on Lough Leane depart from a jetty here. Ask the boatman to take you to Inishfallen Island and O'Sullivan's Cascade, a lovely hidden waterfall in Tomey's Wood, which is almost fairy-like. 'Musts' in the area (cycle, drive or walk) include: the Gap of Dunloe (see **A-Z**); the hill of Aghadoe (for panoramic views); and for walkers and mountaineers, Carrantouhill (see **A-Z**) and the rolling slopes of Mangerton (access from Muckross). Two sections of the Kerry Way in the area also allow you to enjoy some of the less accessible sights and scenery. See **EXCURSIONS 4 & 5**.

Killybegs: Co. Donegal. An important fishing port. Unless you have a phobia about birds the arrival of the fishing fleet, smothered in squawking seagulls, is an impressive sight. Other local industries include fish processing, sail making and the making of hand-woven carpets, a process begun in the 19thC. Carpets from Killybegs have even found their way to Buckingham Palace. The wall of the Catholic church, at the top of the hill, contains the carved memorial slab of Niall Mor MacSweeney, clan chieftain, found near St. John's Point, which is one of only two in Ireland. See **EXCURSION 13**.

Kilrush: Co. Clare. 49 miles west of Limerick city on the N 68. This bustling market town was laid out by the Vandeleur family, whose nearby mansion was burned down in the 1920s. There are some pleasant walks east of the town in Kilrush Woods. The Kilrush Heritage Centre (1000-1800 Mon.-Sat., June-Aug.) focuses on local history, paying particular attention to nearby Scattery Island. Boats leave for Scattery from Cappagh Pier, a mile south of the town. The island, inhabited until the late 1970s, contains the ruins of five churches, a holy well and a 122 ft round tower, reputedly Ireland's tallest and oldest. The tower has one unique feature, an entrance at ground level, which may explain why the island was frequently pillaged by the Vikings. St. Senan, who founded a 6thC monastery here, is said to have been a staunch misogynist, who, according to tradition, even in death displayed his loathing of women by cursing any female who walked on his grave to remain childless. This ironically rather endeared him to many women and until the 1930s they travelled to the island just to walk on his resting place, known as St. Senan's House or Bed.

Kinsale: Co. Cork. The town has played a crucial role in Irish history, being host to the last great stand by the Gaelic Irish against the English. In Sep. 1601 a Spanish force sailed into the harbour and took over the walled town with the local Irish. They were besieged by the English armies of Mountjoy and Carew, but Irish forces marched from the north to join the Munster chiefs in blockading them in turn. A surprise attack was betrayed, however, confusion reigned, and the Spanish force surrendered. It was the final blow to Irish hopes and the Flight of the Earls (see **A-Z**) took place shortly afterwards. St. Multose's Church, built in the 12thC, is still in use. It was here that Prince Rupert proclaimed Charles II King of England. Desmond Castle (The French Prison) in Cork St is a 15thC building first used as the custom house for the medieval port, when the quayside was at the bottom of Chairman's Lane. During the 18thC European wars it became a jail for mainly French prisoners – up to 600 at a time. The Old Courthouse and Regional Museum, Market Sq. (1100-1300, 1430-1700 Mon.-Sat., 1500-1730 Sun.; 60p, child 20p), was originally built in 1600 as the market house. The museum includes ancient town charters and local antiquities. Charles Fort (0900-1700 Tue.-Sat., 1400-1700 Sun., mid April-mid June; 0900-1830 mid June-mid Sep.; £1, child 40p) is a late-17thC 'star' fort overlooking the estuary a short distance outside the town near Summer Cove. Two enormous bastions look seaward and three inland. Kinsale was the base from which James II made his attempt to recover the English crown. When the bid failed at the Battle of the Boyne (see **A-Z**) he fled from the fort to France. Ask the curator about the ghost of the 'white lady'. James Fort, across the estuary from Charles Fort in Castlepark, was the first 'star' fort built to protect the town. It was occupied by the Spanish in 1601 and rebuilt after the Battle of Kinsale. Kinsale is also Ireland's culinary capital. A gourmet festival is held in Oct. and there is a Good Food Circle of 15 restaurants. Just about every restaurant and pub in the town, however, can be recommended. See **EXCURSION 4**.

Kinvara: Co. Galway. 18 miles south of Galway city on the N 67. A picturesque fishing village with breathtaking views of Galway Bay. The annual Crinniu na mBad Festival (The Gathering of the Boats) features the racing of the county's traditional sailing craft, the Galway hooker. The festival commemorates the time when boats crossed Galway Bay from Connemara to bring turf to the otherwise fuel-less villages of The Burren (see **A-Z**). Nearby is the beautifully sited Dunguaire Castle

(0930-1730 mid April-Sep.; £1.60). This 16thC fortified tower has been well restored and there are good guided tours. Its occupants over the centuries included Oliver St. John Gogarty, the renowned author, poet, surgeon and 'wit' (Buck Mulligan in *Ulysses*). Medieval banquets are held here in summer (see **GALWAY CITY-RESTAURANTS**).

Knock: Co. Mayo. 46 miles north of Galway city on the N 17. Since 21 Aug. 1879, when locals claimed to have seen an apparition of the Blessed Virgin Mary, Catholic pilgrims have flocked to this town. It is now recognized as a Marian Shrine and includes the massive Basilica of Our Lady Queen of Ireland, which is capable of holding 20,000 people. The Knock Folk Museum offers a glimpse at 19thC rural life (1000-1800 May-Oct., till 2100 July & Aug.; £1, child 50p).

Larne: Co. Antrim. See **EXCURSION 14.**

Limerick City: Co. Limerick. Pop: 58,000. Tourist Information, The Granary, Michael St, tel: 61-317522. Ireland's fourth-largest city began as a 10thC Viking settlement on an island in the River Shannon, from which the Danes marauded through Munster. The Thomond kings used it as a trading centre, and Muirceartach Mor O'Brien made it his principal seat while high king of Ireland. The city was an early target for the Normans who stormed it in 1175 but it was recaptured by Donal Mor O'Brien, who had it burnt to the ground and later rebuilt. The town received its first charter in 1197, and for the remainder of the Middle Ages served as an English trading colony. In 1690 an attack and besiegement by William of Orange on the Jacobite-held town was defeated by Patrick Sarsfield's troops. A siege the following year, under Ginkel, however, proved more successful and the Jacobites agreed to surrender on the basis of a treaty which guaranteed civil rights to the city's Catholics, and allowed the soldiers to join the French service. Sarsfield and 10,000 troops embarked for France – the beginning of the exile of Irish aristocracy known as the Flight of the Wild Geese (see **A-Z**) – but the civil terms of the treaty were soon violated. Today an urban renewal project is underway in a bid to revive this somewhat economically depressed town. See **LIMERICK CITY, EXCURSIONS 5 & 6.**

Lisdoonvarna: Co. Clare. The town is famous for its unique mineral waters, containing sulphur and lithium, iron and manganese. Here you can sample the revolting sulphur water – 'eggy water' – at the Pump House. People have come here to 'take the waters' since the 18thC. The town is probably best known these days for its annual Matchmaking Festival in Sep. Young and old enjoy the music, late-night pub openings and dances while the serious business of matrimonial offers is carried out on the sidelines. See **EXCURSION 6.**

Lismore: Co. Waterford. This picturesque market town in the Blackwater valley was a major ecclesiastical centre from the 7th to the 14thC. The 7thC monastery founded here by St. Carthach was renowned throughout Europe as a university. Lismore Castle was built by King John in 1185 on the monastic site, and it served as a bishop's residence before passing to Sir Walter Raleigh. He in turn sold it to Richard Boyle, Earl of Cork, and chemist Robert Boyle (Boyle's Law) was born here. It later passed to the dukes of Devonshire. In 1814 the Lismore Crozier and the 15thC *Book of Lismore* were discovered in a hiding place in the castle walls. See **EXCURSION 3**.

Literary Ireland: Ireland's literary tradition can be traced back to the 5thC and the emergence of the monastic writers who went on to produce masterpieces including the *Book of Kells* (see **A-Z**). But Irish legends, stories and epic poems were already enshrined in a vibrant oral culture which had existed for centuries previous, and which continued to be kept alive by the bards and *seanchai* (storytellers). Among Ireland's literary gems are: Brian Merriman's raunchy 18thC *Cuirt an Mhean Oiche* which continued the Gaelic tradition; Jonathan Swift's 17th and 18thC satire; the work of the 19thC novelists, Maria Edgeworth, Somerville and Ross, John Banim, and of course *Dracula*'s Bram Stoker; and the plays of Sheridan, Shaw and that master of wit, Wilde. Though their styles, and subjects, were usually poles apart J. M. Synge (see **A-Z**), W. B. Yeats (see **A-Z**) and Sean O'Casey were the leading figures in Irish literature, drama and poetry early this century, while Joyce (see **A-Z**) was first to enjoy fame, or infamy, in a wave of modern Irish fiction. Samuel Beckett, who actually worked for Joyce at one stage, went on to become one of Ireland's most renowned writers. Brendan Behan (see **A-Z**), Flann O'Brien and Frank O'Connor displayed some of the best in Irish humour (and tragedy), and O'Connor with Liam O'Flaherty and Liam O'Faolain were all masters of the short story. For poetry look to Austin Clarke, Thomas Kinsella and Patrick Kavanagh, or their contemporary counterparts Seamus Heaney, Paul Durcan, Michael Hartnett, Brendan Kennelly and Christopher Nolan. Modern writers John McGahern and John Banville are just two of the authors offering an unsentimental glimpse into Ireland. Continuing in the tradition of Irish playwrights are the magnificent Brian Friel, Tom Murphy and Frank McGuinness. It's a formidable list, and only the tip of the iceberg, but a visit to the Dublin Writers' Museum (see **DUBLIN CITY-ATTRACTIONS 2**) is a good start.

Longford: Co. Longford. See **EXCURSION 10**.

Lough Derg: Co. Donegal. This remote lake near Pettigoe in the Donegal hills is renowned for its cave on Station Island where St. Patrick (see **A-Z**) is said to have fasted for 40 days and nights and had a vision of Hell and Purgatory, before his penance drove the Devil from his last stronghold in Ireland. Only pilgrims are allowed on the island. See **EXCURSION 12**.

Lough Erne: Co. Fermanagh. Upper and Lower Lough Erne encompass 50 miles of navigable water and 154 islands, and are an angler's paradise. A cruiser holiday, boat trip or ferry is the best way to explore this watery wonderland and there are bases at Enniskillen, Belleek, Blaney, Kesh, Killadeas, Lisnarrick and Carry Bridge. There's even an opportunity to travel in a Viking longboat from the Share Centre, Smith's Strand near Lisnaskea. See **EXCURSION 12**.

Lough Gill: Co. Sligo. It is possible to drive a 28 mile circuit of the lake from Sligo town, beginning on the N 4 and turning left after about 1.5 miles before Carraroe church. Along the route are the Tobernalt holy well and shrine where legend says that the marks on top of the Mass rock are of St. Patrick's (see **A-Z**) fingers. Follow signposts for Dooney Rock (Yeats' *The Fiddler of Dooney*), Slish Wood (Yeats' *The Stolen Child*) and of course Inishfree (*The Lake Isle of Inishfree*). Also en route is Dromahair (see **A-Z**).

Lough Gur: Co. Limerick. 16 miles south of Limerick city on the R 512. The area around the lake is one of Ireland's most important archaeological sites. The centre (1000-1800 May-Sep.; £1.60, child 80p) is housed in replica Neolithic dwellings. Its exhibits tell the story of 5000 years of human inhabitation at the lough using an audiovisual presentation and models. Walking tours of the locality's many archaeological features, including crannogs (see **A-Z**), a gallery grave (where 12 bodies dating from c. 2000 BC were found), massive stone circles and a 15thC castle, are probably the best way to see the area. The full historical importance of this region was first realized during the 19thC

Lough Key

when the lake was partially drained. According to legend, the last of the local Desmond chieftains rules beneath Lough Gur's remaining waters, emerging every seven years on a silver-shod horse. See **LIMERICK CITY-ATTRACTIONS**.

Lough Key Forest Park: Co. Roscommon. Northeast of Galway city on the N 4. This 300 hectare park hugs the shores of lovely Lough Key, which was once part of the massive Rockingham estate. Castle Island was the seat of the MacDermotts, princes of Moylurgh, for many centuries. Rockingham's grounds include nature trails, a bog garden and an ugly viewing tower which marks where the house stood prior to being burned down in 1957. Grounds open daily. Shops and restaurant, summer only. Car £4.

Lough Neagh: Northern Ireland. This is the largest lake in Britain and Ireland and covers 153 sq. miles. Because of its similarity in shape to the Isle of Man legend has it that once, when enraged, the giant Finn MacCool scooped out a huge lump of earth and threw it into the Irish Sea. The lough is famous for its eels, which are caught at the Toome fishery in its northwest corner. The lough is navigable and it is possible to cruise from the Lower to the Upper River Bann at Portadown.

Lough Ree: See **EXCURSION 10**.

Louisburgh: Co. Mayo. See **EXCURSION 8**.

Macroom: Co. Cork. 24 miles west of Cork city on the N 22. A bustling market town set in the picturesque Sullane River valley. A gateway is all that remains of Macroom Castle, built by the MacCarthys. In 1654 the castle and town were granted by Cromwell (see **A-Z**) to Admiral Penn, father of William Penn who founded Pennsylvania. About 3.5 miles west are the remains of Carrigaphooca Castle. According to tradition the rock on which it stands was haunted by a 'pooca' or malicious fairy.

Malahide: Co. Dublin. 10 miles north of Dublin city. This pleasant coastal village is a regular winner in the national Tidy Towns Awards. Nearby Malahide Castle Demesne includes, as well as the castle itself, a cottage museum and the Fry Model Railway Museum (castle 1000-1700 Mon.-Fri., all year; 1400-1700 Sat., Sun. & hols, Nov.-Mar.; 1100-1800 Sat., 1400-1800 Sun. & hols, April-Oct.; £2.35, child £1.15).

Malin Head: Co. Donegal. The cliffs rise to 200 ft at Ireland's most northerly point (nearer Glengad Point they rise up to 800 ft). Ali Farren's, a traditional fisherman's pub, is Ireland's most northerly bar. The village of Malin is a picturesque Plantation (see **A-Z**) settlement which still retains its village green.

Mallow: Co. Cork. 22 miles north of Cork city on the N 20. This prosperous town is the largest settlement along the scenic Blackwater valley. Up to a century ago it was renowned as a spa. A half-timbered Elizabethan Clock House and the ruins of 16thC Mallow Castle are the main features of the town centre. Outside the town is 18thC Longueville House, now a hotel, which is famed for its vineyard. Across the river are the remains of an O'Callaghan castle.

Marble Arch Caves: Marlbank, Co. Fermanagh. These spectacular limestone caves lie under Cuilcagh mountain. A 1.5 hr guided tour, which includes an underground boat trip, is available. Tel: 036-582-8855 to confirm they're open; £3, child £1.50.

Markievicz, Countess Constance (1868-1927): Born Constance Gore-Booth in London, she lived at Lissadell House (see EXCURSION 12). She joined the Irish Citizen Army, fighting at Dublin's College of Surgeons during the Easter Rising (see **A-Z**). As she was a woman she escaped execution for her part in it. It was while in prison that she was elected a Sinn Fein MP for Dublin, the first woman elected to Westminster, and on release she sat in the separatist Dail Eireann (see **A-Z**), becoming Minister for Labour. She eventually joined the Fianna Fail party, being elected to the Dail shortly before her death.

Martello Towers: During the early 1800s when the fear of invasion by Napoleon was at its height, a string of observation forts was built around the coasts of Britain and Ireland. The towers had a 360-degree field of vision and were heavily armed – but the invasion never came. Some of the 75 towers built in Ireland have since become homes and museums, among them the Joyce Museum in Sandycove, Dublin (see **Joyce**).

Mitchelstown Cave: Co. Tipperary. 2 miles south of the N 8 between Mitchelstown and Cahir. Discovered in 1833, the cave consists of three large caverns of up to 60 ft in height. The limestone formations include the 30 ft-high Tower of Babel. 1000-1800; £2, child 50p. See EXCURSION 3.

Moher, Cliffs of: Co. Clare. See EXCURSION 6.

Molly Malone: It is uncertain if the Molly Malone buried in St. John's Churchyard in 1734 is the subject of Dublin's unofficial anthem. At the College Green end of Grafton St is a bronze statue depicting one artist's impression of the young woman who, in song at least, wheeled her barrow, crying, 'Cockles and mussels, alive, alive-o'.

Monaghan: Co. Monaghan. Southwest of Belfast city on the A 3. The county town has some remains of a 15thC friary near The Diamond. The nearby ornate Victorian drinking fountain is a memorial to a Baron Rossmore. A museum tracing the history of the St. Louis order and the county is housed in the St. Louis Convent.

Monasterboice: Co. Louth. See **EXCURSION 1**.

Mullet Peninsula: Co. Mayo. 40 miles west of Ballina on the N 59 and R 313. Belmullet marks the entrance to this empty but scenic peninsula. Here only the birds shatter the peace on the many lovely and lonely beaches around Blacksod Bay. Early settlers built forts here and remnants can still be seen at Doonamo Point, Doonaneanir and Portnafrancach. Five miles southwest of Belmullet are the ruins of Cross Abbey, which is traditionally associated with St. Brendan. In the sand dunes of the northwest, a mile from the ruins of Bingham Lodge, is ancient Kilmore, a small circular enclosure with a cross wall and large pillar stone. Legend has it that the people in Kilmore churchyard were buried standing. The ruins of the early Christian St. Dervla's Church and Bed (grave), and some early cross pillars can be seen at Fallmore on the southern tip. See **EXCURSION 9**.

Mullingar: Co. Westmeath. See **EXCURSION 10**.

Nenagh: Co. Tipperary. 25 miles northeast of Limerick city on the N 7. Tourist Information, Kirkham St, tel: 67-31610. The main feature of this market town are the remains of the Butler castle, built c. 1200 by Theobold Fitzwalter, first Butler of Ormond. Its impressive keep is 100 ft high but the last 25 ft were added in the 19thC. In Abbey St are the ruins of a 13thC Franciscan friary.

Newcastle: Co. Down. Tourist Information, Central Promenade, tel: 3967-22222. The town nestles at the foot of Slieve Donard. Amenities include the famous Royal County Down golf course, 5 miles of beach, a bowling green, tennis courts, miniature golf, enclosed warm sea pools and fishing. The promenade has a memorial fountain to Percy French, who wrote the famous song *The Mountains of Mourne*. Beautiful Tollymore Park on the mountain slopes can be reached from Bryansford Rd, northwest of the town. Castlewellan Forest Park, which includes a castle, arboretum and a host of wildlife, is only 4 miles away. See **EXCURSION 15**.

Newgrange: Co. Meath. This restored cairn and passage tomb is over 5000 years old and is regarded as the world's first solar observatory. It is estimated that 18,000 tonnes of stone were needed to build it. It contains many mysterious and well-preserved stone carvings. A small distance away are 12 standing stones, all that remains of a probable 36 stones which once surrounded the cairn. One unique feature of this ancient tomb is the roof-box, positioned to catch the rays of the rising sun during the winter solstice. There is a waiting list of five years to attend this phenomenon. About 100,000 people visit the site every year and long queues for guided tours are common. 1000-1300, 1400-1630 Tue.-Sun., Nov.-mid Mar.; 1000-1300, 1400-1700 mid Mar.-May & mid Sep.-Oct.; 1000-1830 June-mid Sep.; £1.50, child 60p. See **EXCURSION 1**.

New Ross: Co. Wexford. See **EXCURSION 2**.

Newry: Co. Down. See **EXCURSIONS 1 & 15**.

O'Connell, Daniel: (1775-1847): Known as 'The Liberator', he led the nationalist struggle for constitutional reform which led to Catholic emancipation in 1829. He went on to become the first Catholic MP in the British House of Commons and first Catholic Lord Mayor of Dublin. His ancestral home is Derrynane House (see **EXCURSION 5**). He is commemorated by an 1854 bronze figure by Irish sculptor John Henry Foley in O'Connell St, Dublin, just one of the streets named in his honour.

Ogham: An ancient script where notches or lines marked on standing stones represent 20 letters of the Latin alphabet.

Omagh: Co. Tyrone. 34 miles south of Derry city on the A 5. Tourist Information, 1 Market St, tel: 662-247831. The county town and a good base for touring the Sperrin mountains (see **A-Z**). There are a number of lovely forest parks in the vicinity and the Ulster-American Folk Park (1100-1830 Mon.-Sat., 1130-1900 Sun., Easter-mid Sep.; 1030-1700 Mon.-Fri., mid Sep.-Easter; £2.60, child £1.30), complete with a 19thC emigrant ship and American frontier settlement, is nearby in Camphill. Also near Omagh is the new Ulster History Park which, when completed, will include six reconstructed historical sites, such as a Stone-Age house and monastic settlement.

O'Malley, Grace (c. 1530-1603): Born in Co. Mayo into a family of seafarers and pirates, she cropped her hair as a young girl to enable her to sail as a boy to Spain on her father's ship. This earned her the name Grainne Mhaol (bald Grace). Her first husband was another pirate, Donal O'Flaherty, whose family ruled Connemara. For a while Grainne made Clare Island (see **A-Z**) her HQ but when she married Richard Burke she moved to Rockfleet Castle, which guarded a harbour on Clew Bay. In 1539 she sailed up the Thames to meet Elizabeth I, asking for permission to 'invade with sword and fire all your highness' enemies'. It is believed she died in poverty.

Orange Order, The: Founded in Sep. 1795 in Ulster after rioting between Catholics and Protestants over land. Today Loyal Orange Lodges exist across the North, and thousands of Orangemen march on 12 July to commemorate the victory of King William of Orange in the Battle of the Boyne (see **A-Z**), and to demonstrate their continued loyalty to the Protestant faith and the British Crown.

Parnell, Charles Stewart (1846-91): Though the son of a wealthy Anglo-Irish landlord, Parnell was elected Home Rule MP for Meath at the age of 29. He became the leader of the Home Rule and Land League Movement in Ireland, and developed the policy of blacklisting and ignoring absentee landlords and their ruthless agents – a practice that became known as 'boycotting' after one of its victims. Though he managed to win the support of prime minister William Gladstone for home rule, the issue was later defeated in parliament. Three years later this charismatic leader fell from grace when he was cited in a divorce case brought by an Irish MP against his wife, Katherine (Kitty) O'Shea, Parnell's long-time mistress. He was forced out of the party leadership and died shortly after. His Avondale, Co. Wicklow, home is now a forestry centre and open to the public.

Pearse, Padraic (1879-1916): One of the leaders of the Easter Rising (see **A-Z**), executed by firing squad at Kilmainham Jail with his brother Willie and 13 others. Pearse was also an educationalist, and his innovative school at Rathfarnham, Co. Dublin, is now a museum.

Penal Laws, The: Introduced after the Williamite war, these forbade Catholics from: voting; buying land; owning a horse valued at more than £5; celebrating Mass; teaching; educating their children in the Catholic faith; speaking Irish; and playing Irish music. Upon the death of a Catholic man his estate was to be divided equally between his sons, unless one of them turned Protestant. By the middle of the 18thC only 7 per cent of land was in Catholic hands but covert 'hedge schools' flourished, where the Irish language and culture was taught, while Mass continued to be celebrated, often at hidden Mass rocks in the countryside or in secret chapels.

Near Teelin

Dunmore Caves

Butlers Bridge

Lough Swilly

Killarney

Plantations, The: The first Plantations took place during the reign of Mary I when lands in counties Laois and Offaly were confiscated from their Irish owners and given to 'loyal English'. Elizabeth I continued the process and also attempted to 'plant' northeast Ulster, the greatest Gaelic stronghold. It was only when James I 'planted' his fellow Scots here – all Protestant – however, that the Plantation succeeded, and it was these settlers whose descendants stayed loyal to the Crown, becoming Unionists and Orangemen.

Poitin: Illegal Irish 'moonshine', usually made with potatoes.

Portrush: Co. Antrim. See **EXCURSION 14**.

Portstewart: Co. Derry. See **EXCURSION 14**.

Portumna: Co. Galway. 42 miles southeast of Galway city on the N 65. A market town and cruiser base at the head of Lough Derg. Portumna Castle, built in 1609 and destroyed by fire in 1826, is under restoration. Near the castle demesne is Portumna Priory. Originally a Cistercian church stood here but the present structure was built by the Dominicans in the 15thC. Portumna Forest Park, a wildlife sanctuary, includes a marked nature trail.

Powerscourt Gardens & Waterfall: Enniskerry, Co. Wicklow. 13 miles south of Dublin city on the R 755. The 17thC Palladian mansion designed by Richard Castle for the Powerscourts was gutted by fire in 1974 and only a shell remains. The grounds in which it stands, however, are outstanding. The formal gardens were begun in 1731 but a century later the 7th Viscount Powerscourt – who had no heirs and loathed his brother who was due to inherit – decided to deplete the family fortune by creating an elaborate garden. It was designed by Daniel Robertson who supervised the work while being pushed around in a wheelbarrow nursing a bottle of sherry! The nearby waterfall is a great favourite with picnickers. Gardens 0900-1730 Mar.-Oct.; waterfall 1030-1900 (dusk in winter). Gardens £2, child 90p; waterfall £1, child 50p.

Puck Fair: Killorglin, Co. Kerry. This ancient annual fair, held over three days in mid-Aug., may date back to pagan times. On 'gathering day' a large beribboned horned goat is carried to the market square, where it is hoisted onto a platform to preside over the livestock fair and merrymaking. It is lowered and taken away on the final day, 'scattering day'.

Rathcroghan: Co. Roscommon. 13 miles north of Roscommon town on the N 5. This grossly undeveloped area, which was a burial place for the kings of Ireland and Connacht, covers 518 hectares. Over 20 ring forts, burial mounds and megalithic tombs can be found here, and a 6 ft-high standing stone is said to mark the grave of King Daithi, Ireland's last pagan king. The famed Queen Maeve of Irish legends had her home here.

Rathlin Island: Co. Antrim. Ireland's largest inhabited island is located about 6 miles from Ballycastle and 13 miles from the Mull of Kintyre, Scotland. This strategic position has meant a turbulent history, and following settlement by monks it was the site of the first Viking raid in Ireland in AD 795. The island has also witnessed three massacres – one by the Scots and two by the English. Robert the Bruce, King of Scotland, hid from the English in a cave here in 1306. Today the island's inhabitants have a mixture of Scots and Irish heritage, and it is popular with anglers and scuba-divers. Ferry services run daily from Ballycastle, Easter-Sep. See **EXCURSION 14**.

Rathmullan: Co. Donegal. 16 miles northeast of Letterkenny on the R 24. This lovely seaside resort on Lough Swilly was where Red Hugh O'Donnell was captured and taken to be imprisoned in Dublin Castle (see **A-Z**), one of the sparks which ignited a great war between the Gaelic Irish and the English Crown. It was also from here that the earls of Tyrone and Tyrconnell sailed to Continental Europe during the Flight of the Earls (see **A-Z**). A well-equipped heritage centre tells the story of the Flight and its effects. The remains of a 15thC Carmelite friary, whose church was converted into a stronghouse in the 17thC, can also be seen.

Ring of Kerry: The traditional name of the circular road which travels mainly round the coast of the lovely Iveragh peninsula. See **EXCURSION 5**.

Rock of Cashel: The earliest of the buildings which crown St. Patrick's Rock is the perfectly preserved Round Tower. Cormac's Chapel, which was consecrated in 1134, is next in date. The roofless cathedral which joins the two was erected between 1235 and 1270, though its tower is a possible 14thC addition. The bishop's castle which adjoins the cathedral was built in the 15thC, as was the adjacent Hall of the Vicars Choral, through which you enter the complex. Cashel first became a royal seat with the kings of Munster in the 4th or 5thC, and continued as such until 1101 when Muirceartaigh O'Briain handed over the rock to the Church. The guided tour is a 'must'. 0930-1630 mid Sep.-mid Mar., 0930-1730 mid Mar.-May, 0900-1930 June-mid Sep.; £1.50, child 60p, family £4. See **EXCURSION 3**.

Roscommon: Co. Roscommon. 20 miles north of Athlone on the N 61. Ireland's last hang woman, 'Lady Betty', worked at the jail which still stands in the town centre. She had her own death sentence for murder withdrawn on condition that she carried out all the public hangings without payment. Roscommon Castle, located off Castle St, was built by the Norman Robert d'Ufford in 1269. It was razed to the ground by the Irish four years later and rebuilt in 1280. Almost four centuries later it was blown up and never reconstructed. James Harlow's shop on Main

St is a virtual treasure trove, and still retains a colourful old bar to its rear, popular with farmers on mart day. Tom Fox's is one of the few places with traditional music.

Roscrea: Co. Tipperary. 45 miles northeast of Limerick city on the N 7. The road passes between the remains of an Augustinian monastery, built in 1100. On one side is a round tower, capless since 1135 and missing 20 ft since 1798 when a cannon mounted there backfired. On the far side of the road are the remains of the priory, used as an entrance to the early-19thC Church of St. Cronan. In the town centre is a 13thC castle gate and curtain wall, and inside is the lovely Queen Anne-style Damer House, which is now a heritage centre.

Rosslare Harbour: Co. Wexford. 13 miles southeast of Wexford town on the N 25. Wexford's loss was Rosslare's gain, for the silting up of the county town harbour forced a move south and Rosslare is now an important ferry and cargo port. See **Ferries**.

Rosslare Town: Co. Wexford. 11 miles southeast of Wexford town on the N 25. This resort town has been a popular destination for generations. It boasts a beautiful 6 mile strand and a good golf course among its attractions. Lady's Island, a place of pilgrimage, is connected to the mainland by a causeway. It retains the ruins of a Norman castle and an Augustinian priory. In nearby Tacumshane there is an ancient windmill which is still in working order.

Rostrevor: Co. Down. This lovely town edges up the slopes of Slievemartin. It is sited in one of the most sheltered areas of Northern Ireland and Mediterranean plants grow along the seafront. The bell from the 6thC monastery founded nearby by St. Bronagh is preserved at the town's Catholic church, and in the graveyard is the burial place of Paddy Murtagh who was the tallest man in the world, at 8 ft 1 in, until he died in 1861. Above the town is the 40 ton Cloughmore Stone, carried there by a glacial movement. According to local legend, however, the stone was thrown there by giant Finn MacCool from the Cooley mountains across Carlingford Lough. See **EXCURSION 15**.

Roundstone: Co. Galway. A sheltered fishing village at the foot of Errisbeg mountain. It is a popular getaway location, not least because of the splendid beach on Gurteen Bay. Roundstone Musical Instruments at the IDA centre west of the village is worth a visit. See **EXCURSION** 7.

St. Columbcille (AD 521-97): Born into a Donegal royal family, he was baptized Colm and known as Columba. He studied at the monastic schools of Clonard, Co. Meath and Moville Abbey, Co. Down (where he turned spring water into communion wine) and founded his first monastery in Derry. He founded settlements throughout the country, and later, in retribution for a war he had caused, he travelled to Iona to convert the Pictish tribes of Scotland. See **Battle of the Books**.

St. Mullins: Co. Carlow. North of New Ross. An ancient riverside settlement in the picturesque Barrow valley. The place takes its name from an important 7thC monastery founded here by St. Mo-Ling. The remains of Teach Mo-Ling, his main foundation and his burial place, are near the Protestant church. This is also the burial site of the South Leinster kings.

St. Patrick (c. AD 390-461): The son of a junior Roman official in Wales, Patrick was captured at 16 by Irish raiders and sold into slavery to an Antrim chieftain, for whom he herded pigs on Slemish mountain for 6 years, before being called by God in a dream and escaping. He returned to Ireland as a bishop in AD 432, founding his first church in a barn at Saul, Co. Down. Armagh was his HQ as he travelled the country baptizing, ordaining, and encouraging monastic life.

1798 Rebellion: Spurred on by the French Revolution, the United Irishmen was founded by Protestant Theobald Wolfe Tone, who sought French assistance for a rising. In June 1798 rebellions broke out in Wexford and Waterford but were crushed at Vinegar Hill by English troops under Gen. Lake. Disorganized fighting also broke out in other areas before the arrival of Gen. Humbert and his troops at Killala in Aug. The French later surrendered and Tone was captured. He admitted treason and, when refused a request to be shot as a soldier, cut his own throat in prison.

Shannon, The: The longest river, and the largest area of inland waters, in Ireland and Britain. It begins its 250 mile journey in the Cuilcagh mountains, Co. Cavan, flowing southwards through the city of Limerick to the Atlantic. It is navigable for 137 miles, non-tidal for 127 miles and has only six locks.

Sherkin Island: Co. Cork. A mere 10 min boat trip away from the fishing village of Baltimore (see **A-Z**). Its marine station contains a natural history museum and other exhibits. A colourful regatta is held on the 3rd Sun. of Aug. Ferry services run seven times daily during the summer. See **EXCURSION 4**.

Siege of Derry, The (1689): In December 1688 the apprentice boys of the city slammed the city gates on Jacobite forces sent to take over the city. But in April 1689 an enlarged force, led by James himself, marched on the city and attacked Bishop's Gate. For 105 days the city was held under siege, suffering terrible hardships, until at the end of July the ship *Mountjoy* broke through a boom stretched across the river and reached the Ship Quay laden with provisions. The Jacobites lifted the siege on Aug. 1. See **DERRY CITY-ATTRACTIONS**.

Skelligs, The: Co. Kerry. These massive rocks off the Kerry coast are Little Skellig (a bird sanctuary, and breeding ground for 20,000 gannets) and Great Skellig or Skellig Michael. Boat trips to Skellig Michael are made in calm weather from Portmagee and Ballinskelligs, and even the most determined landlubber may find the dramatic journey worth the discomfort and the price (c. £10). As you approach there is no obvious route to the summit but from the tiny landing dock steps cut into the cliff face become visible. This is the ancient route taken by monks to their monastery. A roadway leads to Christ's Saddle, the island's only patch of green; the ruined St. Finian's Abbey; the remaining monks' beehive huts; and two oratories. The monastery was plundered by the Vikings early in the 9thC but continued to be inhabited until the 12thC. See **EXCURSION 5**.

Skerries: Co. Dublin. 17 miles north of Dublin city on the R 127. This seaside town takes its name from the rock islands which lie off the coast: Red Island, now joined to the mainland, site of Ireland's first holiday camp; Colt Island; and St. Patrick's Island, where the saint (see **St. Patrick**) is said to have landed on his way from Wicklow to Ulster. South are Shenick's Island, site of a Martello tower (see **A-Z**), and Rockabill, crowned with a lighthouse, further out to sea. For food try The Slipway or the bar menu at the Stoop Your Head pub, both on the harbour. The Red Bank in Church St is considerably more expensive but one of Dublin's most famous restaurants.

Skibbereen: Co. Cork. Tourist Information, 14-15 Main St, tel: 028-21766. A lively west Cork town which has become the agricultural and industrial centre for the area. Skibbereen is home to a growing community of artists, craftworkers and writers, many from Continental Europe, who use the West Cork Arts Centre on Main St as a focal point. There is a small local folk museum at St. Fachtna's High School. The town newspaper, the *Skibbereen Eagle*, became famous at the turn of the century for a vociferous editorial which ended with the warning, 'The *Skibbereen Eagle* has its eye on the Czar of Russia'! There is a plentiful supply of small restaurants, pubs and coffee shops in the town, including Field's Coffee Shop, Main St, and Katie's Garden Café, a cheap wholefood restaurant behind a shop on North St. See **EXCURSION 4**.

Slieve League: Co. Donegal. These incredible cliffs rise to almost 2000 ft above the Atlantic, affording one of the most panoramic views in Europe, ranging over five counties. The walk is a definite no-no for even the remotely unfit or anyone without a head for heights, as there are some very narrow paths to traverse. Enquire at Teelin for directions or to hire a guide. See **EXCURSION 13**.

Sligo Town: Co. Sligo. Pop: 15,000. Tourist Information, Aras Reddan, Temple St, tel: 071-61201. Sited on both sides of the Garavouge River, the settlement was given in 1235 to Maurice Fitzgerald, who built a castle here and founded a Dominican friary. In a period of 50 years during the 13thC both were destroyed five times, and later castles and abbeys continued to be sacked and gutted by fire during a series of sieges. The busy county town is a good base for W. B.Yeats (see **A-Z**) enthusiasts, golfers and walkers, while its proximity to wonderful beaches, including Rosses Point, makes it ideal for families. The ruins of the 13thC Dominican abbey can be seen on Abbey St, while the Sligo Museum and Art Gallery, Stephen St contains Ireland's largest collection of Jack B. Yeats (see **A-Z**) paintings. There is also a Yeats Museum (1030-1230, 1430-1630 Tue.-Sat., June-Sep.). The nearby Yeats Building at Douglas Hyde Bridge is the HQ of the Yeats Society, and venue for the annual Yeats summer school. The Hawk's Well Theatre on Temple St hosts national and local productions. Haragadon's Pub, O'Connell St, a truly traditional bar (women have only been served here since the late 1970s), is another 'must'. Two miles southwest of the town are the Carrowmore megalithic tombs (1000-1800 June-Sep.; 80p). More than 85 tombs are believed to have survived until the 19thC, when they were demolished by landowners or rifled by amateur archaeologists. Sixty tombs have been located to date. A visitor centre offers an audio-visual display and guided tours. See **EXCURSION 12**.

Sperrin Mountains: Co. Tyrone. The range stretches across the heart of Ulster from Omagh to Cookstown. Among their treasures are almost a thousand Stone-Age standing stones, including the spectacular Beaghmore Circles between Goirtin and Cookstown. The interpretative Sperrin Heritage Centre is at Cranagh (1100-1800 Mon.-Fri., 1130-1800 Sat., 1400-1900 Sun., Easter-Sep.; £1.25, child 50p). You can even try your hand at gold-mining here!

Spiddle: Co. Galway. See **EXCURSION 7**.

Strokestown Park House: Co. Roscommon. Northeast of Galway city on the N 5. Built in 1800, and the home of the Pakenham-Mahon family until the mid-1980s. The main street in the planned village leads to the estate gate. Features of the house include a gallery kitchen (so the lady of the house could oversee work) and a tunnel connecting courtyards so the servants would not be seen on the lawn! 1200-1700 Tue.-Sat., June-mid Sep.; £2, child £1.

Swift, Jonathan (1667-1745): This Dublin-born cleric and satirist, who became the dean of St. Patrick's Cathedral (see **DUBLIN CITY-ATTRACTIONS 1**), is best known as the author of *Gulliver's Travels*. His writings constantly attacked the British Establishment, on behalf of the rights of the Irish, particularly Dublin's poor.

Synge, John Millington (1871-1909): Dublin-born Synge was fascinated with the life of the Aran Islanders (see **A-Z**), and one of his most famous plays, the tragic *Riders to the Sea*, is based there. While most of his work provoked controversy, the first staging of *The Playboy of the Western World* caused a riot. He died tragically young of cancer.

Thomastown: 12 miles south of Kilkenny city on the N 9. The town was formerly a medieval walled settlement, of which the only remains are the castle by the bridge and Sweetman's Castle. The town and surrounding area has become a centre for arts and crafts. A mile southwest is Jerpoint Abbey (1000-1300, 1400-1700 Tue.-Sat., 1400-1700 Sun., May-mid June; 0930-1830 mid June-mid Sep.; 80p, child 30p), founded in the latter half of the 12thC, with some unusual cloister carvings.

Thoor Ballylee: Co. Galway. 22 miles southeast of Galway city off the N 66. A 16thC tower house bought by W. B. Yeats (see **A-Z**) in 1917 and restored for use as his home. It was here that he wrote his collection of poems *The Tower*. He left it for Dublin in 1929 and it fell to 'ruin once again', until it was restored for the centenary of his birth in 1965. It now houses a Yeats Museum. 1000-1800 May-Sep.; £2.50, child 75p.

Tipperary: Co. Tipperary. 24 miles southeast of Limerick city on the N 24. This market town, built by the Normans, is at the centre of the fertile Golden Vale. It featured prominently in both the 19thC Land League campaign and the struggle for independence.

Tory Island: Co. Donegal. The 120 inhabitants of this island Gaeltacht (see **A-Z**) are cut off from the mainland for weeks on end by winter storms; it takes its name from the cliffs, or *tors*, battered by the Atlantic waves. The population swells to about 300 in summer for the salmon fishing and when the school children return. St. Columbcille (see **A-Z**) founded a monastery here, and its round tower and cross still remain. Enquire at Bunbeg or Magheraroarty about crossings.

Tralee: Pop: 13,000. Co. Kerry. Tourist Information, The Mall, tel: 066-21288. This county town is renowned for the Rose of Tralee contest, held every Aug. The *Rose of Tralee* song was written by local man William Mulchinock but the festival is much more than a beauty contest. During the 16th and 17thC the town was the principal seat of the earls of Desmond. Their castle stood where The Mall joins Denny St. The Geraldine Experience, a depiction of the town in medieval times, is worth a visit (1000-1800 Mon.-Sat., 1400-1800 Sun.; £2.50, child £1.50). See **EXCURSION 5**.

Trinity College: TCD. Dublin city. Founded in 1592 by Elizabeth I to consolidate the Reformation through education. The restriction on Catholic students was abandoned in 1873 but the Roman Catholic church maintained its own ban until 1970 on its members being students. Today the majority of the 7000 students are Irish Catholics. Trinity's seven libraries – not all on the site – house almost 3 million books. The impressive Long Room contains many treasures, among them the *Book of Kells* (see **A-Z**), the *Book of Durrow* (7thC), the *Book of Dimma* (8thC) and the *Book of Armagh* (9thC). See **DUBLIN CITY-ATTRACTIONS 1**.

Tullamore: Co. Offaly. Built by the earls of Charleville in the 18thC, and home of Tullamore Dew and Irish Mist liqueurs. Charleville Castle (by appointment, tel: 0506-21279; £3), built in 1798 to a design by Francis Johnston, is considered to be one of the finest Gothic-style houses in Ireland. Boats can be hired for trips on the Grand Canal. The remains of Durrow Abbey, founded by St. Columbcille (see **A-Z**) and origin of the *Book of Durrow*, are 4 miles north on the N 52. See **EXCURSION 10**.

Valentia Island: Co. Kerry. Connected to the mainland at Portmagee by bridge, this homely island is noted for its high rainfall but is still a popular resort. Its capital, Knights Town, has a good harbour and boat excursions can be made to Church Island which has the remains of an oratory and beehive huts. See **EXCURSION 5**.

Waterford City: Co. Waterford. Pop: 40,000. Tourist Information, 41 The Quay, tel: 451-75788. Founded by the Vikings at the beginning of the 10thC. After being conquered by the Anglo-Normans the town grew into a thriving port and became famous for its loyalty to the English Crown. Its world-famous crystal industry was founded in the 18thC, destroyed in the 19thC by high duties, and revived again in 1947. The Waterford Crystal Centre at Kilbarry, 1.5 miles along the Cork road, includes a showroom and video presentation (0900-1700 Mon.-Fri., 0900-1230 Sat.). Free guided tours (adults only), bookable at the tourist office, are also available. The impressive Reginald's

Tower at the junction of The Quay and The Mall was built by the Normans and its thick walls conceal a staircase. It contains the town's Civic and Maritime Museum (1100-1300, 1400-1900 Mon.-Fri., 1000-1400 Sat., May-Sep.; 50p). Nearby in Greyfriars St are the remains of the French Church or Greyfriars. Founded by the Franciscans in the 13thC, the church served as a hospital in the 16thC and was handed over for use as a place of worship to a colony of French Huguenot refugees in 1693. The 13thC Blackfriars or Dominican friary on Bridge St is also in ruins and nearby is the west wall of St. Olave's, all that remains of a Viking foundation. The Protestant Christ Church Cathedral in Cathedral Sq. was built in 1770 (its 700-year-old predecessor was levelled to the ground), while the Catholic Cathedral of the Holy Trinity was completed in 1796. A heritage centre in Greyfriars St includes a model of the original Viking settlement (0930-1730 Mon.-Fri., 1000-1400 Sat., Easter-Oct.). Galley Restaurant River Cruises operate from The Quay to Passage East daily June-Aug., tel: 051-21950/21723. The Munster on Bailey's New St and The Metropole on Bridge St are two of the city's most popular pubs. See **EXCURSION 3**.

Westport: Co. Mayo. See **EXCURSION 8**.

Wexford Town: Co. Wexford. Pop: 14,000. Tourist Information, Crescent Quay, tel: 053-23111. Founded by the Vikings as a base for raids, a flourishing port grew up here and it was the first town to be captured by the Anglo-Normans in 1169. In 1649 Cromwell (see **A-Z**) slaughtered its residents, breaking its terms of surrender, and it was the site of a month-long rebellion in 1798 (see **A-Z**). The town is renowned for its opera festival (see **Events**) and its narrow winding streets and lanes. The huge Westgate at the top of Slaney St is the only surviving town gateway. It was Henry II who ordered the fortification of the town during his visit here in 1172 but on his death the wall, which was only half completed, fell into disrepair. It was not until the local Knights of the Third Crusade returned in the 14thC that the wall, including the Westgate, was finished. Under a recent urban-renewal scheme the tower, walls and adjoining coach house have been renovated. There are plans to house an interpretative centre and museum in the latter. Nearby are the remains of the Abbey of the Holy Sepulchre, or Selskar Abbey, which was destroyed by Cromwell. It was near here that Henry II spent the Lent of 1172 doing penance for the murder of St. Thomas à Becket in Canterbury Cathedral. For food there is a wide range of good pubs and small restaurants to choose from, including the award-winning Bohemian Girl, North Main St, and the Granary Restaurant, Westgate, which specializes in seafood. See **EXCURSION 2**.

Whiskey: Irish whiskey is distinguished from Scottish whisky not only in spelling but because it is distilled three times instead of twice, giving it a smoother, more mellow taste. The word comes from the Gaelic *Uisce Beatha* (pronouced 'Ish-ka Ba-ha'), meaning 'water of life'. At one time there were about 2000 small distilleries operating in Ireland but today there are only two, at Bushmills (see **EXCURSION 14**), and Midleton, Co. Cork, home of the Jameson Heritage Centre, where six brands of whiskey are produced on the same site. Irish pub measures are larger than in Britain and whiskey is usually taken 'neat' or with water, perhaps as a chaser for a pint of stout.

Wild Geese, The: Following the Battle of the Boyne (see **A-Z**) and the Treaty of Limerick, 14,000 Irish troops, who had supported King James, left Ireland and enlisted in the armies of Continental Europe.

Yeats, Jack Butler (1871-1957): One of Ireland's most famed artists. Brother of W. B. Yeats (see **A-Z**) and the youngest son of artist John Butler Yeats, he was also a photographer and writer.

Yeats, William Butler (1865-1939): Born in Dublin, the eldest child of artist John Butler Yeats. A leading figure in the Irish literary revival, his first play, *Countess Cathleen*, launched the Irish Literary Theatre in Dublin in 1899. *On Baile's Strand* was performed at the Abbey Theatre opening in 1904. Rejected in love by Maud Gonne but encouraged by her to join the Irish Republican Brotherhood, Yeats found the inspiration for both his political and love poems. In 1917 he married George Hyde-Lees, an English medium.

Essaranka Waterfall, Co. Donegal

Accidents & Breakdowns: If someone has been injured, tel: 999. If no personal injuries have been suffered there is no obligation to call the police. Exchange names, addresses and insurance details with all involved (including witnesses). If you or the other driver does not own the car, you are obliged to supply the name and address of the company/individual who does own it. Emergency AA telephone boxes are located on many main routes. Towing and repair services are available from local garages. See **Driving**.

Accommodation: Ireland offers a huge variety of accommodation to visitors, ranging from castles to caravans. Bord Failte (see **Tourist Information**) and NITB publish extensive accommodation guides, including self-catering facilities to suit all pockets. Hotels, North and South, are graded A*, A, B*, B and C, and guesthouses A, B*, B and C, but this system is currently under review. All Bord Failte graded and approved premises should display the shamrock sign. The NITB approval sign is a shamrock with a hand at its centre. Many restored town and country houses also provide top-class accommodation. Bed & breakfasts (B&Bs) can be found at almost every turn of the road. Some are 'approved' by the tourist boards but during peak seasons many families 'do B&B', providing travellers with the bare necessities of a clean bed and a good breakfast. Prices start from £10, with en suite costing £2-3 extra, if available. Most accommodation rates are generally slightly higher than comparable British establishments, and prices are higher in summer. Check tourist offices and personal columns of newspapers for special offers. See **Camping & Caravanning**, **Youth Hostels**.

Airports: The principal international airports in the Republic are Dublin, tel: 01-379900, north of Dublin city centre on the N 1, and Shannon, tel: 061-61444, west of Limerick city. Aer Lingus, Ryanair, British Midland and most of the major airlines fly from Dublin to locations throughout Britain and Europe. Facilities include restaurants, two bars and duty-free shopping. A taxi to the city centre costs £12-15, while Bus 41A travels between the airport and Eden Quay (95p). Aer Rianta, the airport authority, runs an express bus service every 20 min to and from Busarus, the main bus station on Store St (£2.30, child £1.15). Shannon has the distinction of being the first airport in the world to operate a duty-free. It is the most westerly air-base in Europe and all transatlantic flights stop here.
There are also regular internal flights from Dublin, and flights from Britain, into Cork, Kerry, Knock (Monsignor Horan international airport), Sligo, Galway and Waterford airports.
In Northern Ireland Belfast international airport, in Aldergrove near Antrim, is the principal airport, tel: 0849-422888. The major airlines operate services here between London, Europe, the USA, Canada and regional airports throughout Britain. An Airbus service operates into the city centre. Flights from locations throughout Britain operate to and from Belfast city airport, tel: 0232 457745. A train service runs into Belfast Central station and there are taxis available. There are flights from Dublin, Glasgow and Manchester into Eglington airport, northeast of Derry city, tel: 0504-810784. Taxis are always available.

An Taisce: The Irish National Trust is committed to defending the country's natural and architectural heritage. Its headquarters are in Tailor's Hall, Back Lane, Dublin, tel: 01-541786, which is the city's oldest surviving guildhall.

Baby-sitters: These can usually be arranged by your hotel/guest-house/B&B. Telephone numbers of local baby-sitters will usually be provided in self-catering accommodation or at caravan parks. There is no State-registered list of child minders in Ireland.

Banks: See **Currency**, **Money**, **Opening Times**.

Beaches: Blue Flags are awarded to beaches which have a consistent high quality of bathing water and coastal environment. These include: Killiney, Co. Dublin; Brittas Bay, Co. Wicklow; Rosslare, Co. Wexford; Clonlea and Ardmore, Co. Waterford; Banna Strand, Co. Kerry; Kilkee and Spanish Point, Co. Clare; Silverstrand, Co. Galway; Keel and Keem, Achill Island; Rosses Point and Rossnowlegh, Co. Sligo; and Rathmullan, Co. Donegal.

Best Buys: Even the smallest of Ireland's cottage craft industries generally produce high-quality attractive products. Pottery is a good purchase almost anywhere but watch out for local potters and factory outlets. Delicate Belleek china is also still a favourite. Despite constant production and industrial problems, Waterford Crystal remains outstanding, while other high-quality crystals include Galway, Cavan and Dublin. Handknits are probably the most popular purchases among tourists but don't just confine your browsing to Aran sweaters (see **A-Z**). Tweeds for both men and women remain good value, and linen is no longer just a favourite for tablecloths – watch out for linen shirts, skirts and jackets. Handcrafted jewellery based on Celtic designs is another good purchase, especially in silver, while Galway's Claddagh ring (see **A-Z**) is a traditional love offering.

Bicycle Hire: Ireland offers both dull lowlands and challenging highlands and hills to cyclists but come prepared for the worst of weather. Bord Failte has mapped out 23 cycling trips, ranging from the 'The Sunny Southeast Corner' to 'The Coast of West Cork'. These are detailed in a brochure called *Cycling Ireland,* available from Bord Failte offices. A list of over 100 appointed Raleigh Rent-a-Bike dealers is given in a BF information sheet on cycling (No. 141).

Bird-watching: Ireland is internationally important for its wintering waterfowl and waders, and its many seabird breeding colonies. A Bord Failte (see **Tourist Information**) information sheet contains a full list of reserves and sanctuaries, and the NITB also publishes a leaflet for bird-watchers.

Border, The: Under the Treaty with Britain in 1921 Ireland was partitioned into two. The Free State, which later became the Republic of Ireland, consists of 26 counties and Northern Ireland of six. Some border roads have been closed off by the security forces, while most others have security checkpoints on both the northern and southern sides. When you cross into Northern Ireland you will usually be stopped by the British Army, asked for ID and requested to open the boot of your car for searching. Sporadic checkpoints are also held within the North, so do not be alarmed if you see armed soldiers with blackened faces lying in ditches by the roadside.

Breakfast: The price of a full Irish breakfast is almost always included in accommodation costs when staying at hotels, guesthouses and of course B&Bs. Generally this meal is substantial enough to tide you through the day. Standards range from the predictable orange juice, cornflakes and fry with tea and toast, to a banquet of fresh juices and fruit, muesli, fish or mixed grill, and home-made breads.

Budget:

Full cooked breakfast		£2-3.50
Lunch, two courses	(pub)	£4-6
	(restaurant)	£4+
Dinner for two with wine		£30+
Guinness (pint)*		£1.50-1.75
Lager (pint)*		£1.60-2
Soft drink (can)		40-50p
Coffee		55p

* The price of alcohol, particularly shorts and mixers, is usually considerably cheaper in Northern Ireland.

Buses:

Republic: There are city bus services in Dublin, Cork, Galway, Limerick and Waterford. Bus Eireann also operates an extensive provincial bus service, tel: 01-366111 or see local directory, and there is a range of coach tours on offer. If you are under 26 and intend using the provincial bus services regularly, invest in a Bus Fare Card (£8). You will need a passport picture and proof of birth date to buy one but it will get you half-price fares. Rambler Passes for bus or both bus and rail are also available (up to £160).

Northern Ireland: Together with city buses, Ulsterbus, tel: 0232-320011 or see local directory, operates an excellent network of buses between most towns, and during the summer runs coach tours from Belfast. A Freedom of Northern Ireland ticket offers 1 or 7 days' unlimited travel on scheduled bus services in Northern Ireland, excluding coach tours (1 day £8, under-16/OAP £4; 7 days £20, under-16/OAP £10).

An Emerald Card offers unlimited bus and rail travel throughout the Republic and Northern Ireland. It can be bought at all major bus and rail centres (8 days £100, under-16 £50; 15 days £160, under-16 £85).

Cameras & Photography: All makes of film are generally available, usually in chemists or large newsagents. Many outlets advertise fast, cheap processing rates and post offices provide a processing service, including free delivery anywhere in the country. Cameras cannot be used in theatres, museums or art galleries. In particular do not attempt to take photographs of security checkpoints or bases in Northern Ireland.

Camping & Caravanning: There are caravan sites near most seaside resorts or popular beaches, with a varying range of facilities. Caravans and mobile homes can usually be hired. Camp sites are not as frequent but farmers and landowners will often allow you to pitch a tent on their land for a small charge. A list of approved camping and caravan sites is available at tourist offices.

Car Hire: Unless arranged as part of a tour package booked outside Ireland, car hire can be very expensive. Occasional cheap deals are

available so enquire locally. Also try consulting *Golden Pages* and *Yellow Pages*.

Chemists: These stock the usual range of drugs, cosmetics and toiletries. Most pharmacists will provide medical advice on minor ailments. Supermarkets sell a small range of medical products, including cold treatments, but rules on selling over-the-counter drugs are tighter than in the USA and Britain, and the bulk of painkilling products are available only on request at chemists. Check listings in the local *Golden Pages* or *Yellow Pages* for late-night pharmacies.

Climate: Ireland's weather is mild, temperate and unpredictable. Come prepared for rain, wind and mist, even in summer, though you may spend your holiday in idyllic sunny conditions.

Comhaltas Ceoltoiri Eireann: An organization of musicians which nurtures and safeguards traditional music, song, dance and storytelling. Its major annual festival, the All-Ireland Fleadh Ceoil, is held in a different venue every year and attracts thousands of musicians and spectators. See **DUBLIN CITY-NIGHTLIFE**.

Complaints: If you are overcharged, find that prices do not correspond to those displayed or are unhappy with the service you have received, ask to see the owner or manager of the premises. If you remain unsatisfied, report the establishment to Bord Failte or the NITB (see **Tourist Information**). The garda taxi office deals with taxi complaints, tel: 01-732222.

Consulates:
Republic:
UK – 38 Merrion Rd, Dublin 4, tel: 01-695211
Australia – Fitzwilton House, Wilton Terr., Dublin 2, tel: 01-761517
Canada – 65-68 St. Stephen's Green, Dublin 2, tel: 01-781988
USA – 42 Elgin Rd, Dublin 4, tel: 01-687122
Northern Ireland:
USA – Queen's House, Queen St, Belfast 1, tel: 0232-328239

Conversion Chart:

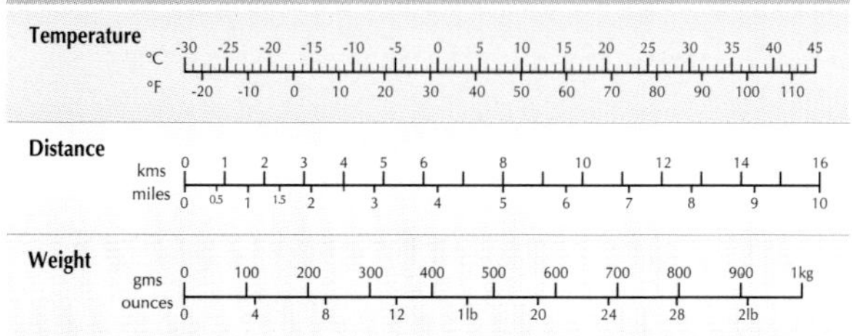

Crack: Not the drug but a much-loved word in Ireland meaning 'fun' or 'a good time' – usually involving drink, music and conversation – as in 'the crack was good'.

Credit Cards: See **Money**.

Crime & Theft: Mainly an urban problem. The usual advice applies. Take precautions against pickpockets and bag-snatchers in cities. Never leave valuables or luggage in cars. Avoid leaving even small items like cassettes and sunglasses visible in cars, and use a steering-wheel lock. Make use of designated car parks; do not park on wasteland. Carry traveller's cheques instead of cash and keep the numbers safe. Keep valuables in the hotel safe. See **Consulates**, **Emergency Numbers**, **Insurance**, **Police**.

Rosses Point, Co. Sligo

Cruising Holidays: Ideal for fishing, bird-watching (see **A-Z**), sightseeing or just relaxing. Well-equipped boats can be hired to cruise the Shannon, Lough Key, Lough Derg, the River Barrow and part of the Grand Canal. Approved hire operators can be found in Carrick-on Shannon, Co. Leitrim; Athlone, Co. Westmeath; Banagher and Tullamore, Co. Offaly; Killaloe, Co. Clare; and Portumna, Co. Galway. A brochure, *Cruising Ireland*, is available at Bord Failte (see **Tourist Information**) offices. See **Sailing Holidays**.

Currency: The unit of currency in the Republic is the punt (£), which is divided into pence (p). In Northern Ireland the unit of currency is sterling (£) and pence. They are not interchangeable, though sterling coins will be accepted at face value in the Republic.
Coins: 1p, 2p, 5p, 10p, 20p, 50p and £1
Notes: £5, £10, £20, £50, £100
There may still be £1 notes in circulation. See **Money**.

Customs Allowances:

Duty Free Into:	Cigarettes (or)	Cigars (or)	Tobacco	Spirits	Wine
EC	300	75	400 g	1.5 *l*	5 *l*
UK	300	75	400 g	1.5 *l*	5 *l*

DART: The DART (Dublin Area Rapid Transit) is a regular train service (every 10-20 min) which runs 0700-2330 round Dublin's coast between Bray to the south and Howth to the north. Iarnrod Eireann (Irish Rail) and Dublin Bus run feeder services to stations. It is a pleasant way to see Dublin if you travel outside the rush hours (0830-0930, 1645-1800). Monthly, weekly saver and family tickets are on sale at stations, the price depending on the route. A day or 10-journey ticket is usually good value. For timetable and fare enquiries, tel: 363333 (0900 -1715 Mon.-Fri.).

Disabled People: Increasing efforts are being made to facilitate disabled people. A number of holiday cottages and houses included in Bord Failte's *Guide to Self-Catering Accommodation* have been adapted for wheelchair use. Further details can be obtained from the Irish Wheelchair Association. The National Rehabilitation Board, 25 Clyde Rd, Dublin 4, tel: 684181, publishes a comprehensive guide to Dublin which is a 'must' for disabled visitors. See **Health**, **Insurance**.

Drinks: Tap water is safe to drink everywhere and there is also a wide selection of sparkling and still mineral waters on sale, the best known being Ballygowan and Tipperary. Irish blended teas are regarded as the best in the world, and the Irish are the most prolific tea-drinkers in Europe. In general most pubs serve good-quality tea and coffee, and it's often a safer bet than the house wine.
It is Guinness (see **A-Z**) which remains the most famous of all Irish beverages. Sister stouts Murphy's (Cork) and Beamish (Dundalk) are also available and locals will swear to their superiority but connoisseurs claim they do not travel well. Lagers are increasingly popular, though expensive, and a wide range of popular foreign brands is brewed under licence. Real ale fans should try Hilden, produced at Lisburn, while down south Smithwick's, Bass or McCardle's may be a satisfactory alternative. Irish coffee and hot whiskey (whiskey, hot water, sugar, lemon and cloves) are popular winter drinks. See **Poitin**, **Whiskey**.

Driving: Road rules in both the Republic and Northern Ireland are identical to Britain: drive on the left, overtake on the right, give way to the right at roundabouts and wear seat belts. In Northern Ireland the speed limit in towns is 30 mph, 60 mph on country roads and 70 mph on dual carriageways and motorways, unless indicated otherwise. The only difference in the Republic is that the maximum speed limit is 55 mph but this is under review. See **Accidents & Breakdowns**, **Parking**, **Petrol**.

Drugs: There is a drugs problem in some urban areas of Ireland, particularly Dublin. Penalties for importation, possession and dealing in drugs are severe.

Eating Out: Some of the best – and worst – food in the world can be discovered when eating out in Ireland. Fresh vegetables, seafood, home-baking, prime Irish beef and lamb are just some of the delights on offer. The larger cities also have a variety of ethnic restaurants, ranging from Chinese, Italian, Greek and Mexican to Japanese, Vietnamese and Russian. Hot lunches, with a main course for about £4, are available in most urban pubs, and in Northern Ireland in particular some restaurants offer their best value at this time. High tea, usually a fry with bread, scones and cakes, is available in many northern hotels and restaurants around 1800. For dinner, probably the best way to eat is off table d'hôte menus which usually offer five courses from £15-25. Many restaurants in the Republic also have a good-value three-course tourist menu, from £6-12, including a glass of house wine. Meanwhile, few towns, no matter how small, are without at least three 'chippers' and a Chinese takeaway. See the **NIGHTLIFE** or **RESTAURANTS** topic pages for named cities. See **Breakfast**, **Food**.

Electricity: The supply is 220 V AC (50 cycles) and British equipment can be used without adaptors. Plugs are 3-pin flat or 2-pin round.

Emergency Numbers:

Police, ambulance, fire	999	
	Republic	*NI*
Rape Crisis Centre	01-614911	0232-249696
Samaritans	01-727700	0232-664422

Equestrian Holidays: A special brochure detailing trails, residential centres, stables and hunting contacts is available from Bord Failte (see **Tourist Information**). Holidays range from exploring rural byroads in a horse-drawn caravan to the Lough Derg Gourmet Ride, based at Ballycormac House in Borrisokane, Co. Tipperary. There is a NITB bulletin on horse-riding and pony-trekking facilities in the region.

Events:

17 March: St. Patrick's Day, parades in most cities and towns in the Republic.
May: Lord Mayor's Show, Belfast; Belfast Civic Festival; Belfast City Marathon.
June: Dublin Street Carnival, street entertainment, face-painting, music and funfair for a weekend; *16:* Bloomsday (see **A-Z**).
July: Strawberry Fair, Enniscorthy, Co. Wexford; Carroll's Irish Open Golf Championship; *12:* Battle of the Boyne (see **A-Z**) commemorations and Orangemen's Day, Northern Ireland.
August: Dublin Horse Show, Royal Dublin Society, Ballsbridge; Puck Fair (see **A-Z**), Killorglin, Co. Kerry; Oul' Lammas Fair, Ballycastle, Co. Antrim.
September: All-Ireland hurling and football finals, Croke Park, Dublin; Waterford International Festival of Light Opera.
October: Dublin Theatre Festival; Dublin City Marathon; Cork Guinness Jazz Festival.
October/November: Wexford Opera Festival.

Ferries:

Dublin: B&I has a daily service to and from Holyhead in Wales. The Isle of Man Steam Packet Company operates a ferry to Douglas.
Dun Laoghaire: Sealink ferries connect daily with Holyhead.

Rosslare: B&I has a ferry route to Pembroke and Sealink a service to Fishguard.
Cork: Swansea–Cork Ferries operate between these two cities.
Larne: Sealink operates daily sailings to and from Stranraer, and P&O European Ferries runs a daily service to Cairnryan.
Belfast: There are regular sailings to and from Douglas, Isle of Man, June-Sep. Contact the Isle of Man Steam Packet Company. A new Seacat hydrofoil capable of carrying cars and passengers operates to Stranraer.

Fishing: Just about every British and European angler can vouch for Ireland's attraction as a fishing destination, be it deep-sea, coarse or salmon fishing. Permits are only required for sea trout and salmon fishing. For up-to-date regulations and requirements, check with the local tourist office or fisheries board. There is no close season for coarse fishing in Northern Ireland. The Department of Agriculture's *Angling Guide* offers details of department-owned fisheries and other useful tips. The NITB also publishes invaluable information bulletins on game and sea fishing.

Food: Irish salmon, sea trout, oysters and other seafood are among the best in the world. Bacon, or corned beef, and cabbage has been a staple Irish dish for generations, with of course, potatoes. Ulster champ is a delicous mashed potato and onion mixture, while its equivalent in the South is colcannon, where shredded kale or green cabbage is also added. Soda bread, brown and white, is a long-time favourite. It is made using sodium bicarbonate. See **Breakfast**, **Eating Out**.

Garda: See **Police**.

Genealogy: The Genealogical Office, 2 Kildare St, Dublin, tel: 618477/611626, is a good starting point for anyone researching their family history. Arrive early as there is usually a queue (1000-1230, 1400-1630 Mon.-Fri.). Bord Failte (see **Tourist Information**) publishes an information sheet, No. 8 *Tracing Your Ancestors*, which lists other centres that keep records. You may face some difficulties as many records were destroyed when the Four Courts was shelled during the 1922-23 Civil War. If you wish to hire a specialist research company contact the Association of Professional Genealogists, 22 Windsor Rd,

Dublin, tel: 966522. In Northern Ireland the Ulster Historical Foundation, 68 Balmoral Ave, Belfast BT9 6NY and the Irish Heritage Association, 162a Kingsway, Dunmurry, Belfast BT17 9AD, organize heritage holidays for groups or individuals. Other organizations that can help you trace your roots include the General Register Office, Oxford House, 49-55 Chichester St, Belfast BT1 4HL and the Presbyterian Historical Society, Church House, Belfast BT1 6DU.

Golf: Just about every area boasts at least one 18-hole golf course, and most are open to visitors so enquire locally. The NITB's Information Bulletin 17 on golf lists details of courses, fees and facilities. Among the best-known are: Portmarnock and Royal Dublin, Co. Dublin; Lahinch, Co. Clare; Ballybunion, Killarney, Tralee and Waterville, Co. Kerry; Royal Portrush's Dunluce course, Co. Antrim; Rosses Point, Co. Sligo; and Connemara near Ballyconneely, Co. Galway.

Health: Visitors from all EC countries are entitled to the same free medical treatment as Irish citizens by presenting an E111 form. This can be obtained from your local health authority before travelling. Non-EC visitors have to pay full costs.

Horse-racing: One of Ireland's favourite pastimes. The country boasts 28 courses. Some of the major annual racing fixtures include:
Mid-Jan.: Ladbroke Hurdle, Leopardstown.
Mid-Feb.: Vincent O'Brien Gold Cup, Leopardstown.
Easter: Jameson Irish Grand National, Fairyhouse.
Late April: Spring Festival, Punchestown.
Mid-May: Irish 2000 Guineas, Curragh.
Late May: Goff's Irish 1000 Guineas, Curragh.
Late June: Budweiser Irish Derby, Curragh.
Late July/Aug.: Galway Races.
Mid-Aug.: Heinz '57' Stakes, Leopardstown.
Late Aug.: Sand races, Laytown Strand, Laytown.
Early Sep.: National Stakes and Moyglare Stud Stakes, Curragh.
Late Sep.: Jefferson Smurfit Memorial Irish St. Leger, Curragh.
Mid-Oct.: The Million, Curragh.

Insurance: Travel insurance to cover you against personal accident, medical expenses, theft and loss of property is strongly recommended. Your travel agent should be able to recommend a suitable policy. See **Crime & Theft**, **Driving**, **Health**.

Laundries: Coin-operated laundries and service washes are usually only available in larger towns and cities, and are more widespread in Northern Ireland. They can usually be found in areas frequented by students, e.g. Rathmines, Dublin. Many hotels offer a laundry service.

Lost Property: In the Republic a visit to the local garda station where you lost the item is usually worthwhile. It is also common in Ireland to hand in items at a nearby shop for safekeeping or to leave a name and address in case the owner returns. The central lost property office for Dublin city is at Harcourt Sq. garda station, tel: 732222. If you think you lost something on a bus or DART train, contact Dublin Bus at 59 Upper O'Connell St, tel: 720000. Take along a passport or form of identification. In Northern Ireland enquire at your hotel or the tourist office for the best local procedure. See **Insurance**.

Money: Major credit cards are accepted almost everywhere and you should have no difficulty changing traveller's cheques. Some places in the Republic will accept British sterling but you are unlikely to get the full exchange rate. See **Crime & Theft**, **Currency**.

Music: All types of live music are on offer in the larger urban centres: classical, rock, jazz, country, traditional and heavy metal. Ask at the local tourist office about venues. Even the smallest village will generally have some kind of musical entertainment, usually traditional or Irish country. Concerts, gigs, music festivals and recitals are listed in the 'What's On' sections of local and national newspapers, or in listings magazines like *In Dublin*. See **Events**.

Newspapers: There are four Irish national daily papers in the Republic: *The Irish Times, The Irish Press, The Irish Independent* and *The Cork Examiner*. British papers are available and *The Star* has its own Irish edition. The *Press* and *Independent* both publish evening papers: the *Evening Press* and *Herald*. Sunday's Irish papers are *The Sunday Press, The Sunday Tribune, The Sunday World* (the closest Ireland comes to a British tabloid), *The Sunday Independent* and *The Sunday Business Post* (a business- and finance-oriented publication). The daily northern newspapers are the Unionist-oriented *Belfast Newsletter*, and Nationalist *Irish News*. The more middle-of-the-road *Belfast Telegraph* is an evening publication. In addition, most areas have their own local weekly newspaper.

Nightlife: Every city has a choice of discos, nightclubs, cabarets, cinemas and theatres but in the smaller towns most entertainment revolves around the pubs. See the **NIGHTLIFE** topic pages for the named cities.

Opening Times: In general:
Republic:
Banks – 1000-1230, 1330-1500 Mon.-Fri.
Post offices – 0900-1700 Mon.-Sat.
Offices – 0900-1700 Mon.-Fri.

Shops – 0930-1730, late-night shopping in urban areas Thu. & Fri. Some rural towns have half-day closing one day during the week.
Pubs – 1030-2330 Mon.-Sat. (2300 in winter), 1230-1400, 1600-2300 Sun. Some pubs with special licences, usually around dock areas or close to a livestock mart, open early in the morning, often from 0630.
Northern Ireland:
Banks – 1000-1730 Mon.-Fri. In some towns banks close 1230-1330, while in small villages the banks only open 2-3 days a week.
Offices – 0900-1700 Mon.-Fri.
Shops – 0930-1730 Mon.-Sat. There is usually late-night shopping on Thu. and Fri. but many towns have a half-day or closed day during the week.
Pubs – 1130-2300 Mon.-Sat., 1230-1430, 1900-2200 Sun. Some bars do not open on Sun.

Orientation: Buy an indexed street map for any city you intend spending time in. An indexed road map is also essential. When seeking directions avoid asking for the N 1, R 5, N 6, etc. Instead, ask directions to the Cork road, Belfast road, etc.

Parking: Car parks are expensive in most cities – up to 80p an hour in Dublin and Belfast – but you are unlikely to find a legal parking space on a street after early morning. There are, however, free car parks in most towns and cities if you have time to seek them out. Some towns and cities (e.g. Cork) have a parking disc system in operation. This means that to park along streets you must first purchase a book of discs from a shop. In Dublin, if a youngster offers to watch your car, say yes and tip them £1 when you return. Your car will be untouched – unfortunately it won't be if you refuse the offer! In Northern Ireland control zones, usually in town centres, are indicated clearly by yellow signs. Unattended cars left here are treated as a security risk. See **Driving**.

Passports & Customs: British citizens born in the UK travelling from Britain do not need passports, though it is advisable to bring some form of photo identification. Nationals from other countries must have a valid passport, while some (not EC countries, USA, Canada, Australia or New Zealand) also need visas. Details are obtainable from Irish consulates, embassies or tourist offices. Value-Added Tax (VAT) makes most goods and services more expensive in Ireland. Visitors from outside the EC can reclaim the tax paid through the Cashback system, which allows you to reclaim VAT paid at airports and ferry ports (for a handling fee). Ask for a Cashback form when you buy goods.

Petrol: Both unleaded and leaded petrol are available. Many city garages are self-service. The price is quoted in pence per litre and unleaded is cheaper. Maximum prices are set by the Irish government each month and most garages charge the full price. Petrol is cheaper in Northern Ireland, as you will gather by the number of petrol stations on the border. See **Driving**.

Police: The Republic's police force is called An Garda Siochana (literally 'the keepers of the peace') and performs all the duties of a national police force. One officer is a garda, more than one are gardai (pronouced 'gard-ee'). They are unarmed except in exceptional circumstances. Apart from some of the islands, most areas will have a police station in close proximity. In Northern Ireland the Royal Ulster Constabulary (RUC) is the police force and most are armed. Because of the security risk, RUC stations are completely barricaded in and surrounded by surveillance equipment.

Post Offices:
Main post offices: O'Connell St, Dublin; Oliver Plunkett St, Cork; Castle Pl., Belfast.
Republic: Postcard to EC countries 28p; Closed letter 32p; Airmail 52p.
Northern Ireland: 1st class to EC countries 24p; 2nd class within Britain 18p; Airmail 39p.

Public Holidays:
General: 1 Jan.; 17 Mar. (St. Patrick's Day); Good Fri. (not statutory but usually observed in most areas); Easter Mon.; Dec. 25; Dec. 26.
Republic: June bank holiday (Mon. after 1st June weekend); Aug. bank holiday (Mon. after 1st Aug. weekend); Oct. bank holiday (Mon. after

last Oct. weekend).
Northern Ireland: May Day holiday (Mon. after 1st May weekend); Spring holiday (last Mon. in May); 12 July (Orange Day).

Pubs: There are around 12,000 pubs in Ireland and it's usually the crack (see **A-Z**) which sets one above another. In rural areas, if you stay around long enough, you will be introduced to 'after-hours', an illegal but enjoyable extension of drinking time. See **Drinks**, **Opening Times**.

Railways:
Republic: Irish Rail (Iarnrod Eireann) operates daily services from Dublin's Heuston and Connolly stations to Cork, Limerick, Tralee, Galway, Westport, Waterford, Sligo and other destinations, with numerous stops en route. It is time-consuming and often expensive, however, to travel by train from the west or northwest to the south. Interail tickets, bought in another country, can be used here, while 8- or 15-day Rambler tickets are good value if you intend doing a lot of train travel. A Railfare card, £8.50 for the under 26s, gets half-price fares.
Northern Ireland: There are three main rail routes in Northern Ireland which operate from Belfast Central station, tel: 0232-230310: north to Derry via Ballymena and Coleraine; east to Bangor along the shores of Belfast Lough; and south to Dublin via Lisburn, Portadown and Newry (which is regularly delayed by bomb hoaxes).

Religious Services: Enquire at the nearest tourist office or locally.

Sailing Holidays: For beginners there are sailing courses, for experts yachts to charter. Unspoilt waters, breathtaking scenery and hundreds of sheltered anchorage spots make this an idyllic type of holiday. The coastline from Cork Harbour to the Dingle peninsula remains the most popular area. A Bord Failte (see **Tourist Information**) brochure, *Sailing Ireland*, provides a wealth of information. See **Cruising Holidays**.

Shopping: See **Best Buys**.

Smoking: Recent legislation in the Republic has banned smoking in public buildings, cinemas, buses and DART trains. Smoking carriages are still available on Irish Rail trains. All restaurants must provide a nonsmoking area but pubs remain a smoker's haven.

Sport: Hurling, played with a small hard ball and flat *camans* (wider than a hockey stick), and Gaelic football, a mixture of soccer and rugby, are played under the auspices of the Gaelic Athletic Association on both sides of the border. All-Ireland finals are held in Dublin's Croke Park (see **Events**). Both rugby and soccer (even before the arrival of Jack Charlton!) are popular sports. Tennis, golf (see **A-Z**) and water sports are also widely enjoyed. See **Fishing**, **Horse-racing**.

Taxis:
Republic: Plentiful in most urban centres, except during the Christmas season and busy weekends. Most rural towns have hackney services. Check in the local directory for telephone numbers.

Northern Ireland: In Belfast and Derry the black taxis are sectarian, and operate like minibus services into either Catholic or Protestant areas. In Belfast cabs into Catholic areas operate from the Smithfield area of Castle St and into Protestant areas from North St. Ordinary taxis operate from Donegall Sq. and other ranks throughout the city. Black cabs from Derry's Foyle St go into Catholic districts. Regular taxis include Autocabs, tel: 0504-45100, and Quick Cabs, tel: 0504-260515.

Telephones & Telegrams: There are direct-dial services from just about everywhere and a good supply of telephone boxes, though these are often vandalized or out of order in the Republic. Post offices supply a telegram service and many offer a fax service.

Television & Radio:
Republic: The state-owned Radio Telefis Eireann runs two television channels. A third Irish channel is also in the pipeline. All the British channels, including Sky, are available on cable in most areas.
Northern Ireland: In many areas both the British and Irish channels are available. All areas have local radio stations, while it is usually possible to pick up broadcasts from Britain.

Time Difference: Ireland uses GMT. The clocks go forward 1 hr in late Mar. and back 1 hr in late Oct.

Tipping: A service charge is included on most hotel and restaurant bills. Otherwise a 10% tip is adequate if the service merits it. Tip pub waiters and waitresses (not bar staff) up to 50p depending on the size of the order, and hotel porters 50p per bag. Taxi drivers get 10-15%. Remember, however, that all tipping is optional.

Toilets: Public conveniences are few and far between and most are to be avoided. Everyone uses toilets in department stores, pubs and hotels, few of which object. In Irish *mna* is ladies and *fir* is gents.

Tourist Information: The Irish Tourist Board (Bord Failte) has its UK bureau at 150 New Bond St, London W1Y 0AQ, tel: 071-4933201.

The Northern Ireland Tourist Board's (NITB) office is at 11 Berkeley St, London W1X 6BU, tel: 071-4930601. For addresses of tourist offices in Ireland, turn to the appropriate town entry in the excursions or the historical/cultural gazetteer.

Transport: See **Airports**, **Buses**, **DART**, **Ferries**, **Railways**, **Taxis**.

Traveller's Cheques: See **Money**.

Walking: Just about every county or region has a mapped-out and signposted long-distance walk, e.g. Ulster Way, Wicklow Way. Enquire at local tourist offices for details.

What's On: See **Events**.

Youth Hostels: An Óige, the Irish youth hostelling organization, has hostels scattered throughout the country. Members of other national youth hostelling organizations are entitled to use these hostels. Membership for over 18s is £7.50. Further details can be obtained from An Óige, 39 Mountjoy Sq., Dublin, tel: 01-354749.

Mount Usher Gardens, Co. Wicklow

Bewley's Oriental Café, Dublin

Killarney

This book was produced using QuarkXPress™ and Adobe Illustrator 88™ on Apple Macintosh™ computers and output to separated film on a Linotronic™ 300 Imagesetter

Text: Louise Ni Chriodain
Photography: Douglas Robertson
Electronic Cartography: Bartholomews

First published 1993

Published by HarperCollins Publishers
Printed in Hong Kong
ISBN 0 00 435908-9

Guidebook information is subject to being outdated by changes to opening hours, prices, and by fluctuating restaurant standards. Every effort has been made to give you an up-to-date text but the publishers cannot accept any liability for errors, omissions or changes in detail or for any consequences arising from the use of information contained herein.
The publishers welcome corrections and suggestions from readers; write to: The Publishing Manager, Travel Guides, HarperCollins Publishers, PO Box, Glasgow G4 0NB.

Dunmore Caves, Co. Kilkenny